# Fair Trade and the Citizen-Consumer

# Fair Trade and the Citizen-Consumer

## Shopping for Justice?

Kathryn Wheeler
*University of Essex, UK*

First published 2012 by
PALGRAVE MACMILLAN

Palgrave Macmillan in the UK is an imprint of Macmillan Publishers Limited, registered in England, company number 785998, of Houndmills, Basingstoke, Hampshire RG21 6XS.

Palgrave Macmillan in the US is a division of St Martin's Press LLC, 175 Fifth Avenue, New York, NY 10010.

Palgrave Macmillan is the global academic imprint of the above companies and has companies and representatives throughout the world.

Palgrave® and Macmillan® are registered trademarks in the United States, the United Kingdom, Europe and other countries.

ISBN 978–0–230–30142–9

This book is printed on paper suitable for recycling and made from fully managed and sustained forest sources. Logging, pulping and manufacturing processes are expected to conform to the environmental regulations of the country of origin.

A catalogue record for this book is available from the British Library.

A catalog record for this book is available from the Library of Congress.

10  9  8  7  6  5  4  3  2  1
21  20  19  18  17  16  15  14  13  12

Printed and bound in Great Britain by
CPI Antony Rowe, Chippenham and Eastbourne

*In loving memory of Grace Wheeler (Grandma) and
Geraldine Smart (Nana)*

# Contents

# List of Tables, Box, Figures and Graphs

## Tables

## Box

## Figures

## Graphs

# Acknowledgements

This book began its life as another project and therefore special thanks must go to my supervisors, Professor Lucinda Platt and Dr Sean Nixon, whose intuitive insights and guidance were a constant source of support. Many thanks also to Dr Peter Gurney and Professor Rob Stones who offered many interesting ideas and suggestions, as well as to the Sociology Department at Essex, which has provided a stimulating environment to study and work. I would also like to thank Professors Alan Warde and Mark Harvey for their encouragement, as well as the anonymous reviewers for their suggestions. Special thanks must also go to Professor Miriam Glucksmann who very kindly gave me the time away from our current project to finish this book.

I am very grateful to all of the participants in this research project – the residents of Chelmsford who participated in this research in 2008, and the members of the Fairtrade Towns from Lund and Berkeley, as well as the representatives from the national fair-trade organisations in the UK, USA and Sweden, and speciality coffee experts, who were interviewed in 2011. Without their willingness to discuss their consumption behaviour and commitment to varied social practices, this book quite simply would not have been possible. I would especially like to thank Alfred and the Chelmsford Fairtrade Action Group who gave me access to their minutes and allowed me to attend their meetings. I must also thank Karen Potter who very kindly agreed to help me transcribe my interviews for a nominal fee.

Thanks must go to my family, friends and colleagues who have offered much moral support both throughout my research years and beyond. I owe a huge thank you to my parents, Jacqui and Mick Wheeler, who have patiently and lovingly supported me throughout my years at university and beyond. Not only have they demonstrated an unwavering belief in my ability to get the book completed, but they have also proofread and commented upon my many drafts, and provided office space when I needed it. I would like to thank my mum for acting as my focus-group assistant for the majority of the groups and my dad for getting me interested in fair-trade in the first place. Thanks also to my big brother, Alex Wheeler, who has provided vital IT and technical support! Thank you to the Ziemes for putting me up during my fieldwork in Sweden.

I would also like to *especially* thank Jennifer Bullen, who went above and beyond the call of duty by reading and commenting upon the entire manuscript twice, as well as acting as the assistant for several of my focus-group discussions. Her insightful comments challenged me, and the book has been substantially improved because of her input. Her kindness was only outweighed by her courage in the last months of her life. She is sorely missed.

Special thanks must also go to Luke Branch for his understanding, love, patience and shoulder to cry on. His constant support and encouragement have made me find the strength to get up every morning and face the challenges of the day. I know that I could not have completed this book without him, and for this, and many other things, I express my eternal love and gratitude.

I would like to acknowledge the financial support of the Economic and Social Research Council who funded the research on the 1+3 scheme, and the Sociology department at the University of Essex whose Research Endowment Fund contributed towards my trip to Berkeley.

Finally, the publishers and I wish to thank the following for permission to reproduce copyright material:

- Sage Publications Limited for Wheeler, K. (2012) 'The Practice of Fairtrade Support', *Sociology*, Vol. 46(1): 126–41, which is reproduced in a revised and extended format in Chapter 5.
- The Fairtrade Foundation for the use of the FAIRTRADE label (Figure 3.1).
- Fair Trade USA for the use of the Fair Trade Certified label (Figure 3.2).
- The World Fair Trade Organization for the WFTO logo (Figure 3.3).

# List of Abbreviations and Acronyms

| | |
|---|---|
| ASI | Adam Smith Institute |
| ATO | Alternative Trading Organisation |
| CA | Consumers' Association |
| CFAG | Chelmsford Fairtrade Action Group |
| CSR | Corporate Social Responsibility |
| DFID | Department for International Development |
| ECRA | Ethical Consumer Research Association |
| EDM | Early Day Motion |
| EU | European Union |
| FLO | Fairtrade Labelling Organisation |
| FFTS | Föreningen för Fairtrade Sverige |
| FTF | Fairtrade Foundation, UK |
| FTrF | Fair Trade Federation, USA |
| FTUSA | Fair Trade USA |
| IMF | International Monetary Fund |
| LO | Swedish Trade Union Confederation |
| LSA | Ligue Sociale d'Acheteurs |
| NCL | National Consumers' League |
| NGO | Non-Governmental Organisation |
| NHS | National Health Service, UK |
| OCA | Organic Consumers Association |
| RA | Rainforest Alliance |
| SIDA | Swedish International Development Cooperation Agency |
| TUC | Trades Union Congress |
| WFTD | World Fair Trade Day |
| WFTO | World Fair Trade Organization |
| WTO | World Trade Organization |

# 1
# Introduction: The Rise of the Fair-Trade Citizen-Consumer

> The idea that shopping is the new politics is certainly seductive. Never mind the ballot box: vote with your supermarket trolley instead. Elections occur relatively rarely, but you probably go shopping several times a month, providing yourself with lots of opportunities to express your opinions. If you are worried about the environment, you might buy organic food; if you want to help poor farmers, you can do your bit by buying Fairtrade products; or you can express a dislike of evil multinational companies and rampant globalisation by buying only local produce. And the best bit is that shopping, unlike voting, is fun; so you can do good and enjoy yourself at the same time.
>
> *The Economist* (2006)

Calls for consumers to use their shopping choices to make a difference to social and environmental causes have become increasingly prevalent in contemporary society. We are faced with a diverse array of ethical labels when we enter the supermarket, each one offering us the opportunity to use our status as consumers to enact our citizenly duties. Consumers are regularly told that they are co-responsible for global poverty, environmental degradation and public health (to name but a few), and that by making the right choice, they can alleviate the suffering of hard-working producers, save a rainforest or reduce the burden on public spending. Consumers are constructed as powerful actors in the global market society whose individual choices have the capacity to shape social, political and economic systems. This book challenges this account of the consumer as an autonomous and individualist chooser and instead argues that consumption is a collective and complex process that is embedded within routine and normative practices. Consumption is performed in the course of pursuing daily practices and is thus subject to situational and institutional forms of collective constraint. Rather than the consumer operating in a vacuum, his/her behaviour is shaped and coordinated by infrastructures of provision and social conventions. To explore these ideas, this volume offers a detailed case study of fair-trade[1] consumption and support and reveals how the fair-trade citizen-consumer has been called to action and publicly represented as an individual, at the same time as market interventions are editing the choices available to consumers and collective cultures of fair-trade support are flourishing. This book offers an international perspective on the growth of the fair-trade movement in the UK, Sweden and the USA, with a close focus on fair-trade consumers living within a Fairtrade Town in the UK.

Fair-trade is the most well-known ethical consumer label across the globe, with roughly six in ten consumers recognising this label in a survey of 24 countries (FTF, 2011a). The fair-trade model presents itself as a simple solution to the problems of poverty created by unfair trading relations. Fair-trade provides market access to marginalised producers through the development of long-term trading partnerships that enable producers to support their families and livelihoods. Producers receive a minimum price for their crop or product, which is intended to cover the cost of sustainable production, and an additional social premium for investment in social, environmental or economic development projects. The use of this premium must be democratically decided upon by producers within the farmers' cooperative or between workers on a plantation. By choosing a fair-trade coffee or chocolate, which may or may not be more expensive than their regular brand, consumers are told they can help to make a difference to the lives of families in the developing world who will now receive a 'fair' price for their produce. The global chain between the producer and the consumer is shortened as the active choice of a consumer in one corner of the world is connected to the improved livelihood of a producer in the other corner.

There has been a striking increase in the consumption of fair-trade goods across the world, with global sales quadrupling in value between 2005 and 2010 (FLO, 2011a). Existing accounts of the 'fair-trade consumer' by the fair-trade movement, policy makers and academics tend to assume that the decision to purchase a fair-trade product is the conscious choice of a 'citizen-consumer' who wants to register their support for producers in the developing world or, more politically, to 'vote' for fairer trade through their consumption (Bennett, 2004; Carter, 2001;

Goodman, 2004; Lamb, 2008; Lyon, 2006; Micheletti, 2003; Nicholls & Opal, 2005; Scammell, 2000; 2003; Shaw, Newholm & Dickinson, 2006; Soper, 2004; 2008). By contrast, this book argues that much of fair-trade's market growth in recent years can be accounted for by the expansion of fair-trade goods into mainstream retail outlets; the development of collective cultures and practices, which motivate and sustain fair-trade consumer behaviour among not only committed fair-trade supporters but also an increasingly 'non-activist' consumer-base; and the efforts of a range of intermediary actors who construct and mobilise the 'citizen-consumer' in order to encourage public debate and to legitimise their own role in speaking on behalf of the consumer.

The fair-trade movement has developed according to different tempos across the world, with the mainstream provisioning of fair-trade goods occurring later in some countries than others. In many ways, mainstream availability of fair-trade was pioneered in the UK, and it is for this reason that this book focuses much of its attention on the UK market. Following the commitment from the Co-operative retail group, who in the year 2000 launched their own-brand Fairtrade chocolate, most other major supermarkets and retail outlets in the UK, with differing levels of commitment to the fair-trade movement's aims – Asda, Boots, Debenhams, Sainsbury's, Marks & Spencer, Morrison's, Tesco and Waitrose – now offer their own-brand fair-trade lines. There have also been a number of high-profile 'fair-trade switches' in the UK where entire product lines have been converted to Fairtrade. For example, in 2006, Sainsbury's switched to selling only Fairtrade bananas, and in 2007 they announced their decision to switch their own-brand coffee and tea to Fairtrade-only lines, and in 2009 the nation's favourite chocolate bar, Cadbury's Dairy Milk, became Fairtrade-certified. Sainsbury's sales of Fairtrade goods accounted for one third of Fairtrade retail sales in the UK in 2008 (Sainsbury's, 2009), and the switch by Cadbury tripled the sales of Fairtrade cocoa (FTF, 2009a). In other countries, we see similar trends, albeit several years after the UK, with, for example, Coles (Australia), Carrefour (France), Coop Nordic (Scandinavia) and Wal-Mart (USA) all launching their own-brand fair-trade products since 2006. The 100 per cent switch is currently less common outside the UK, although there are some examples, such as the Hilton and Scandic hotel group, which converted all its coffee to fair-trade in 2006, and Ben and Jerry's, which committed to a 100 per cent fair-trade policy in 2011, as well as fair-trade espressos served in Dunkin Donuts and Starbuck's.

Alongside the displays of support for the fair-trade movement from mainstream retailers and brands, the growth of fair-trade sales have also been influenced by an ever-growing network of Fairtrade Towns (as well as Fairtrade schools, universities, churches and workplaces). A Fairtrade Town is defined as 'a community which has made a commitment to supporting fair-trade' in which the residents have significant levels of awareness and understanding of the fair-trade concept and should regularly buy and use fair-trade products (FTF, 2002: 1). One of the key aims of the Fairtrade Towns movement is to encourage local councils/ municipalities, businesses and retail outlets to make the switch to fair-trade products, often by removing non-fair-trade alternatives. Launched in 2000 following the efforts of a group of committed fair-trade supporters in the small Lancashire town of Garstang in the UK, this active grassroots campaigning-network has grown significantly, with over a thousand Fairtrade Towns across 24 countries around the world (at the time of writing). Fairtrade Towns provide the opportunity for individuals and groups to join together in a collective movement for change inspired by the notion of consumer power. In a 2009 report commissioned by the Fairtrade Foundation (FTF) to examine the impact of the European Fairtrade Towns initiative, it was claimed that

> Fairtrade Towns have an incredible and quite unique power. They bring the challenges facing developing world producers and the promise of positive action to make a difference into the immediate locale and everyday life of ordinary citizens. In the midst of a thriving Fairtrade Town campaign Fairtrade stops being 'out there' for people and becomes the cup of coffee they're offered in their local hairdresser, a new Fairtrade Mark sign in the store they visit several days a week or a chocolate sample they're offered in their local shopping centre. In other words, it becomes something they can hardly fail to notice and will almost certainly pause for thought about.
>
> Taplin (2009: 11)

However, we would be wise to respond cautiously to the claim that the Fairtrade Towns movement, and indeed the fair-trade switches by large corporations discussed above, has made fair-trade something that 'ordinary citizens ... can hardly fail to notice'. Somewhat paradoxically, an important consequence of these forms of collective mobilisation and provisioning has been the growth of the 'accidental' fair-trade consumer who consumes fair-trade but does not necessarily support or even recognise the fair-trade movement's aims or claims.

As fair-trade products have moved into mainstream markets, academic and policy attention has tended to focus upon the veracity of the claims of the fair-trade movement – in particular whether it is really able to improve the lives of disadvantaged producers in the developing world (Barrientos & Dolan, 2006; Dolan, 2008; Jaffee, 2007; Lyon, 2006; Lyon & Moberg, 2010; Raynolds, Murray & Wilkinson, 2007). This research reveals that the fair-trade model is far from perfect and, in some cases, no better than trade through 'conventional' trading routes. For example, in her study of a fair-trade cooperative in Guatemala, Lyon points out that the earnings farmers receive from fair-trade enable them to 'maintain their families but not necessarily get ahead' (Lyon, 2006: 458). In another example, Dolan's ethnographic study of the cut flower industry in Kenya highlighted how the emphasis placed upon equality and partnership by the fair-trade movement is not necessarily recognised as such among producers – they often confuse fair-trade with charity or experience fair-trade regulations as 'an instrument of authority and control' (Dolan, 2008: 298). Although the fair-trade movement began as an aid to local development and as a challenge to global trading rules through the use of alternative trading networks, as the movement has moved into the mainstream this project has, for some, come under threat. Jaffee (2007) suggests that the involvement of transnational corporations is threatening the principles of the fair-trade model because these organisations are not really committed to changing their practices but use fair-trade in order to improve their public image. Meanwhile, Renard and Perez-Grovas (2007) argue that the involvement of transnational corporations in the fair-trade scheme has generated changes in the national initiatives (organised under the Fairtrade Labelling Organisation [FLO]) that are pursuing a more market-oriented approach that is to the detriment of small producers. For those who want to see greater benefits for producers, working with big corporate brands and supermarkets is seen as the best way to achieve this objective. But for those who see fair-trade as 'a counter-hegemonic political project' (Low & Davenport, 2006: 315), the paradox of growth has been that fair-trade is anchored 'within the same mainstream sector many sought to avoid' (Barrientos, Conroy & Jones, 2007: 54). Raynolds, Murray and Wilkinson's (2007) edited collection examines the impact of fair-trade's market success on its movement commitments, and reveals how the pursuit of sales volumes as an end in itself has made it more difficult for the movement's aims to be realised. Focusing on the businesses, producers and social movements who are promoting, experiencing and challenging the increasingly market-driven approach to fair-trade, their collection remains quiet about the impact of mainstreaming upon the consumers who will knowingly or unknowingly be consuming ever-more fair-trade products.

It is surprising that so little attention has been given to the consumer, especially in light of the fact that most people's contact with the fair-trade movement in the developed world is likely to be through fair-trade marketing initiatives (like Fairtrade Towns, the fair-trade promotional period and creative displays in supermarkets), which highlight the important role that consumers must play in a 'citizen's movement for change' (FTF, 2009b). Fair-trade organisations, like the Fairtrade Foundation (FTF) in the UK or Fair Trade USA (FTUSA), and organisations that are supportive of the wider movement (such as Oxfam, the Cooperative movement and various Christian development charities) play an important role in motivating public debate about fair-trade. It is these organisations that are responsible for constructing and mobilising the consumer as a citizen because it enables them to speak on behalf of this figure when they engage in advocacy work (Clarke et al., 2007a). In their 'Charter of Fair Trade Principles', the Fair Trade Advocacy network (a coalition of three international fair-trade organisations) reveals how they rely on being able to demonstrate they have widespread consumer support in order to be able to engage in their advocacy work (Fair Trade Advocacy Office, 2009: 4 & 5). As Clarke et al. (2007a) argue, the fair-trade movement is only able to have an influential voice in the global debate on international trade by representing the multiple acts of fair-trade consumption as indicative of widespread public support. But what do the consumers really think? And what actually drives their consumption behaviours? I argue that if we are to fully interrogate the fair-trade phenomenon and such representations of consumer support, attention must be paid to those who buy fair-trade products, intentionally or unknowingly, and their opinions of the fair-trade movement's aims and claims. This book provides such a consumer perspective.

## Fair-trade consumption, practice theory and the citizen-consumer

The study of fair-trade consumption offers an exciting opportunity for sociological research because it provides a connection between so-called spectacular consumption, that is, consumption that connects to individuals' tastes and lifestyles and is spoken about with reference to theories of freedom and choice, and 'ordinary consumption', that is, consumption that requires little reflection and often occurs while conducting our daily routines (Gronow & Warde, 2001).[2] On the one hand, there are a number of individuals who do consciously and reflexively consume fair-trade goods because they have a commitment to the aims of the fair-trade movement and recognise the field of consumption as an additional sphere in which they can communicate their values and political voice. These 'fair-trade supporters' are likely to be organised into Fairtrade Town (or school, church, university or workplace) networks and be involved in activities that extend beyond individual consumption – for example, campaigning to shift systems of collective provisioning to fair-trade within local places and spaces. On the other hand, because of the success of the actions of these fair-trade supporters and the larger fair-trade movement in intervening in the market, fair-trade products are now widely (and often solely) available in a diverse range of locations, particularly within the UK. Therefore, individuals who have no real commitment to the fair-trade movement are increasingly consuming fair-trade products without necessarily being aware that they are doing so. Those who happen to live in Fairtrade Towns or visit supermarkets and public buildings that stock more fair-trade items are likely to be regularly drinking fair-trade coffee or eating fair-trade bananas but are unlikely to be using these fair-trade items in order to express their 'vote' for the fair-trade movement. Their routine or 'ordinary' consumption has little to do with conscious choice and more to do with 'contextual and collective constraint' (ibid.: 4). This book will argue that it is necessary to separate forms of support for the fair-trade movement from the actual consumption of fair-trade goods if we are to fully understand the fair-trade phenomenon.

In order to achieve this, I apply elements from a practice-theoretical perspective so as to embed the act of fair-trade consumption into its social context and web of social relations (Halkier, 2010; Warde, 2005). A 'theory of practice' approach to consumption emphasises the routine nature of much of our consumption behaviour and points out that it is rarely completely reflexive but neither is it completely constrained. Rather consumption is a complex process that is subject to contingent variations. Consumers (both fair-trade and non-fair-trade) are motivated by a complex multitude of logics and moralities, making a consistent performance across space and time difficult to maintain. Our dispositions towards consumer goods are influenced by cultural conventions and shared meanings, cultural representations, institutional frameworks and systems of provision. Consequently this book explores how these various elements come together to shape and coordinate fair-trade consumption behaviour or 'choice'. Moving away from accounts of abstract individual choice, the reader will learn that reflexivity is a much more 'situated' phenomenon (Adams & Raisborough, 2008), and is thus enacted and empowered by various kinds of local, national and transnational social practices. How fair-trade consumption is publicly represented by national and international organisations, the availability and accessibility of fair-trade goods across various locations, and the social norms that surround the fair-trade consumer 'choice', must all be taken into consideration if we are to understand how and why fair-trade consumption is or is not accomplished in practice.

Not everyone will have the same degree of commitment towards, understandings of or opportunities to access fair-trade goods, but by examining the circumstances under which individuals or groups learn about fair-trade, and perhaps go on to support it, this book argues that we are able to gain a clearer idea of what being a fair-trade supporter might entail. An individual's dispositions towards fair-trade consumption are developed through their immersion in organised practices – for example, many of the fair-trade supporters I spoke with first learnt about and came into contact with fair-trade through their membership at the local church or Co-operative society (or some other organised network), and they connected their support of fair-trade with these already-existing commitments. I suggest that attention must be paid to an individual's 'career' of fair-trade support if we are to understand the meanings and motivations behind fair-trade consumption. Indeed, those who had not been involved in practices of fair-trade support were less likely to be committed to fair-trade and more likely to organise their consumption according to different logics with alternative moralities. By widening the focus beyond consumption acts and paying attention to the context within which these acts occur, we will see how consumption is often not the most important way for an individual to register their support for the fair-trade movement.

The representation of fair-trade consumption as a form of individual political participation or citizenship presents an important arena for sociological exploration. For hundreds of years, the sphere of consumption has been used as a tool for the expression of political voice. However in recent years, appeals to the figure of the citizen-consumer have become increasingly prevalent – for example, within UK policy debates around the provision of public services in which the mantra of individual choice has been pervasive (see Malpass et al., 2007b; Needham, 2007), and also within debates around wider forms of sustainable and healthy consumption practices that call upon citizen-consumers to change their behaviour in order to achieve a public goal. While what follows will be a discussion of consumer-citizenship as exemplified within fair-trade discourses, the issues raised do have wider implications.

First, attempts to encourage citizen-consumers towards particular types of behaviour tend to place a great deal of emphasis on the importance of providing information to individuals so that they can choose wisely. However, as we will see, this approach assumes that consumers'/citizens' behaviour is infinitely malleable and ignores the importance of an individual's existing commitments and practical concerns, as well as the local environment in which they are operating, all of which are likely to limit the 'choices' open to them and their ability or willingness to actually receive/absorb, as well as act upon, the information provided. Southerton, Warde & Hand (2004) have spoken of the 'limited autonomy of the consumer' and highlight how consumption is socially constrained by one's economic and cultural resources, social norms and technical infrastructures or 'choice-sets'. The implications of such an approach are that 'strategies for changing consumption depend ultimately on the transformation of practices' rather than providing more information or incentives to individuals (ibid.: 33). For Kjærnes, Harvey and Warde (2007), it is equally important to question how the role of the 'consumer' may actually vary within different socio-political contexts. In their study of consumer trust in food across six European countries, the authors discovered significant variations in levels of consumer activism, which could be related back to how state regulation and market responsibility are differently institutionalised in different countries – with consumers in Norway least likely to engage in consumer activism owing to their high levels of trust in state institutions to regulate the market, and consumers in the UK most likely to identify with the active consumer model. It is for this reason that this volume explores how fairtrade has developed in different countries (UK, Sweden and USA) and the role of socio-political contexts in the construction of the citizen-consumer, as well as focusing upon how fair-trade consumer behaviour is embedded in social practices.

Secondly, and closely related to the first point, this book encourages us to reconsider the passivity that is attributed to those who do not (knowingly) engage in citizen-consumer activity compared to those who do. It is often assumed that those who do not engage in a topic or practice of interest lack the necessary information or understandings in order to participate, rather than interest being directed to their own practices and priorities. Uniquely, this study pays attention to 'non-fair-trade supporters' in the UK, who were likely to have consumed fair-trade at some point but were often unaware of fair-trade when they were shopping and instead spoke about the ways in which their consumption was ordinarily ethical by virtue of the fact that it was connected to their commitments to their family and friends. When asked about fair-trade, the majority of non-fair-trade supporters could recognise the moral value of trying to help producers receive a fair price for their crop; they were, however, often quite critical of the suggestion that consuming fair-trade was the only way to be a responsible citizen and sceptical that changing their individual consumption habits would have much impact upon poverty in the developing world. The moral, practical and political challenges made by non-fair-trade supporters are taken seriously because these individuals are, after all, fair-trade consumers whether they like it (or know it) or not, and it is therefore interesting to hear what they think rather than dismiss them as inert or irrelevant. Of course, directing attention to a group of individuals who are defined through being outside of a particular circle forces the researcher to confront a difficult methodological problem of recruitment (because non-fair-trade supporters are more diffuse than a group of 'anti-activists'), but every attempt ought to be made to gather their views because they enable us to interrogate the assumed passivity of non-participation. This approach has the potential to inform consideration of non-participants in studies of citizen engagement more generally.

In what follows, I highlight an important tension within the consumer-citizenship model, which on the one hand promotes the power of individual choice, but on the other hand uses this to institutionalise forms of collective purchasing. I also demonstrate the importance of separating forms of support for the fair-trade movement from the actual consumption of fair-trade goods. When consumers and supporters of fair-trade are taken to be the same and the only voices that are heard are those that combine the two (as exemplified in the earlier quotation from Taplin), I argue that we miss a great deal. On the one hand, the fair-trade supporter may not actually (consistently) purchase fair-trade, and may engage in a number of campaigning activities beyond what is required of the relatively passive citizen-consumer (in an activist context); on the other hand, consumers of fair-trade goods may not even be aware of fair-trade and far less be explicit supporters of its aims or claims – indeed, they may have specific critiques of the fair-trade movement and reasoned scepticism, which are not given a voice when consumers are conflated with supporters. We also miss a key contradiction in the citizen-consumer model, which takes non-supporters to be 'blank sheets' to be imprinted with the principles and practices of consumer-citizenship at the same time as these individuals are unknowingly consuming fair-trade and thus represented as already possessing these qualities.

While this book is about fair-trade consumption, it affects the way we think about the malleability of consumer behaviour, the morality (or ethics) of consumption and forms of political participation more generally. It investigates the perceived differences between the supporter and the non-supporter, and considers how individuals' engagements in particular social practices in specific cultural contexts are likely to influence their dispositions towards consumer goods and political/moral campaigns. Littler (2009; 2011) has argued that 'radical' forms of consumption, like fair-trade, ought not to be celebrated uncritically as a positive force for social change but neither should they be dismissed without recognising the political potential 'of the very enthusiasm people can bring to ethical consumption' (Littler, 2011: 33). Fair-trade does generate 'resources of hope' for some consumers, but as academic commentators it is important also to explore how this relates to wider political systems of trade injustice and to interrogate the possibilities and limitations of a consumerist strategy for achieving structural changes to global inequalities.

## Research design and structure of the book

This research project is based upon a selection of qualitative methods (nine focus-groups, participant observation, documentary research and 19 in-depth individual/couple interviews) conducted between January 2008 and February 2009 in a Fairtrade Town in the UK (Chelmsford). I supplemented this in-depth study with ten additional interviews conducted in April and June 2011 in Berkeley Fair Trade Town (CA, USA) and Lund Fairtrade City (Sweden) respectively, as well as attending the International Fair Trade Towns Conference in November 2011 where I met fair-trade supporters from all over the world. The material gathered in Chelmsford within the UK context forms the bulk of research presented in Chapters 5 to 8, following the author's in-depth case study of fair-trade supporters and non-fair-trade supporters living within this Fairtrade Town. I chose to base the research within Fairtrade Towns because it both gave me access to committed fair-trade supporters and provided the opportunity to explore how the distinctive features of different towns impacted upon the way fair-trade supporter networks developed and were promoted. In Chelmsford, I conducted focus groups and interviews with non-fair-trade supporters because these individuals have been largely ignored in the existing accounts of fair-trade consumption. I found in the course of my research that these non-fair-traders were often consuming fair-trade without being aware of it, yet there remained the question of what it was that these individuals perceived was stopping them from using/supporting fair-trade. The broadening of the research to account for international variations in fair-trade support in 2011 enabled me to reflect upon the generalisability of this in-depth case-study and draw out some important variations in the practice of fair-trade support between countries. The qualitative data is complemented by quantitative analysis of a question on the UK National Omnibus Survey (2002–5), which asked individuals to rate the effectiveness of buying fair-trade goods relative to other individual political and ethical actions, such as paying taxes or donating to charity. Using a 'sequential-mixed design' (Teddlie & Tashakkori, 2009), each phase of data collection built upon and informed the execution and analysis of the other phases.

Chapter 2 explores the existing research into fair-trade consumption in more depth, paying particular attention to how the conditions of late modernity and globalisation (Beck, 1994; Giddens, 1991) have been used as principal explanatory forces underlying individuals' motivations to use their consumption in political ways. The chapter challenges this position by exploring the 'making' of the fair-trade citizen-consumer and demonstrating how this figure has emerged, not solely because of changing market conditions, but through the concerted efforts of a range of intermediary actors with distinct objectives. This chapter sets the scene for the discussion that follows by arguing that the abstract figure of the fair-trade citizen-consumer must be re-evaluated in order to take account of the specific contexts in which fair-trade consumption is achieved.

Chapter 3 examines the development of the international fair-trade consumer movement, with an in-depth focus upon the movement in the UK, Sweden and USA. Existing studies of the fair-trade movement tend to present it as a relatively homogenous movement across socio-political contexts. However, this chapter shows that there are distinct differences in the way the fair-trade consumer is mobilised and how conceptions of consumer power are institutionalised within the three countries. Having said this, it is possible to detect common promotional strategies within the international movement, and Chapter 4 focuses on two of the major promotional tools used in all three countries – the Fairtrade Towns movement and the fair-trade promotional period. Both these strategies are shown to operate as powerful market devices (Callon, Méadel & Rabeharisoa, 2002), which engage diverse actors – fair-trade organisations, local and national government, NGOs, businesses, local activists and the media – who together shape the qualities and availability of fair-trade goods in a world of similar commodities. Particular attention is given to the collective cultures that develop around the notion of fair-trade consumer power and their role in legitimising fair-trade choice-editing. I also explore the consequences of these promotional campaigns among those who do not count themselves as fair-trade supporters.

Chapter 5 presents the findings from the in-depth interviews with residents in Chelmsford. After introducing the theory of practice approach to consumption (Halkier, 2010; Warde, 2005), I trace the 'careers' of four committed fair-trade supporters, focusing on how the actions of these individuals work to extend the practice of fair-trade consumption and their existing commitments to ethical and political campaigns. The outward-looking practices of these fair-trade supporters are then compared to a narrative from a couple who have 'resisted recruitment' to the practice of fair-trade support because of their commitment to a yogic-vegetarian lifestyle. This chapter demonstrates that there is much more to being a fair-trade supporter than merely buying fair-trade goods.

Chapter 6 addresses the often-ignored social identity of the fair-trade citizen-consumer and considers the politics of inclusion and exclusion that this identity can evoke. Building on a long tradition in cultural sociology, it asks whether fair-trade consumption is used by fair-trade supporters as a form of class distinction revealing their superior taste over others. While work by Varul (2008b) has argued that fair-trade consumption is understood as a form of class distinction, this chapter reveals a more complex picture based on the difficulty of categorising morality and ethical judgements by social class. Using Sayer's (2005a) concept of 'lay normativity', I argue that fair-trade consumption is often valued in and of itself regardless of its association with any social status group. The relation between fair-trade, social class and morality is further complicated by a blurry boundary between the exclusivity and ordinariness of fair-trade consumption in view of the changes to systems of fair-trade provisioning and practices of fair-trade support that are expanding the availability of these goods at comparable prices. But that does not mean to say that social class is irrelevant, as I demonstrate.

Chapter 7 presents the findings from the National Omnibus Survey in order to explore how individuals rate the effectiveness of fair-trade consumption relative to other individual actions, such as donating to charity, paying one's taxes or putting pressure on politicians. Although consumption is represented as an important and new form of political participation, almost no attention has been given to how effective citizens believe this action to be. The findings from the survey are supplemented with views from respondents in Chelmsford who reveal some important challenges to the concept of individual consumer power.

The final chapter draws together the various arguments and reflects upon their implications for institutions that promote and support fair-trade consumption, as well as existing and future sociological debates on (ethical) consumption practices. It highlights the possibilities and limitations of the fair-trade citizen-consumer, at the same time as it critiques models of individual consumer 'choice' and fair-trade choice-editing.

# 2
# Constructing the Fair-Trade Citizen-Consumer

> The sheer enormity of global poverty can make people feel powerless. But your choices and your point of view are taken very seriously, by both business and politicians. Your voice can make a difference in the global trade debate – as both voter and consumer:
> * Vote with your wallet – buy fairly traded goods.
>
> *Trade Matters*, DFID (2005: 36)

> Fairtrade is not just about buying and selling. It is about creating a global family. One that links citizens in the rich world with farmers and workers in Peru or Burkina Faso or India. ... It is that bringing together of people which is the defining feature of Fairtrade – and one reason why so many people warm to it. Because it is putting people back into the heart of trade and chipping away at deeply ingrained injustices.
>
> Harriet Lamb, Executive Director of the Fairtrade Foundation (2008: 2)

There has been a growing interest in addressing the potential fair-trade consumer – whether as subjects of government policies, as customers of retail outlets, or as citizens of a global society. By purchasing a fair-trade product ordinary people are told that they can make a difference to global poverty and reconnect with more personal trading relationships that a global capitalist system has undermined. Much of the existing academic literature surrounding the growth of fair-trade consumption has tended to suggest that changes in contemporary society, such as the shift of power away from nation-states and the increased reflexivity of people's lifestyle choices, can help us to understand the increased popularity of fair-trade products (Bennett, 2004; Goodman, 2004; Lyon, 2006; Micheletti, 2003; Murray & Raynolds, 2007; Scammell, 2003). Allusion to a new figure, the citizen-consumer, who uses their individual purchasing power to challenge unfair trading relations, appears as the driving force behind the growth of the fair-trade movement. Fair-trade calls on individuals to contest the traditionally acquisitive and selfish sphere of consumption and act as citizens with responsibilities and duties in the global world, thereby merging the apparently dichotomous roles of self-interested consumer and politically minded citizen.

However, on closer inspection the opposition of the spheres of consumption and citizenship is not as straightforward as popular representation suggests. Citizenship and consumption are multifaceted concepts, which have not always been polarised in terms of their perceived levels of civic engagement but rather have been configured in different relationships with one another in different contexts and in relation to different products and services. One need only look at a selected number of organised consumer movements between the eighteenth and twenty-first centuries to realise that consumers have often been called upon to use their consumption to challenge particular social and political situations. This chapter pays attention to the particular ways in which citizenship and the consumer have been framed and how the 'fair-trade citizen-consumer' has been mobilised in relation to selected conceptions of both citizenship and consumption. I argue that it is important to take into consideration the role of intermediary actors (consumer organisations, governments, NGOs) and socio-political contexts in producing and sanctioning particular forms of participation and consumption and in according them meaning as acts of citizenship.

## Fair-trade, globalisation and reflexivity

There has been a tendency to understand the rise of fair-trade consumption as a response to the conditions of late modernity and global capitalist systems. At a time when Free Trade and neo-liberal policies are increasingly blamed with widening the gap between rich and poor, fair-trade appears as a 'modern-day market-based "Robin Hood" … redistributing income from the consuming North to the producers in the South' (Goodman, 2004: 897). This section will focus on the ways in which narratives of globalisation and appeals to increased consumer reflexivity have been variously used to account for the growth of the fair-trade movement.

## Globalisation and new roles for consumers

In a global economic system, we all rely on producers in the developing world to provide us with some of our most basic commodities, and yet these producers are often living in conditions of poverty that are unimaginable for the consumer in the Western world. As the opening quotations to this chapter reveal, the fair-trade movement is presented in the context of the negative effects of globalisation and the perceived failure of the free trade movement to provide real and long-lasting benefits to producers. Murray and Raynolds describe the fair-trade movement as 'the new globalisation', which seeks to 're-frame globalisation from below' (Murray & Raynolds, 2007: 6). Globalisation is said to have led to a 'race to the bottom' where transnational corporations are competing to exploit both people and the environment for the lowest possible input costs (ibid.). The IMF, World Bank and the World Trade Organisation (WTO) have come under attack in recent years (e.g. anti-globalisation protests at the WTO meeting in Seattle in 1999) for their promotion of neo-liberal policies and their failure to provide real access for many developing nations to the markets of the developed world – for example, Global Exchange (2008) points out that many trade talks go on behind closed doors, meaning that developing countries are subject to 'agreements' they were not aware were being discussed and, for those talks that do take place in public, developing nations are often unable to represent their interests because of a lack of trade personnel. The fair-trade model attempts to address these imbalances in information and power in the current global market-system by agreeing minimum prices for crops and developing transparent and direct relationships with producers. This had led some to argue that 'Fair Trade is a sustainable, market-based solution to global trade failures' (Nicholls & Opal, 2005: 19), although some research suggests that the fair-trade model does not always operate according to these ideal principles (Dolan, 2008; Jaffee, 2007; Lyon & Moberg, 2010).

It is argued that because transnational corporations now operate outside of nation-state regulations (although in reality this is an oversimplified account of the relationship between national governments and multinational corporations: see Jensen, 2006), consumers now uniquely have 'the power and duty to safeguard both fair economic distribution and the natural environment' (Sassatelli, 2006: 230; see also Scammell, 2000; Soper, 2008). Naomi Klein's influential book, *No Logo*, used this idea to introduce a new brand of politics – which she has termed 'anticorporatism' – where consumers, on discovering the 'truth' behind global logos and their treatment of their workers and the environment, have enough 'outrage' to 'fuel the next big political movement' (Klein, 2000: xviii). Soper points out that companies' reliance on our loyalty to their brands reveals 'the growing subversive potential of consumption' (Soper, 2008: 202). Similarly Miller (1995) has argued that consumption is the 'vanguard of history', indicating a shift in political power away from production towards consumption and suggesting that the IMF and political parties of the left and right 'are increasingly the agents, not of international capitalists so much as international shopping' (Miller, 1995: 3).

It is within this context that the prototypical 'fair-trade consumer' emerges who is urged to exercise his/her responsibilities as a citizen of the global world by purchasing fair-trade. Individuals are increasingly told by fair-trade organisations, and those other agencies that appeal to the potential fair-trade consumer (e.g. government, businesses, NGOs, the media), that as the consumers of global capitalist products they hold some responsibility for the conditions under which those products were produced. In order to implicate the consumer in global chains of responsibility, fair-trade advertising plays an important role in symbolically reducing the distance between consumers and producers, and seemingly making caring-at-a-distance a 'reality' for more affluent consumers (Goodman, 2004; Raynolds, 2002; Wright, 2004). With close-up images of fair-trade farmers and vignettes describing their family life, consumers can begin to 'know' these people and empathise with their situation. As Harriet Lamb (Executive Director of the Fairtrade Foundation) remarked, in one of the opening quotations to this chapter, fair-trade is about creating a 'global family' and 'bringing people together'. However, as Barnett, Cloke, Clarke & Malpass (2005) point out, we should not assume that once chains of global relations are made visible it automatically becomes easier for all consumers to act upon them.

In an analysis of ethical consumption campaigns by the Ethical Consumer Research Association (ECRA) and the Fairtrade Foundation (FTF), Clarke et al. draw attention to the rhetorical importance of the discourse of globalisation, which implies a number of key changes in contemporary society and calls upon the empowered consumer to regulate economic institutions – to become 'citizens of the world by virtue of their status as consumers' (Clarke et al., 2007a: 243). The authors suggest that by drawing attention to consumers' responsibility for systems of global exploitation and by calling on consumers to use the global market in order to act upon these responsibilities, ethical consumer organisations turn the discourse of globalisation, which traditionally highlights the dominance of companies over individuals and local places, into an affirmative narrative of consumer empowerment. However, Clarke et al. also point out that the audience for this type of information tends to be rather self-selecting, providing narrative and informational resources for those who are already interested and have some sympathy with the fair-trade movement's aims, rather than for the generic 'consumer'. I pay further attention to the implications of this finding later, but for now it is enough to point out that the empowered global citizen-consumer, who is motivated to take responsibility for the global implications of their consumption, is not just anybody.

### Reflexive consumers

The use of discourses of globalisation to understand the rise of fair-trade consumption is very often accompanied by allusions to an increasingly 'reflexive' consumer. Giddens (1990; 1991) and Beck (1992; 1994) have suggested that the conditions of late modernity – globalisation, space-time distanciation, detraditionalisation, individualisation – have created a climate in which a highly reflexive self emerges. Reflexivity is the capacity of an individual subject to direct their awareness towards themselves, reflecting upon their own practices, and constantly examining and reforming these practices in the light of incoming information (Giddens, 1990: 38). While reflexivity is not a new human capacity, Giddens suggests that it is radicalised in late modernity because, as tradition loses hold, individuals are increasingly forced to negotiate their identity from a huge diversity of options in which the 'dialectical interplay of the local and the global' are embedded (Giddens, 1991: 5). Individuals living within the conditions of late modernity have 'no choice but to choose how to be and how to act' (Giddens, 1994: 75).

For both Giddens and Beck, there is a concern with how these changes alter the possibilities for political participation. For Beck, individuals become distrustful of the traditional political system, feeling they are limited in their actions in this sphere, and new demands for political participation emerge *outside* the political system in the form of a 'new political culture' governed by social movements (Beck, 1994: 185). As our traditional understandings of politics shift in late modernity, and as individuals must negotiate their own identities through their self-reflexive lifestyle choices, politics can increasingly be understood as a 'politics of life decisions' (Giddens, 1991: 215). 'Life politics', or 'sub politics' as Beck (1994) terms it, brings to the fore moral questions about how we ought to live our lives, and these moral issues are articulated both collectively, by governments and social movements, and individually in everyday lifestyle choices. In this way, the reflexive project of the self becomes intimately entwined with life-political issues as individuals attempt to construct a coherent biographical narrative and maintain a sense of ontological security.

It is this increased capacity for the reflexive monitoring of our actions that some writers have suggested can help us to understand the emergence of fair-trade consumption (Bennett, 2004; Goodman, 2004; Lyon, 2006; Micheletti, 2003; Murray & Raynolds, 2007; Scammell, 2003). The consumer is imagined to use the emerging global reflexive space to engage in a form of 'self-directed life-politics', which draws on his/her 'ability to self-actualise while constructing a morally justifiable form of life in the context of global interdependence' (Lyon, 2006: 456). Micheletti's work on political consumerism provides the most extensive application of the notion of life-politics to understand 'new' forms of politicised consumption, like fair-trade. She argues that changes in the political landscape have politicised consumption so that our everyday lives as consumers 'are increasingly intertwined with global politics' (Micheletti, 2003: xi). She suggests that because consumers have to rely on the global marketplace for the provision of goods, most consumers are forced to trust the retailers and corporations we depend upon for our daily existence. However, this leaves us vulnerable, especially when we are told about the bad practices of global corporations. In the face of our lack of control over production processes, citizens are prompted to 'take politics in their own hands ... creating new arenas for responsibility-taking' (ibid.: 5). Onto the political landscape emerges a new figure, the 'citizen-consumer', who combines his/her role as consumer and citizen to develop 'new coalitions to solve problems of risk society and global injustices' (ibid.: 16).

Important to draw out here is how consumption and citizenship are imagined to hold *new* and *powerful* associations in the late modern/ global society. Indeed, many discussions of fair-trade consumption have become synonymous with consumer-citizenship. We can see how this discourse draws heavily on ideas of 'life politics' where consumers are imagined to find new opportunities to engage with political and moral questions in their daily lifestyle choices in the late modern world. Given the significance placed upon the figure of the citizen-consumer, the next section will explore how these two traditionally opposing identities have become hyphenated.

However, in closing this section on reflexivity, the reader should be made aware that the 'reflexivity thesis' has 'been greeted with a cacophony of critical voices' because of its tendency to lift individuals out of the social relations they are embedded within and to ignore a whole range of material, cultural and affective factors that are likely to constrain or enable an individual to construct their self-identity (Adams & Raisborough, 2008: 1169). If we follow through the implications of the reflexivity thesis to the extreme, we are left with the suggestion that all individuals upon becoming aware of the existence of global inequalities will act upon this information by using their consumer power to construct a morally justifiable self-identity. This explanation (although exaggerated) ignores the fact that people from different social situations with different experiences are likely to be differentially motivated to act. Adams and Raisborough have suggested that what is needed is a more 'situated' account of reflexivity, which acknowledges that attention needs to be given to how reflexivity emerges in specific and localised contexts rather than constructing 'a seemingly universal, disembedded and disembodied self' (ibid.). Indeed, if we look at the small number of empirical studies that have reported on the socio-demographic characteristics of ethical consumer behaviour we persistently find that the propensity to engage in this behaviour is stratified according to social class, income, level of education and gender, as well as being influenced by individuals' existing attitudes, practices and commitments, and the cultural contexts in which it is carried out (Co-op, 2007; Cowe & Williams, 2001; De Pelsmaker et al., 2007; Dickson, 2005; European Commission, 1997; Littrell & Dickson, 1999; Newholm, 2005; Pirotte, 2007; Tallontire, Rentsendorj & Blowfield, 2001; Varul, 2008a; 2008b). Those who *knowingly* engage in ethical consumer behaviour are likely to have particular characteristics and forms of knowledge that predispose them to use fair-trade products, but not all individuals are equally willing or able to take part in a 'self-directed life politics' in an emerging global reflexive space.

## The rise of the citizen-consumer

The request for consumers to 'vote with their wallet' made by the Department for International Development (DFID) in the opening quotation to this chapter, suggests that citizens are being called upon to use their purchasing choices as a way of demonstrating their responsibility to distant strangers. The use of the word 'vote' seems to imply a democratic process often associated with the rights of citizens within a nation. The authors of a recent study into the rise of the citizen-consumer point out that consumption and citizenship have traditionally been understood to sit at opposite ends of the political spectrum, with the consumer indulging their individual, private wants in the marketplace and the citizen being an outward-looking figure who embraces the public interest (Clarke et al., 2007). In recent years the citizen-consumer has become an increasingly utilised concept and has been widely applied to the fair-trade consumer (Carter, 2001; Clarke et al., 2007a; Lamb, 2008; Micheletti, 2003; Scammell, 2000; 2003; Soper, 2004; 2008). Indeed, Harriet Lamb explicitly refers to fair-trade consumers as 'citizens in the rich world'.

For some, fair-trade represents 'the founding of a nascent international moral economy', or a 'novel morality', with its promotion of a 'critical consumer culture which challenges the individualistic, competitive and ethically impoverished culture of capitalism' (Fridell, 2006: 86; Goodman, 2004). However, historians of consumer movements have demonstrated how consumers have regularly been called upon to tackle important social and political issues. Thus, it is not the case that newly reflexive consumers have 'discovered agency and morality only in recent battles for fair trade' but rather that 'consumers and social movements have throughout modern history played an integral role in the creation of global markets and imperial systems' (Trentmann, 2007: 1080). This section begins by highlighting some of the continuities between fair-trade consumer activism and other organised consumer movements between the eighteenth and twentieth centuries. It will show how different visions of consumer power have been regularly mobilised in the pursuit of moral and political objectives. In particular, it focuses on the ways in which coalitions of interest groups have come together at specific points in time in order to construct an image of the citizen-consumer. I go on to argue that the rise of the 'fair-trade citizen-consumer' identity must likewise be understood as the contingent outcome of a coalition of intermediary actors, with various objectives, operating within distinct socio-political contexts.

## Fair-trade as a continuing morality

In 1790s, a pamphlet was launched by a coalition of Quakers and abolitionists that encouraged people to take action against the slave trade by abstaining from the use of slave-grown sugar (Midgley, 1992; Sussman, 2000). This pamphlet went into 25 editions and 50,000 copies were printed in four months (Sussman, 2000: 38). At the height of this campaign, around 300,000 families were abstaining from using slave-grown sugar. The mobilisation of a consumerist strategy to challenge the economic and moral imperative for slavery was novel and was made possible because of a growing political and cultural awareness that consumption was a force that drove the economy. Sussman suggests that the growth in the agency and power of individual consumers can be attributed, in part, to the shift from mercantile capitalism to free-market capitalism, as well as the growing popularity of Adam Smith's economic theories, which stressed the important role of (luxury) consumption in sustaining the economy. The consumer was granted new moral responsibilities and powers in the emerging free-trade capitalist market, and the abolitionists used these conditions to their advantage to convince their readers that 'consumption involved ... the "fundamental right" to be able to choose' (Sussman, 2000: 43). The British consumer was placed 'at the head of a chain of actions', with the slave traders and plantation owners as mere 'agents' of the consumer (ibid.: 41).[1] Discussions of fair-trade consumption have given great explanatory power to the emerging global capitalist system and the rise of consumer reflexivity; however, the slave-grown sugar campaign reveals how similar conditions (the emerging free-market economy) were utilised by social and political activists in order to construct an active (reflexive) consumer identity over two hundred years ago. Having said this, although it may appear that the slave-grown sugar campaign represents an early example of fair-trade activities through its mobilisation of a citizen-consumer to care for distant others, Trentmann has cautioned of the danger of constructing 'pure moral antecedents out of ambivalent past traditions' (Trentmann, 2007: 1097). We cannot ignore the imperialist morality that imbued the campaign, nor the stark gender, class and 'race' hierarchies through which the campaign was played out.

Moralities of consumptions 'are always specific to time and cultural context, and are mediated by other existing traditions' (ibid.: 1097). For example, the National Consumer's Leagues, which emerged in the late nineteenth and early twentieth century in Europe and America, exhibited differences in the ways they organised their campaign and addressed the citizen-consumer. The Consumer's Leagues were predominantly female-led organisations seeking to improve labour conditions for workers through the promotion of ethical shopping (Atley, 1978; Black, 1887; Breckman, 1991; Chessel, 2006a; 2006b; Coffin, 1991; Cohen, 2003; Sklar, 1998). In America, the American National Consumers' League (NCL) grew out of the socialist tradition and encouraged middle-class women to shop only at those approved employers that offered fair working conditions for their staff – the NCL produced 'white lists' (Sklar, 1998). Later, the NCL developed a White Label, which was attached to women's undergarments to certify that the product had been produced under conditions that adhered to state factory law and did not involve forced overtime or child labour, representing a similar 'buycott' strategy to fair-trade labelling initiatives today.[2] This consumerist strategy was used by the NCL as the first stepping stone to lobbying for wider reform and policy interventions. In France, however, the Ligue Sociale d'Acheteurs (LSA) drew its support from a Social Catholic base[3] and had a membership that was skewed towards the upper and middle classes (Chessel, 2006a; 2006b). The workers the LSA sought to help were only ever imagined as workers and not as consumers, meaning that the reform suggestions proffered by the organisation were somewhat out of step with the reality of working life for women.[4] Unlike the American NCL, which lobbied the US government directly for reform changes, the LSA acted more indirectly by using consumer activism as an 'opportunity to affect the mentality and social action of Catholics' as well as playing a role, principally through research into working conditions, in the wider movement to reform labour legislation (Chessel, 2006a: 93). Therefore, the different social make-up of these Consumer's Leagues within distinct social and political contexts had an important impact on the forms of campaigning available to the leagues and the type of citizen-consumer they attempted to appeal to.

Throughout modern history, the consumer has offered 'an ideal broad-based constituency' who could be mobilised to address and reform social and political problems (Cohen, 2003: 21–2). However,

> consumers did not rise effortlessly as an automatic response to the spread of markets but had to be made. And this process of making occurred through mobilisation in civil society and the state as well as in the commercial domain, under conditions of deprivation, war and constraint as well as affluence and choice, and articulated through traditions of political ideas and ethics.
>
> Trentmann (2006: 6)

The organised consumer movements discussed thus far have relied upon a coalition of interested individuals and groups who appealed to the figure of a consumer that they themselves had constructed in line with their own concerns and in response to their immediate socio-political context. The movement organisers had an explicit aim – whether that was ending the slave trade within the Empire, or reforming labour policy – and they each used their figure of the 'citizen-consumer' to create popular support for these aims and/or to influence government policy.

A good example of the construction of the 'citizen-consumer' by an organised consumer movement can be found in the Co-operative movement in Britain in the nineteenth and twentieth centuries.[5] The Co-operative movement is particularly important when we come to consider how it configured the knowledge about its aims with the identity of the consumer. The Co-operative movement did not seek short-term political changes at the level of the state but rather sought to build a cultural revolution that would realise the transformative potential of the movement in the long term. The Co-operative movement's 'ultimate ambition was to reintegrate the economy into the common social life of the people' to create a cooperative commonwealth, and in order to do this there was a need to create a feeling of community among its members (Gurney, 1999: 143). Retail co-operatives were member-owned businesses whose distribution of profits was related to member's purchases rather than upon their ownership of shares – the innovative 'divi'. The 'divi' was an important way of securing the loyalty of the co-operative consumer,[6] and the movement placed a strong emphasis on the provision of social and cultural activities, principally education (lectures and reading rooms at libraries), because it was hoped that the working classes could become empowered and equipped with the tools to transform existing social, economic and political relations. Working-class, married women were particularly important to the creation of a social life around the store both as daily shoppers[7] and as organised members of the Women's Co-operative Guild. The store also arranged recreational activities, like the Co-operative festival, which provided entertainment for the whole family and helped to promote the Co-operative movement and working-class members' loyalty to it.[8] The movement organisers sought to construct an active community of consumers who would support the collective campaign for a co-operative commonwealth. While this utopian commonwealth was never realised, by the outbreak of the First World War Co-operative membership had reached well over three million (Gurney, 1996: 18).

Although civil society organisations, governments and individuals construct a particular image of the 'consumer' in order to promote their specific agendas, it does not necessarily follow that individuals understand their consumption in the same way as these intermediary actors represent it. There is often a gap between the campaign language and both the consumer's motivation for engaging in the campaign and the consumer's organisation of their consumption. So, for example, Sussman argued that on a textual level slave-grown sugar became synonymous with the flesh and blood of the slave, with a suspicion that commodities produced under conditions of intolerable cruelty 'retained traces of the violence with which they were appropriated' (Sussman, 2000: 13–14).[9]

On the one hand consumers abstained from consuming slave-grown produce as part of a 'moral and spiritual commitment to the welfare of the slave' (ibid.: 37), but on the other hand there was an awareness of 'the dangerous repercussions' the ingestion of slave grown sugar could have. In the same vein, Hilton's (2003) account of the Consumers' Association (CA)[10] reveals how the founders of this consumer-testing organisation attached an idealistic vision to their rational direction of consumption and production. They believed it would be possible to create a better society with consumers acting as a counterweight to industry, forcing bad manufacturers to improve their standards and enabling good ones to prosper. However, although the activist milieu of the CA were committed to consumerism as a social movement, the majority of the subscribers to *Which?* had little knowledge of the wider aims of the organisation (Black, 2004).

We have seen through this brief examination of four organised consumer movements that fair-trade consumption does not really represent a 'novel morality', as Goodman (2004) and others have argued, but rather a 'continuing morality'. The emergence of the new political economy of the free market did not demoralise the economy and trade (Thompson, 1991) but rather provided new ways of thinking about consumption and morality. Fridell's suggestion that fair-trade is an attempt to 're-moralise' the theory of trade and consumption seems to imply that everything after free trade and before fair-trade has been unable to connect with those lost traditional values of entitlement, fairness and community. But, as this discussion has demonstrated, the assumption that consumption is an automatically selfish and apolitical sphere cannot be sustained because the identities of the consumer and citizen have regularly been stitched together, creating linkages between the political and commercial domain (Nixon, 2008). Indeed, the doctrine of free trade was in fact championed by working-class, radical, feminist and peace movements because of its potential to foster reciprocity and goodwill across the globe (Trentmann, 2007). It is surprising therefore that such little attention and recognition has been given to earlier consumer movements in discussions of fair-trade consumption today, given that they pioneered the types of consumer mobilisation so frequently invoked by fair-trade organisations, such as boycotts, buycotts, consumer education, provision of social and cultural events, and so on. Consumption has long been targeted as an arena for the expression of political concerns. But the citizen-consumer had to be 'made' by various intermediary actors in specific socio-political, cultural and economic contexts rather than this figure emerging automatically because of changing societal conditions (Trentmann, 2006). This process of making-up the citizen-consumer as a public figure does not always match how consumers understand and organise their consumption. It follows that any examination of the rise of the 'fair-trade citizen consumer' must address both this process of mobilisation and the different ways individuals use and give meaning to fair-trade goods in their daily lives.

## Mobilising the fair-trade citizen-consumer

Fair-trade consumption has only become aligned with citizenship because various commercial, civic, academic and political institutions have mobilised the fair-trade consumer in this way. While it may be the case that not all individuals who consume fair-trade necessarily understand their actions as a form of citizenship, the citizen-consumer remains an important figure through which to publicly represent fair-trade and to recruit supporters (Clarke et al., 2007a). Miller and Rose (1997) have suggested that organisations that promote consumption use 'productive' techniques to mobilise and 'make-up' 'the consumer' – they focused on the forms of 'psy-expertise' used by advertisers in the 1950s. The 'consumer' is thus an active achievement of the various knowledge systems and intermediary actors who connect 'human passions' with the specific qualities of particular consumer goods and use this knowledge 'to act upon consumer choices' (Miller & Rose, 1997: 4). The importance of paying attention to both the role of intermediary actors and the socio-political context in the construction of consumer identities is demonstrated effectively by Liz Cohen's (2003) *A Consumer's Republic*. Although citizens and consumers are often considered as opposites, Cohen points out that 'no simple distinction between these roles [has] held true over the course of the twentieth century' (Cohen, 2003: 8). Rather they were 'ever-shifting categories that sometimes overlapped [and] often were in tension' (ibid.). Cohen focuses on different periods of American history – in particular, the New Deal Era (early 1930s), the Second World War and the post-war era (which Cohen labels the 'Consumer's Republic) – and in each of these periods draws attention to how specific contexts enabled particular configurations of the relationship between consumers and citizens to develop. Her work encourages us to pay close attention to the role of business interests, labour concerns, protest movements[11] and governmental policies in shaping the historically contingent and shifting relationship between consumption and citizenship.

Following this, it is therefore important to situate the emergence of the fair-trade citizen-consumer into the wider socio-political context that has attributed powers to consumers – in particular, the privatisation of public services in the UK and USA, which marked a moment when the 'consumer' became a much more important political figure (Kjærnes, Harvey & Warde, 2007: 95). The neo-liberal policies of the Thatcherite Conservative government in the UK and the Reagan Administration in the USA in the 1980s appealed to the consumer enshrined in neoclassical economics as a rational-economic actor regulating services in a market free from state intervention.[12] This moment, marked by the diffusion of the economic doctrines of the New Right, drew the 'consumer' 'into the limelight of public debate' (ibid.). The continual references to 'the consumer', in both economic and political language, 'has provided a major impetus to a notion that consumers are increasingly active and powerful', which has led a number of powerful organisations to direct their attention to this figure at the close of the twentieth century (ibid.). In this moment, when the 'consumer' was conceptualised as a powerful figure across all major institutions, from government to consumer organisations, producers and multinational corporations, the idea of the fair-trade citizen-consumer began to gain strength. The citizen-consumer was called upon to recognise the changing structure of contemporary society, which could no longer rely on political intervention to control the economy and redistribute wealth through a public welfare state and was subject to the control of world economic institutions (like the World Bank and the IMF) who answered to the demands of multinational corporations. Interest groups, like Oxfam, Traidcraft and the World Development Movement, increasingly appealed to and used this figure of the citizen-consumer to promote their demands for fairer trading rules with government institutions and businesses and to gain legitimacy for their own advocacy work. The fair-trade consumer was thus mobilised as a citizen of the world who 'voted' through their purchases and whose interests were represented by the intermediary actors – NGOs, consumer organisations, social movements – who played a key role in their construction.

In their analysis of the ethical consumption campaigns, Clarke et al. (2007a) explore this 'making' of the fair-trade consumer and suggest that the relationship of this type of consumption to forms of political engagement is 'a contingent achievement of strategically motivated actors with specific objectives in the public realm' (Clarke et al., 2007a: 231). They suggest that the mobilisation of the fair-trade citizen-consumer identity is achieved by organisations like ECRA and the FTF, who both provide information to already-interested individuals and generate information about the fair-trade consumer in order to make this figure visible in the public realm. On the one hand, ethical consumer organisations produce a number of publications, like *The Ethical Consumer*, and coordinate campaigns like Fairtrade Fortnight, which attract a 'self selected' audience who are already concerned about the implications of their everyday consumption and who use these resources to sustain their engagement with fair-trade. On the other hand, the same organisations that are responsible for providing information and narrative storylines to fair-trade consumers are also responsible for generating information about the 'fair-trade consumer' and making this figure visible in the public realm. By collecting survey data detailing the potential size of the ethical consumer market and representing this as indicative of individuals' active consumption choices, it is possible to attract media coverage, which is an important way these organisations can raise awareness about issues and establish 'the legitimacy of their own claims and the validity of their own arguments' (ibid.: 241). Organisations like Traidcraft, Oxfam, the FTF and Christian Aid are engaged in advocacy work with governments and corporations, which relies on them being able to show they have 'broad-based popular support for the sorts of changes they are promoting', such as unfair trading rules and cancelling Third World debt (ibid.). Their survey data, which details the various acts of fair-trade consumption, provides them with this. In this way, Clarke et al. suggest that 'it is acts, not identities or beliefs, which matter in mobilising the presence of "ethical consumers" in the public realm' (ibid.). What is important is to show that fair-trade products are being bought, which can then be represented as indicative of the active choices of thousands of consumers who support efforts to challenge fairer trading rules, even if in practice all those people who buy fair-trade do not understand their consumption in this way or fit the image of the citizen-consumer.

This section has suggested that the alignment of fair-trade consumption with conceptions of citizenship serves a particular agenda of those organisations that promote fair-trade consumption and is made possible because of the wider socio-political context that has attributed power to the figure of the 'consumer'. However, it is also made possible because it assumes particular versions of the 'citizen' and 'consumer'. Both citizenship and consumption are contested categories that mean different things to different people in different contexts. Their conceptual separation has been maintained through the use of ideal-typical formulations of the consumer and citizen that fail to reflect the complexity of these two identities. While citizenship is imagined to be an egalitarian, public and collective action and consumption is imagined to be a selfish, private and individualist action, scholars of both citizenship and consumer studies reveal a much more complex picture of these two spheres (Heater, 1999; Janowitz, 1994; Miller, 1998; Sassatelli, 2007; Soper & Trentmann, 2008).

## Traditions of citizenship and the elusive 'consumer'

Heater identifies two traditions in the history of discussions on the nature of citizenship – 'the civic republican style, which places its stress on duties, and the liberal style, which emphasises rights' (Heater, 1999: 4). It is the former of these that tends to be placed as a counterweight to consumption. Civic-republicanism comes from the model of ancient Greek society and was expounded in the writings of Aristotle. The civic republican tradition calls for the balance between 'freedom and rights for the individual on the one hand and commitment and duties to the community on the other' (Heater, 1999: 72). It assumes the active participation of all citizens who 'share in the civic life of ruling and being ruled' (Aristotle, 1948 cited in Heater, 1994: 45). It has been argued that consumption eroded this tradition of citizenship because its 'transnational and fluid forces' ran counter to the organising principles and mentality of republican citizenship, which was based in small territories and communities (Soper & Trentmann, 2008: 3). The acquisitive nature of consumption, with its focus on personal pleasure, was seen to operate in direct opposition to the participation in public life demanded by the republican tradition.

Liberal citizenship, on the other hand, with its emphasis on citizens' rights and its separation of the public and private spheres, appears to sit more easily with the ideal-typical formulation of the consumer as an individualist chooser. Heater argues that it is this liberal interpretation of citizenship 'that has shaped our current civic style' (Heater, 1999: 44). Liberal citizenship places few obligations upon the individual – mainly the payment of taxes – and accepts that the citizen has little attachment to their nation-state and their fellow citizens. When thinking of liberal understandings of citizenship, it is fair to say that Marshall's *Citizenship and Social Class* (1950), which traces the gradual extension of citizenship rights from the civil, to the political, and finally to the social sphere, has been the most influential work. However, Marshall, like the majority of texts on citizenship, paid little attention to the role of consumption in the development of these rights. Hilton's (2003) examination of the value-for-money movement in post-war Britain – where consumers were directed to make informed consumption choices so that they could become a third force in society organised to defend their rights to safe and high-quality products – seems to fit quite closely with this liberal approach to citizenship.

If we are to suggest that consumption is opposed to forms of civic participation and citizenship, it matters which tradition of citizenship we place it against. If consumption is understood as individual economic rational action, then its separation from citizenship is partially maintained in the civic republican tradition but it is not sustained in the liberal tradition. Soper and Trentmann point out that it is important to be aware of the persistence of these different interpretations of citizenship when thinking about consumption because 'these two traditions continue to provide protagonists with their main vocabularies in debating whether consumption is good or bad for public life' (Soper & Trentmann, 2008: 4).

If we look at the work of Horowitz, who has traced the anxieties surrounding affluence in American social thought from 1875 to 1979 (Horowitz, 1985; 2004), we can recognise the endurance of these two traditions in shaping the ways consumption has been represented and understood. Horowitz's work draws attention to the persistent characterisation of consumption as a 'social problem' and a fear that the 'self-indulgence of consumers' and 'a rising or changing standard of living' have endangered the 'health of America' (Horowitz, 1985: xvii). He discusses how various social commentators – from David Henry Thoreau and Alexis de Tocqueville in the nineteenth century to Lewis Mumford in the 1930s and Rachel Carson in the 1970s – have adopted a moralistic position in their calls for restrained consumption and the pursuit of more 'authentic', non-material needs in the path to achieving the good life. However, not all individuals were imagined to be equally as likely to succumb to 'the dangers of decadence' or to lose their 'self-control', and for example much of the moralist critique was directed at those in lower working-class positions (Horowitz, 1985: xi). By the 1970s, Horowitz argues that there emerged a 'post-moralist vision', which emphasised 'the liberatory and democratic possibilities of consumer culture' (Horowitz, 2004: 3). This post-moralist position offered a more 'celebratory' view of consumption, highlighting the opportunities it provides for self-realisation, protest and hedonism.[13] While the moralist position developed its critique of consumption by appealing to a republican ideal of citizenship, in which citizens (with particular socio-economic characteristics) who engage in selfish consumer behaviour fail to respect their duties to one another for the good of society as a whole, the post-moralist position seems to draw on a more liberal tradition that values the rights of individual consumers to pursue their individual needs and remarks upon the positive benefits of this for developing bonds between individuals in society.

Horowitz is careful to make the reader aware that we have not actually witnessed a transition from moralism to post-moralism, not least because he suggests that moralism resurfaced in the 1990s when the environmental and simple living movements provided a fresh wave of consumer critique, but rather that the 1970s represented a particular period when celebratory perspectives on consumption flourished and challenged much of what had come before it. Similarly, Sassatelli (2007) does not highlight a particular period during which consumption has been subject to either 'apocalyptic' or 'celebratory' views, but suggests we can find both perspectives in accounts of consumption to differing degrees from the birth of consumer society onwards. For Sassatelli, it is because the sphere of consumption can be both celebrated and denigrated that it is possible for it to emerge as a site of politics. Connections between consumption and ideas of democracy and individual rights and duties continue to be found throughout the eighteenth to twenty-first centuries, particularly demonstrated through the existence of a number of organised consumer movements, including the fair-trade movement, that have used consumption as a mechanism to challenge specific social, political, cultural and economic conditions.

Having discussed how differing understandings of citizenship have shaped attitudes towards consumption, it should have become clear to the reader that 'the consumer' cannot really be understood as a purely rational economic actor indulging in their individual wants in the marketplace, but rather is a figure that only comes into being in relation to specific practices and objects. Writers in the fields of sociology, anthropology and cultural studies have given a great deal of attention to the different faces of the consumer and have attempted to understand this figure by paying close attention to the ways individuals use and give meaning to goods within a web of social relations. Indeed, Gabriel and Lang (2006) have introduced the concept of the 'unmanageable consumer' in order to highlight the multiple identities of this figure – in a review of literature in the field of consumption, these authors identify the consumer as chooser, communicator, explorer, identity-seeker, hedonist, victim, rebel, activist and citizen. Importantly, consumption scholars have only been able to identify the multiple personalities of 'the consumer' because they have placed consumption acts into the contexts in which they occur concentrating on individual and social motivations (Bourdieu, 1984; Douglas & Isherwood, 1979; McCracken,

1988; Miller, 1998; Willis, 1978), the places and spaces of consumption (Jackson & Thrift, 1995; Low & Davenport, 2007; Malpass et al., 2007a; Nixon, 1996; Zukin, 2008) and the institutions that mediate acquisition and use (Chatriot, Chessel & Hilton, 2006; Miller & Rose, 1997; Nixon, 2003; Sassatelli, 2006). These studies reveal how consumption is 'informed by a variety of different logics' – for example, consumers may act in order to maintain social relationships, to communicate their values, to shape and express their identity, or because they are influenced by hedonistic desires. Thus, the reasons behind consumption 'are many and anything but univocal or coherent' as the ideal-typical formulation of 'the consumer' as a rational economic actor has suggested (Sassatelli, 2007: 54). Consumption can only be understood as a social phenomenon that occurs within ordinary social practices, and therefore any attempt to categorise 'the consumer' as a universal figure fails to recognise this.

It is argued that the fair-trade consumer is unique because s/he challenges the image of the consumer as a passive, private and wasteful actor by engaging in an active, public and purposeful act. Sassatelli points out that there has been an enduring tendency to view consumption through a series of dichotomies – for example, rational/irrational, active/passive, public/private – which risks making consumer culture into a 'fetish concept' rather than an object of study (ibid.: 122). Therefore, in light of the fact that consumption is informed by a 'variety of logics', it seems unlikely that the fair-trade consumer's motivations for using fair-trade will only reflect the imagined shift from private to public action. Rather, depending upon who does the consuming and where and when they do it, fair-trade consumption could be both a public and a private action, and could encompass motivations that are not entirely in keeping with the popular representations of fair-trade consumerism. For example, an individual may buy a fair-trade product because they believe it tastes better than other available options rather than because they want to support producers in the developing world; or individuals may buy fair-trade because it both tastes better and communicates their ethical taste and distinction (Varul, 2008b); or indeed, as the discussion in the Introduction made clear, they may buy fair-trade without being aware of it because of changes in the way that fair-trade products are distributed in mainstream retail outlets – they may simply want a banana.

Interpretations of consumption and citizenship are 'less substantial and solid than their representation in the liberal social imaginary suggests' (Clarke et al., 2007: 4). Instead of acknowledging this elusiveness and diversity, the organisations that promote fair-trade and the existing accounts of fair-trade consumption hang a great deal on very specific formulations of the citizen and consumer, which employ the dominant narratives of globalisation and reflexivity to imply both the novelty of the construction and its salience in the global world. Clarke et al. have suggested that, from the perspective of those organisations promoting ethical consumption, it does not matter why people buy fair-trade or who does so, but rather what matters is the ability to show that fair-trade products are popular and that consumption figures are growing. This is one consequence of the mainstreaming of fair-trade that was discussed in the Introduction. However, while from a campaigning perspective the motivations of actors may be a matter of indifference – as long as they buy – from an academic perspective it is important to interrogate and challenge the received perspective, which attributes conscious choice to consumers and elides consumption and support to better understand exactly who the fair-trade supporters actually are. The fact that the audiences for ethical consumption campaigns are likely to be those who are already disposed to support certain causes, means this question is not irrelevant to fair-trade organisations themselves; and, as I show in Chapter 4, they address this particular audience very directly at the same time as constructing a generic 'fair-trade consumer' for them to promote.

## Conclusion

This chapter began with two quotations from DFID and the FTF, each of which called upon the potential fair-trade consumer/supporter to use their consumption as a way of demonstrating their responsibility to their fellow citizens and 'voting' for fairer global trading rules. It was suggested that these quotations were indicative of a wider set of academic and policy debates, which have represented the growth of the fair-trade movement as the consequence of globalisation and late modernity and which has enabled thousands of reflexive consumers to use their consumption as a tool to exercise their political power, at the same time as constructing themselves as responsible global citizens/ethical subjects. Although a number of academic studies have argued that fair-trade consumption challenges the selfish individualism traditionally associated with the sphere of consumption, this chapter has shown that the fears of the acquisitive consumer undermining the public duty of the citizen have not always been well founded. We have seen that both citizenship and consumption are more complex than their popular representation suggests, and that the different traditions of citizenship have been used to provide very different accounts of the impact of consumption upon society. Fair-trade consumption has become aligned with notions of citizenship through the efforts of a range of intermediary actors with specific objectives in the public sphere. The construction of the consumer as a citizen, and the representation of the various acts of fair-trade consumption as the active choices of citizen-consumers by organisations like the FTF work to sustain the support of the already-interested fair-trader; to enable these organisations to claim they have widespread public support; and to create a normative vision of consumer responsibility in the wider public realm. While the majority of existing research has operated with a very abstract image of the fair-trade consumer as a newly reflexive, citizen-consumer operating according to the same logic across space and time, this chapter has suggested that this image needs to be re-evaluated in order to account for the specific contexts in which fair-trade consumption emerges. The chapters that follow explore these issues in greater depth.

# 3
# The International Fair-Trade Consumer Movement

There is a growing body of research that has revealed significant variations in the organisation of fair-trade production systems within and between countries in the developing world (Barrientos & Dolan, 2006; Dolan, 2008; Jaffee, 2007; Lyon & Moberg, 2010; Raynolds, Murray & Wilkinson, 2007). However, academic research exploring fair-trade consumption within a comparative context is limited. To my knowledge Varul (2009) offers one of the only examples of such a study. Varul examined how the fair-trade market is organised in the UK and Germany, and suggested that fair-trade consumers understand their decision to purchase fair-trade differently in these national contexts because of differing infrastructures of provision, histories of colonialism and visions of the consumer. In the UK, the privatisation of public services has led to an image of the consumer as an autonomous agent who exercises their right to free choice and in so doing regulates the market. The fair-trade consumer in the UK is able to access fair-trade goods in mainstream retail outlets and understands fair-trade as a business relationship based on a notion of equal exchange. By contrast, in Germany, there is an emphasis placed upon the rational planning of consumption and the consumer is an agent who is guided by expertise from the established agencies who are responsible for ensuring that fair-trade farmers are protected. The fair-trade consumer in Germany accesses fair-trade goods through alternative retail outlets (the World Shop) and understands fair-trade as something that educates producers and provides them with social welfare (i.e. a guaranteed set of rights). The national context of fair-trade consumption informs the way that people are able to think about their responsibilities to distant others and influences the ways in which they are able to construct themselves as ethical consumers. As we saw in the previous chapter, different cultural, political and economic contexts have an important impact upon the way citizen-consumers are mobilised. Indeed, recent comparative research across six European countries found that there were significant differences in the levels of consumer activism and consumer trust, suggesting that notions of consumer power are differently instituted within varying socio-political contexts (Kjærnes, Harvey & Warde, 2007).

This chapter will begin with a general historical overview of the fair-trade movement and how it has developed internationally from its roots in Mennonite and Brethren affiliated activities in the 1940s in the United States to the establishment of 19 Fairtrade labelling organisations across 26 countries today (FLO, 2011b). In so doing, it provides an important backdrop to the chapters that follow. It will then focus more specifically upon fair-trade in a comparative context, by considering the similarities and differences of the movements within three countries. This chapter will consider the growth of the fair-trade movement in the UK, Sweden and USA, paying particular attention to how the movement developed in the UK given that the majority of the data presented in the chapters that follow were gathered within the UK context. Sweden has been chosen as a comparative case study because of its social-democratic welfare regime (Esping-Andersen, 1990), which arguably makes it 'an unlikely place for political consumerism' (Micheletti, 2010: 119). However, as Micheletti herself discovered, green labels are relatively popular among the Swedes, so it seems likely that fair-trade labels will be too. The US is chosen because it represents the largest potential market for fair-trade products in the world at present,[1] and because of the distinctive way in which the Fair Trade certified label has been promoted and challenged as it has developed alongside the more movement-driven alternatives. By providing an overview of fair-trade within the USA and Sweden, I highlight to the reader the distinctiveness and generalisability of the UK case study.

## The growth of the international fair-trade movement

Nicholls and Opal (2005) suggest that the growth of the fair-trade movement can be charted into four key waves, and this section will outline each of these waves in turn, expanding upon them in order to take account of other important developments within the movement. The reader should note that this section offers the dominant and often-told narrative of the growth of the fair-trade movement and is, as such, less attuned to the national specificities and varying trends that will be the focus of the second half of the chapter. The first wave identified by Nicholls and Opal places the roots of the fair-trade movement in the period just after the Second World War when a range of North American and European organisations sought to help disadvantaged groups through the creation of alternative trade networks. In the US in the 1940s, faith-based missionary workers affiliated to the Mennonites and the Church of Brethren began importing artisan and craft products, which were sold in churches and through the Alternative Trading Organisations (ATOs) now known as SERVV and Ten Thousand Villages. These early activities used trade as a way of alleviating the poverty of refugees and struggling communities, and were motivated by religious commitment (Littrell & Dickson, 1999; Rosenthal, 2011). The ATO model spread to Europe, and the developmental charity Oxfam started importing and selling crafts made by Chinese refugees in Hong Kong in the late 1950s (Dankers, 2003: 5).

The second wave of development came when the ATOs in Europe established a network of World Shops in many cities in order to sell these craft products, as well as coffee and tea (Jaffee, 2007). The first of these World Shops opened in the Netherlands in 1969 (Bowes, 2011a), and it is estimated that there were around 4000 such shops within Europe, USA, Japan and Australia in 2007 (Krier, 2007). By the early 1980s, new trading groups had formed that were also engaged in the creation of alternative trading routes but were associated with secular movements on the political left. In the UK, Twin Trading was founded in 1985 by the Greater London Council to generate markets for products from Socialist countries, such as Cuba, Vietnam and Nicaragua. In 1986, Equal Exchange became the first US for-profit alternative trade company with an 'overtly political approach', which distinguished it from other ATOs at the time (Rosenthal, 2011: 160). These solidarity groups viewed 'the creation of alternative trade networks as part of a much larger critique of capitalism and the global economic system' (Jaffee, 2007: 13). Given the spread of these alternative trading networks and World Shops, the European Fair Trade Association was set up in 1987, as was the International Fair Trade Association in 1989, now the World Fair Trade Organisation (WFTO).

The turning point in the movement came in 1988, when the Max Havelaar Fairtrade label was created by Solidaridad, a Dutch Christian development aid organisation,[2] following the request of Mexican coffee farmers for better coffee prices rather than aid. This certification model enabled *alternative* trade to become *fair* trade, with the opportunity it offered small-farmer co-operatives to move beyond the marginalised world shops and into the mainstream market. In developing a certification scheme, it became possible for 'naturally sympathetic retail businesses, such as Co-operative Group in the UK and Wild Oats Markets [now Whole Foods] in the USA' to support fair-trade, thus marking the third wave of the movement's development (Nicholls & Opal, 2005: 20). Coffee was the first certified Fairtrade product and, despite the movement's history of certifying artisan craft products, as the labelling movement moved forward it tended to focus predominantly on agricultural products. The establishment of notable Fairtrade brands, such as Divine and Cafédirect, played an important role in bringing fair-trade goods onto the mainstream market. The labelling initiative quickly spread across Europe, so that by 1992 the Fairtrade Foundation in the UK and TransFair in Germany had been established, followed by a number of other national initiatives, including Rättvisemärkt in Sweden in 1996. By 1997, the Fairtrade Labelling Organisation (FLO) was launched to coordinate the efforts of the growing number of national initiatives. In the same year, TransFair USA (now Fair Trade USA) was established, as were certification schemes in Canada and Japan, bringing the total number of national initiatives to 17 (Jaffee, 2007: 15). In 2002, the international Fairtrade certification mark was launched to help facilitate awareness raising activities and cross-border trade (see Figure 3.1), although, Fair Trade USA (FTUSA) has not adopted the international label and continues with its own logo (see Figure 3.2). In addition to the Fairtrade certified labelling scheme, the WFTO launched their own logo in 2004, which can only be used by businesses that are 100 per cent committed to fair-trade principles, thus differentiating themselves from businesses that only offer single fair-trade lines (see Figure 3.3). While there may be some differences between FLO and the WFTO about how to implement fair-trade in practice, they do share a common vision of 'Fair Trade principles', which can be found in their joint charter released by the Fair Trade Advocacy Office (2009) (see Chapter 1).

*Figure 3.1*  International Fairtrade certified label

*Figure 3.2*   Fair Trade Certified label (USA)

*Figure 3.3*   World Fair Trade Organization logo

The fourth wave of the movement's development is marked by the entry of traditional mainstream businesses, such as Tesco, Sainsbury's, Sam's Club, Wal-Mart and Starbucks, whose distribution and size can help us to understand increasing fair-trade sales figures over time. Global sales of Fairtrade certified products in contemporary society are

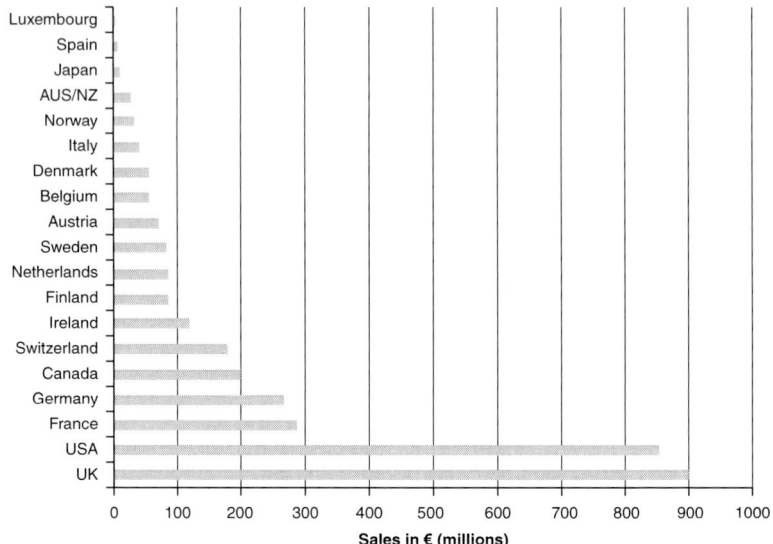

*Graph 3.1*   Fairtrade-certified sales in 2009

witnessing impressive growth; between 2008 and 2009, sales grew by 15 per cent, which amounted to approximately €3.4 billion worldwide (FLO, 2010). Graphs 3.1 and 3.2 show the overall global sales of certified Fairtrade goods in 2009 and the per capita spend on Fairtrade goods in the same year, respectively. As we might expect, the levels of fair-trade consumption and the profiles of fair-trade activities vary in different countries (see Krier, 2007), and it will be important to consider how fair-trade has developed and been institutionalised within different national contexts in order to understand why this is so.

Although Nicholls and Opal's 'four waves' offers a useful way of thinking about general trends in fair-trade, they pay little attention to the varying development of fair-trade in different countries, nor do they consider the growing number of other ethical certification schemes that exist alongside fair-trade. For example, an important part of the fair-trade tale is the emerging development of fair-trade markets in Asia and Africa, which challenge the presumed North-to-South trading relationship (David & Kim, 2010; Otero, 2007). Rather than highlighting the distance between consumer and producer, such fair-trade activities can take advantage of the proximity between the two parties and use principles of localism to market these goods. Fair-trade does not exist in a vacuum, and it is important to highlight other organisations and

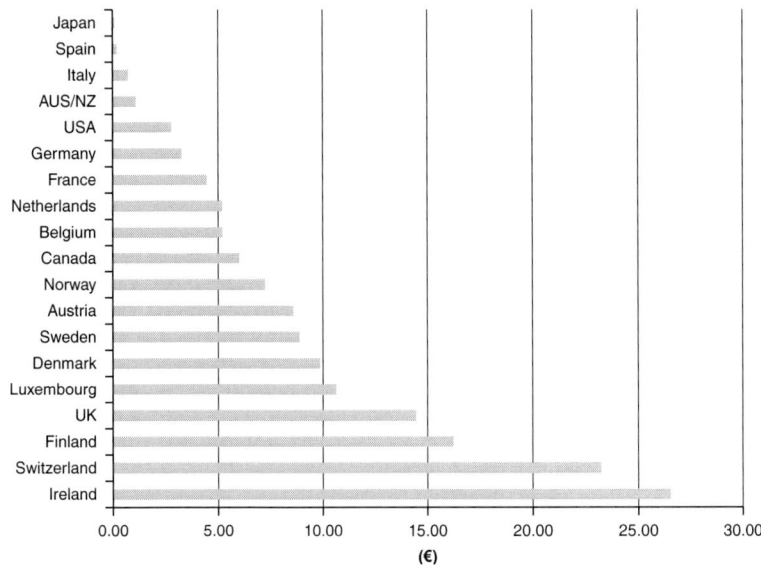

*Graph 3.2*   Per capita expenditure on Fairtrade in 2009 (€)
*Source*: Author-generated graphs using figures from FLO (2010: 12) and World Bank Development Indicators Database (2010).

initiatives that offer an alternative to the Fairtrade certified seal. Perhaps the most successful of these has been the Rainforest Alliance (RA), whose organisation was founded in 1986 to address the destruction of tropical rainforests. Today, the RA certifies coffee, cocoa, tea, bananas, flowers, juice, mangos and wine, as well as paper and wood, and has a long list of corporate members (such as Chiquita, Kraft, Unilever, Tetley, Nestlé, Mars). Unlike fair-trade it does not guarantee a minimum price, but it does claim to alleviate poverty because all workers on RA certified farms receive 'decent wages, respectable housing and healthcare, and their children have access to education' (RA, 2011a). Another popular scheme (particularly in the Netherlands) is Utz Certified, which originated through the efforts of Dutch supermarket chain, Ahold, and works with existing brands, such as Douwe Egberts, to implement sustainability programmes for coffee, tea and cocoa (Utz, 2011). There is a global association called ISEAL that works to develop codes of good practice for social and environmental certification and the RA, FLO and Utz Certified are all members of this body. Other innovations include 'Direct Trade', which is becoming increasingly popular in the specialty coffee sector and involves roasters forming direct relationships with farmers, enabling them to trade fairly without going through a third-party certification system.[3] Beyond fair-trade practices, we have also seen growing support for organic and local products, highlighting a competition among the ethics of consumption that ought not to be overlooked.

It is important to be aware of these broader developments, as well as the specific national variations in the growth of the fair-trade consumer movement, in order to fully understand the context within which fair-trade goods emerge and are sustained. The tale that tends to be told is one of generality, which draws undifferentiated examples from the growth of the movement in Europe and USA to present a relatively homogenous account. However, as Graphs 3.1 and 3.2 show, there are considerable variations between these countries in terms of their consumption of fair-trade goods that are not addressed when the broad overview is given. In what follows, I pay attention to national specificity as I present an account of the development of fair-trade in the UK, Sweden and USA.

## Fair-trade in the United Kingdom

The Fairtrade Foundation (FTF) was established in 1992 by the Catholic Overseas Development Agency, Christian Aid, Oxfam, Traidcraft (a Christian ATO), the World Development Movement and the National Federation of Women's Institutes. However, as intimated above, fair-trade activities and companies were in operation before the Foundation launched, notably Traidcraft plc, which began its operations in 1979, and was a Christian response to poverty through trade. Working with over 100 producer groups in 30 countries today, this organisation relies on an extensive network of local activists (called Fair Traders) who buy Traidcraft products to sell at their church stall or other events. This grassroots network continues to be an important force in the movement today. The solidarity organisation, Twin, also began trading fair-trade products in the 1980s and was responsible, along with Equal Exchange, Oxfam and Traidcraft, for the establishment of the now leading, gold standard Fairtrade coffee and hot drinks company, Cafédirect, in 1991 (following the collapse of the quota system imposed under the International Coffee Agreement in 1989). The FTF's operations are funded by the income from licence fees paid by companies for the use of the Fairtrade mark, as well as from government grants and member contributions from Comic Relief, DFID, the European Union, Oxfam, Shared Interest, United Reform Church, Impetus Trust and Triodos Bank (FTF, 2010a: 8).

The first labelled Fairtrade certified product to hit the supermarket shelves was Green & Black's Maya Gold Chocolate in 1994, and this was shortly followed by Cafédirect coffee and Clipper tea. Fair-trade products continued to trickle onto the market in the five years that followed, including the now popular and producer-owned Divine chocolate company in 1998. However, it was not until 2000 that the movement really started to take off, with the major support of the Co-operative Retail Group, which aligned their involvement with fair-trade with their history of ethical trading.[4] In this year, the Co-op, after introducing fair-trade bananas in all of their retail stores, 'engineered a paradigm shift in the whole market' by launching the UK's first own-brand fair-trade milk chocolate bar (Bowes, 2011b: 126). As Bowes notes, this action 'established the format and set the pattern for a decade of rapid and sustained [fair-trade] growth' (ibid.). Following the Co-op's lead over the next five years, all the major supermarket retailers in the UK had launched their own-brand fair-trade products, enabling millions of people to access fair-trade products through mainstream channels. It is important to highlight that fair-trade in the UK tends to be organised around the Fairtrade-certified logo, unlike in the USA where there exists a real tension between different organisations about how best to support producers through fair-trade.

Alongside this major retailer support emerged the grassroots Fairtrade Towns movement whose significance for the growth of the movement in the UK cannot be overstated. The first Fairtrade Town was established in Garstang in 2001 and it has grown to over 500 towns in just ten years. Bringing together local activists (often Traidcraft Fair Traders) with local government and businesses, to increase the availability and awareness of fair-trade within communities, it has proved a huge success (see Chapter 4 for more details). One of the key activities of these town groups has been to campaign for changes in public procurement policies, as well as demanding that Fairtrade-certified products be stocked in local stores. The existence of consumer pressure through these networks legitimates changes to institutional policies (Littler, Barnett & Soper, 2005), giving them 'permission to care'.[5] The Fairtrade Towns movement has spawned a host of other Fairtrade 'place' initiatives, so that there are now 6683 Fairtrade Faith groups, 547 Fairtrade schools (with a hundred more working towards the status), 139 Fairtrade universities and a growing number of Fairtrade workplaces (FTF, 2011b: 15).

A report by Globescan (2009) revealed that UK consumers are the most likely to have seen Fairtrade labelled goods, with 90 per cent of those questioned agreeing that they had seen fair-trade goods often or occasionally. This figure drops to 64 per cent in Sweden, and 33 per cent in USA. The UK has the largest market for fair-trade goods, with sales of certified Fairtrade products in 2009 amounting to €897,315,061 (FLO, 2010). Although the growth in the movement is often represented as the result of thousands of individual consumers 'voting' for fairer trade, it should not be forgotten that the growth of fair-trade in the UK is a tale of increasing mainstream market domination through supermarkets and businesses. In 2006, Sainsbury's (soon followed by Waitrose) announced that all of their bananas would be converted to Fairtrade by 2007, meaning that shoppers would automatically become fair-trade consumers when performing their weekly shop. By 2007, Sainsbury's had announced its intention to switch its own-brand tea and coffee to 100 per cent Fairtrade certified (soon followed by Marks & Spencer), and in 2008 Tate & Lyle announced that all its retail sugar would be switched to Fairtrade. The nation's favourite chocolate bar, Cadbury's Dairy Milk, became Fairtrade certified in 2010, and the list of Fairtrade switches now includes Nestlé KitKat and Mars Maltesers. High-street coffee chains, Pret A Manger, EAT and Starbucks all offer Fairtrade-only product lines. These mainstream switches have led to criticism from some sections of the movement. In particular, following Nestlé's introduction of Partners' Blend freeze dried coffee in 2005, there were angry exchanges from within the European fair-trade movement (Moberg & Lyon, 2010), given the long-running consumer boycott of this company following its baby milk marketing tactics in the developing world.

These high-profile Fairtrade-certified switches have important implications for our understanding of fair-trade consumption acts as indicative of reflexive and conscious choice. As indicated in Chapter 2, the persistent representation of fair-trade consumption as an individual choice ought to be viewed in the context of the privatisation of public services within the UK, which celebrated the active citizen-consumer as a way of regulating the market. This consumer is understood as an autonomous citizen governed at a distance through a variety of discourses, and is distinctive from the fair-trade consumer in Germany who, according to Varul, is informed and guided by established authorities and expertise to shop rationally (Varul, 2009: 185). These various discourses have been selectively employed by the fair-trade movement in the UK to demonstrate that they have mass support for their model of trade and a legitimate voice in their advocacy work (Clarke et al., 2007a). For, if sales of fair-trade are increasing, it must mean that more people are choosing fair-trade because they see it is the right thing to do. As this book demonstrates, this is not necessarily the case as on the one hand established brands are editing the choices that are available to ordinary consumers, and on the other the fair-trade movement calls on a growing number of 'self-selecting' fair-trade supporters to sustain the representation of the fair-trade consumer as voting for trade justice. That the fair-trade movement within the UK is engaged in advocacy work and has close links with trade justice organisations is important because it is not something that was found in Sweden, where the close relationship between the state and civil society meant that fair-trade consumption was not linked to a wider critique of government trade and policies, as it has been in the UK. For example, during Fairtrade Fortnight 2008, fair-trade supporters were encouraged to send trade justice postcards to the prime minister to ask him to use his influence in G20 meetings to make all trade fair through structural interventions, suggesting that fair-trade support in the UK is about more than merely consuming fair-trade. The reason for this difference will be discussed after we have explored the growth of the fair-trade movement in Sweden.

## Fair-trade in Sweden

In 1969, the first World Shop (*Världsbutik*) opened in Sweden in Gothenburg under the name *Alternativ Handel* (Alternative Trade), and it is still in operation today. More shops followed and focused on providing trading routes for countries like China, North Vietnam and Tanzania (Högberg, 2011). In 1973, unfair trading issues became a key focus of the churches' annual developing-weeks (*u-veckor*), and a number of individuals were given the opportunity to sell fairly traded goods on church stalls (ibid.). An importing organisation, Sackeus AB, was established in 1976 by the Christian development organisation Diakonia, the Swedish Church and the Lutheran World Federation, to supply the churches with goods for sale, including 'church coffee' (*kyrkkaffe*). These committed Christians set up their own fair-trade stores, commonly known as *U-landsbodar*, and in 1986, a national association of World Shops for Fair Trade was formed, which was known as *Världsbutikerna för Rättvis Handel*.[6] In 2007, Krier reported that there were 44 World Shops in Sweden, compared to 117 in the UK, 280 in the USA and 836 in Germany. So unlike Germany, where World Shops are the most important distribution channel for fair-trade goods (Varul, 2009), Sweden has a relatively low proportion of World Shops. That is not to say that these distribution channels are unimportant, however, as the continued involvement of a national association attests, but for further expansion there was a need to reach beyond this niche market and into the mainstream.

In 1996, the National Fairtrade Labelling initiative, Rättvisemärkt, offered just this opportunity.[7] Fairtrade in Sweden consists of two separate organisations: one that deals with the sales of Fairtrade goods and the licensing of the Fairtrade mark, and one that focuses on public relations and informational and awareness-raising campaigns. The former, now known as Fairtrade Sverige AB since 2009, is owned by the Swedish Church and the Swedish Trade Union Confederation (LO),[8] while the latter, known as Föreningen för Fairtrade Sverige (FFTS), has 45 member organisations from different sections of Swedish civil society, including Caritas, Diakonia, Forum Syd, Swedish Cooperative Centre, Save the Children, Red Cross Youth, the LO and the Workers' Education Association. Funding for these two organisations is generated by licensing and member fees and grants from the Swedish International Development Cooperation Agency (SIDA), the Swedish Consumer Agency and the European Union (FFTS, 2010a: 27). In 2003, the Swedish organisation changed its label to the international Fairtrade Mark (Figure 3.1), and in 2010 it changed from its Swedish name, Rättvisemärkt, to Fairtrade.

Cafe Organico[9] was the first Fairtrade certified product to go on sale in Sweden in 1997, and this was soon followed by tea, cocoa and bananas. However, sales of Fairtrade were sluggish for the first few years, and the label struggled to penetrate into the market and into consumer awareness (FFTS, 2007: 1). Whereas the Co-operative movement has been a key actor in the development of fair-trade in the UK and the USA, in Sweden it was slow to invest; writing in 2006, Björner revealed how Coop Nordic was experiencing falling sales and was unwilling to promote fair-trade products for which they believed there was a 'weak demand' (ibid.: 59). Having said this, Coop Nordic did launch their own-brand Fairtrade products under their Änglamark brand, and in 2009 made a commitment to double sales of Fairtrade labelled goods over the next three years (FFTS, 2010b: 16). In many ways, 2006 was the year when the fair-trade movement began to really gain momentum in Sweden, as a number of Swedish brands began to offer Fairtrade lines; these included Dansisco sugar, Zoegas coffee and the coffee retail chain Barista. In addition, the renowned hotel chain Scandic and Hilton adopted a 100 per cent Fairtrade policy in 2006, and the first Fairtrade City was established in Malmö. However, grocery stores in Sweden are yet to make a commitment to fair-trade in the same way they have in the UK, with no chains adopting a 100 per cent fair-trade policy (FFTS, 2010b: 5). It is interesting to note that 82 per cent of fair-trade products available in Sweden were also certified as organic (excluding sports balls, flowers and cotton) (FFTS, 2011), and the organic label is often promoted over the Fairtrade label in retail outlets.[10] As in the UK, there is no real competition between the Fairtrade-certified label and other fair-trade brands, with the majority of campaigning activities or 'switches' organised around the Fairtrade-certified mark.

Since 1999, the FFTS has offered a formal training course for (young) people to become 'Fairtrade Ambassadors', which involves paying to attend a 14-hour course to learn about fair-trade and how to promote it with the hope that these individuals will then go out and do just that by getting involved with FFTS' member organisations, or awareness-raising campaigns (such as Fairtrade City and Fairtrade Fokus). As of 2011, over 3000 people have been through such a programme, including the Swedish Minister for EU Affairs, Birgitta Ohlsson (FFTS, 2011). There are also 46 Fairtrade cities within Sweden, which, unlike the grass-roots movement in the UK, was initiated by the FFTS as a way for the municipalities to get involved with fair-trade. The city campaigns are led by a paid member of staff from the municipality and are very much focused on public procurement. Sales of fair-trade have been increasing in Sweden but it lags behind other parts of Europe. Nevertheless there is a real desire to become a 'world leader' for fair-trade, which would be in keeping with Sweden's strong commitment to justice, environmental and international issues (FFTS, 2010b: 5).

As already indicated, an important difference in the Swedish fair-trade movement, when compared to their UK counterparts, is the lack of political lobbying conducted by this movement towards state policy. The organisation was described to the author as 'not political' and more focused upon fair-trade products than the 'bigger picture'. For the Swede, buying fair-trade was about making 'sure that this product is produced according to human rights, dot and nothing more'.[11] In order to understand this position, it is necessary to consider the political culture and context in which fair-trade has emerged in Sweden. When Boström and Klintman (2006) explored the development of organic standards and labelling in Sweden and the US, they found that differences in the political and organisational structures of the two countries impacted on the way organic labelling was institutionalised. The political culture in Sweden is often described as social-democratic, with its universalist welfare state and strong labour movement, as opposed to the liberal regimes we find in the US and UK (Esping-Andersen, 1990; Salamon & Anheier, 1996). Both Boström and Klintman (2006) and Micheletti (2003) have argued that Sweden seems an unlikely place for political consumerism to emerge because the state ought to take responsibility for the welfare of individuals without the need for them to turn to the market for a solution. Indeed as Chapter 2 highlighted, the rise of the 'citizen-consumer' is often placed into the context of neo-liberal welfare regimes and a socio-political context that frames the consumer, rather than the state, as holding the power to regulate the market through individual choice. Having said this, these authors show how green and organic labels have successfully been brought onto the Swedish market because of the cooperation between state and civil society actors.

The development of civil society in Sweden followed a different path than in other countries (Trägårdh, 2007). 'Anglo-American citizenship theory' – which portrays civil society as an autonomous entity that is 'distinct and prior to the state' and therefore an important institution to protect citizens from the power or 'tyranny' of the state (ibid.: 14) – dominates popular understandings of civil society. However, in the Swedish case it is argued that the universal welfare state has fostered trust between the state and its citizenry. Wijkström and Zimmer suggest that Nordic civil society organisations 'are accepted partners of neo-corporatist arrangements instead of being engaged in pluralistic pressure politics and lobbying activities' (Wijkström & Zimmer, 2011: 11). It therefore seems likely that the absence of political campaigning within the Swedish fair-trade movement[12] can be understood with reference to the distinctiveness of the political culture of cooperation within which it is embedded. In this context, it is not surprising that the Fairtrade City campaign in Sweden is managed by employees within local state departments, rather than among grassroots activists as in the UK, and its key focus is on the public procurement of Fairtrade goods. In a liberal regime, like the USA, and to a certain extent the UK, it is likely that there will be more conflict between and within the state and civil society, and thus 'protest mobilisation matters' more in this context (Boström & Klintman, 2006: 175). The Swedish case encourages us to consider how institutional configurations of responsibility across different social contexts shape the role and mobilisation of the 'citizen-consumer'. Rather than adopting an individualised model of consumer reflexivity, which assumes that we find the same tendencies everywhere, it is important to pay attention to how 'state and markets do, or might, operate' because this can 'reveal different perceptions of the consumer role in different countries' (Kjærnes, Harvey & Warde, 2007: 107).

### Fair-trade in the USA

The fair-trade movement in North America 'developed according to a different tempo than in Europe, although along parallel lines' (Barrientos,

Conroy & Jones, 2007: 54). Certified Fair Trade products took a lot longer to reach the US market, and for a long time it was through the ATO-led model that consumers had access to fairly traded goods. The early ATOs, such as Ten Thousand Villages and SERVV, which were motivated out of religious commitment to alleviating poverty, operated on a not-for-profit basis and sold fair-trade goods through Third World Shops and a catalogue service. Equal Exchange, a worker co-operative founded in 1986, was the first for-profit venture, and its focus was primarily upon foodstuffs rather than crafts (Rosenthal, 2011). In 1994, the work of the growing number of ATOs in the US led to the creation of the Fair Trade Federation (FTrF) whose membership comprises of businesses who are 'fully committed' to fair-trade (FTrF, 2011).

In 1992, following the success of the labelling initiative in Europe, Equal Exchange launched its own fair-trade seal for coffee, but was unable to successfully manage this venture and after a year the label idled (Rosenthal, 2011). However, there was still a desire to pursue the labelling model within the US, and after a second seal attempt (led by the Sustainable Coffee Coalition) failed, a group led by Oxfam America and the Institute for Agriculture and Trade Policy (an organisation exploring the impact of trade policy upon farmers in the US and overseas) met in 1995, and after a short period Transfair USA was established (Barrientos, Conroy & Jones, 2007). Their operations are funded by the licensing fees, as well as grants from a range of organisations from faith groups to philanthropists like Paul Newman, and company foundations like the Ford Foundation and Levi Strauss Foundation, as well as the United States Agency for International Development.[13] The Fair Trade label initially focused primarily upon coffee, and labelled Fair Trade coffee hit mainstream retail stores in 1999. Jaffee (2007) notes that larger coffee retailers were initially unwilling to participate, and although Starbuck's agreed to serve Fair Trade coffee in all their US stores in 2000, following a year-long campaign by the activist organisation, Global Exchange, it amounted to just 1 per cent of their total volume of coffee sales. Nevertheless, the commitment from Starbuck's encouraged other specialty coffee roasters to follow, such as Green Mountain Coffee Roasters, who are now the world's biggest purchaser of Fair Trade coffee and a financial supporter of the Fair Trade Towns campaign (FTUSA, 2011a). Transfair USA continued to pursue fair-trade partnerships with large commercial retailers, with Dunkin Donuts, Procter & Gamble and Kraft offering Fair Trade lines in 2004, followed by Wal-Mart, Costco, Sam's Club and McDonalds (in New England stores) in 2005. Unlike the UK, no supermarket retailer has made a 100 per cent commitment to Fair Trade – although Whole Foods did launch a 'Whole Trade' concept in 2007 that comes close to the UK model but which importantly includes not just Fair Trade but RA certification as well. Having said that, Dunkin Donuts does offer an exclusive Fair Trade espresso coffee and Ben & Jerry's announced in 2010 that by the end of 2011, all the ingredients in its range of ice creams that can be Fair Trade would be.

The pursuit of mainstream Fair Trade has led to some tension within the fair-trade movement in the US between those ATOs who believe that only businesses that are 100 per cent committed to fair-trade with direct links to producers ought to be allowed to enter the Fair Trade model rather than those perceived to be 'greenwashing' their image through their association with Fair Trade certification on single product lines (see Jaffee, 2007; Raynolds & Long, 2007; Rosenthal, 2011). While it is certainly the case that this tension exists everywhere, it is also the case that this tension reveals itself most clearly within the US market, given the distinctive history and organisation of ATOs and labelling schemes within this context. Indeed, Transfair USA's decision to change its name to Fair Trade USA in 2010 has highlighted this quite effectively. Critics, including the Organic Consumer's Association (OCA) and Dr Bronner's Magic Soaps (a 100 per cent Fair Trade company) have condemned this action, which they feel 'attempts to legally claim, as an exclusive brand, a term that encompasses this broad movement far beyond its specific work' (OCA, 2010). The FLO labelling model is not the only social and fair-trade certification label in the US market, with the Institute for Market Ecology 'Fair for Life' scheme offering an alternative for products that have a majority of Fair Trade certified ingredients or materials, and the FTrF offering their seal to those organisations that are fully committed to fair-trade principles (similar to the scheme offered by the WFTO). The tension between mainstream and alternative retailers is a difficult one to resolve, given that mainstream retailers are likely to be dealing with higher volumes of fair-trade commodities than the smaller ATOs. The real issue remains whether these different approaches offer differential benefits to the farmers and producers within the scheme, and indeed whether the consumer is aware of this. Jaffee's (2007) excellent overview of fair-trade coffee in the US market begins to address these issues, and suggests that the pursuit of mainstream Fair Trade is threatening the capacity of the movement to secure benefits for producers. Why it should be that the tension in the movement reveals itself most clearly in the US, can perhaps be explained with reference to their distinctive political culture, which Boström and Klintman characterise as 'polarised' and 'confrontational'. In this climate, there are likely to be 'more fundamental controversies … [and] debates between coalitions that use separate frames that disagree on basic purposes and concern' (Boström & Klintman, 2006: 167).

As I write this chapter, there is a new twist in FTUSA's tale: they undertook to renounce their membership of FLO as of 31 December 2011, in view of the existence of 'different perspectives on how best to achieve [their] common mission' (FLO, 2011c). Their new approach, 'Fair Trade For All', addresses one of the long-held controversies in the movement regarding the certification of co-operatives over larger estates and plantations that use hired labour to produce coffee, sugar and cocoa crops. Where this development will lead will be important for academics, activists and policy makers to follow. Interestingly, one of the three strands of their new approach, which aims to double sales of Fair Trade by 2015, highlights the need to 'ignite the consumer movement' through the Fair Trade Town and University model, as well as the use of a 'Fair Trade Month' promotional period (FTUSA, 2011b) – these two promotional strategies will be the focus of the next chapter. The first Fair Trade Town in the US was Media, Pennsylvania in 2006, and there are currently 22 other towns that have achieved this status. The Fair Trade Towns network is housed in FTUSA's offices but is a partnership between the FTrF and FTUSA, with financial support from the Lutheran World Relief and the Ford Foundation, and more recently Green Mountain Coffee Roasters. FTUSA's need to 'ignite the consumer movement' reveals an important part of the development of the fair-trade movement in the US, when compared to the growth of the movement in the UK. As Katie Barrow, PR Manager at FTUSA, told me:

> We started just going after businesses and getting all these businesses involved, but we didn't have the consumer push and in the UK it really started with the consumer push and then the businesses got involved. So we're kind of behind with the consumer push and that's why we've been focusing so much energy on the Fair Trade towns.[14]

While FTUSA were engaged in expanding the supply of Fair Trade goods in mainstream retail outlets, they focused their attention on businesses rather than on building grassroots consumer networks. It was felt that other organisations, such as Oxfam America, United Students for Fair Trade and Co-op America (now Green America), would be the 'foot-soldiers for building the grassroots'.[15] But because of the tensions within the mainstreaming model, this has not necessarily happened.

Rosenthal notes that in the 12 years since FTUSA began certifying products, sales have 'multiplied by a factor of more than 100, yet consumer interest and the number of NGOs engaged in fair-trade has not kept pace' (Rosenthal, 2011: 166). It is perhaps for this reason that awareness of fair-trade among the American general public sits at just 33 per cent compared to 90 per cent in the UK (Globescan, 2009). In addition, competition from the RA certification represents a serious threat in the US, with 48 per cent of consumers recognising this label, compared to a 37 per cent average across the 15 countries surveyed (ibid.). Without a strong consumer push for, or awareness of, fair-trade compared to other certification systems, the US movement will be unable to communicate its distinctive message. Rather than the citizen-consumer emerging automatically with increasing availability of fair-trade goods in the USA, fair-trade organisations and businesses must mobilise and 'make-up' this figure through various promotional tactics.

## Fair-trade in cultural context

Having provided an overview of the development and history of fair-trade in the three countries, we can see that distinct differences have emerged in the ways that fair-trade consumption and support are represented and understood, as well as in how fair-trade goods are distributed. In the UK, grassroots support for the fair-trade model developed from an early stage among Christian Fair Traders who were readily mobilised into action, along with other local campaigners and activists, within the fast-growing Fairtrade Towns networks. Mainstream support of Fairtrade was established in the early 2000s, and it has continued to grow, so that 100 per cent Fairtrade-certified policies are fast becoming a normal part of everyday life. The fair-trade consumer/supporter is imagined as a global citizen regulating the market through their consumption choices as well as engaging in political and trade justice lobbying. In Sweden, on the other hand, although early support for fair-trade can be found in the church networks and World Shops, the grassroots support did not develop in the same way as in the UK. Consumer awareness of the movement had to be carefully managed through national initiatives like the Fairtrade Ambassador scheme, which formally trains consumers to be active fair-trade supporters within their social networks, and the Fairtrade City programme, which is overseen by municipal employees rather than local activists. Major retailers and existing brands' adoption of Fairtrade has lagged behind other European countries so that there are few 100 per cent Fairtrade policies, although Fairtrade options are available in most retail stores. Swedes seem to view the purchase of fair-trade as a way to ensure that products are produced in accordance with human rights, but there is limited lobbying around trade justice issues, suggesting that the political culture of a country influences the way fair-trade citizen-consumer support is realised. The social-democratic Swedish state, marked by cooperation between civil society and the state, offers an important comparison to the liberal regime within the US, which is marked by underlying tensions and debate surrounding how best to support farmers in, and certify products from, the developing world. In the US, certified Fair Trade developed much later than within Europe, and it concentrated on encouraging mainstream businesses to switch part of their activities to Fair Trade, at the same time as the ATO-led business model was flourishing. This tension appears to have divided the movement and has left consumer support for fair-trade lagging behind the grassroots activism we find in the UK. Although major retailers and businesses do offer Fair Trade, no supermarket retailer has pledged a 100 per cent Fair Trade line. With competition from other ethical labels and competition between the two Fair Trade labels, the fair-trade movement in the US now needs to mobilise the citizen-consumer to take action.

By utilising a comparative perspective, it is possible to see that the opportunities for mobilising the fair-trade citizen-consumer are likely to differ within the three countries. This is important to highlight because the fair-trade consumer is often portrayed in the same way across different contexts without acknowledging that systems of provision, shared structures of knowledge and institutional frameworks shape how consumers are enabled to support fair-trade in their daily lives. This chapter has also demonstrated that fair-trade cultures are not static across time, but are constantly evolving and are instituted across the economic processes of production, distribution, exchange and consumption in different ways within different spatial and historical contexts (see Harvey, 2007). In what follows it will be important for the reader to remember that the current mainstream availability of Fairtrade and strong grassroots support for the movement across a number of organisations and businesses is somewhat distinctive to the UK context. At the same time, it is important not to overstate the differences between the UK and elsewhere, given that we can find similar promotional tactics and marketing messages across this international movement, and some similar trajectories of fair-trade development over time. Rather, we ought to adopt a more nuanced account and recognise the contingent and shifting nature of the citizen-consumer identity by paying close attention to the role of different actors in diverse cultural contexts in the mobilisation of this figure. The next chapter explores two such common promotional tactics – the Fairtrade Town and the fair-trade promotional period – in order to demonstrate how local, national and international discourses interact to construct the fair-trade citizen-consumer in different ways.

# 4
# Promoting Fair-Trade

A 'market device' is defined as the 'material and discursive assemblages that intervene in the construction of markets' (Muniesa, Millo & Callon, 2007: 2), and it is the contention of this chapter that fair-trade is a powerful market device. It calls upon a whole host of actors – fair-trade organisations, NGOs, activists, retailers, businesses, the media, local and national government, community organisations and so on – who together work to qualify the characteristics of fair-trade goods and reconfigure the position of these goods within a world of similar commodities. Callon describes the market as a dynamic process in which 'calculative agencies compete and/or co-operate with one another ... [so that] each agency is able to integrate the already framed calculations of the other agencies into its own calculations' (Callon, 1998: 32). This approach encourages us to think of both fair-trade and the citizen-consumer as contingent and shifting constructs that are constantly being defined and redefined through the interplay between different actors and organisations that may have different or even competing objectives. This chapter takes two popular promotional campaigns – Fairtrade Towns and fair-trade promotional periods (like Fairtrade Fortnight and World Fair Trade Day) – in order to show how the 'fair-trade consumer' is constructed and mobilised as a citizen-consumer, with specific attention paid to the range of actors and organisations involved in this process in diverse cultural contexts. As the previous chapter made clear, fair-trade switches are becoming a common feature of fair-trade provisioning in the UK, and to a lesser degree in Sweden and the USA. This chapter pays particular attention to the institutionalisation of collective fair-trade purchasing and asks how this choice-editing has been made possible through an evolving and complex set of interactions.

In Chapter 2, it was noted that there are two common strategies employed by consumer organisations, like ECRA and the FTF, when mobilising and representing the ethical consumer (Clarke et al., 2007a). First, they provide a 'self-selecting' audience with narrative resources to help them to understand and extend their engagement with fair-trade (or ethical trade). Second, they carefully represent the collective acts of fair-trade consumption so as to provide legitimacy for them to speak on behalf of the consumer when advocating for trade justice. We will remember that it was this second strategy that led Clarke et al. to suggest that 'it is acts, not identities or beliefs, which matter in mobilising the presence of "ethical consumers" in the public realm' (Clarke et al., 2007: 241). In a similar vein, Goodman (2004) has argued that fair-trade is more of a consumer-dependent movement than a consumer-led one because fair-trade organisations have to actively promote fair-trade products and seek out consumers to support their cause. Although it is vital to acknowledge the role of consumer organisations and trade justice organisations in shaping public understandings of fair-trade, it is also important not to lose sight of the role of other actors, including the fair-trade consumer/supporter, in this process. One thing is certain, that the consumer is not alone when choosing between products but is supported by a range of market professionals and devices, as well as being informed and guided by peers and social networks. The qualification of goods depends upon 'the joint work of a host of actors and there is no reason to believe that consumers do not participate, like the other actors concerned, in the objectification of those qualities' (Callon, Méadel & Rabeharisoa, 2002: 203). It is this 'joint work' that will be the focus of this chapter.

## The Fairtrade Towns movement

When a small town in Lancashire, Garstang (with a population of just over 4000 people), declared itself the world's first Fairtrade Town in 2000, it took the FTF by surprise (Lamb, 2008). Organised by residents and campaigners living within the town, this was a concept that originated from the grassroots. Headed by the local Oxfam group and supported by a number of local churches, the local school and youth group and in collaboration with local dairy farmers, this campaign succeeded in persuading 90 per cent of local shopkeepers, churches, workplaces and schools to sign a pledge that they would use or sell fair-trade and local products on their premises (see FTF, 2002). With such widespread public support, a public council meeting was held in 2000, and the motion was passed to make Garstang a Fairtrade Town. The event attracted the attention of the regional and national media, as well as the then Under Secretary of State for International Development, George Foulkes, who said:

> I want to try to ensure that the initiative is followed in many other towns and cities throughout the whole of the United Kingdom and beyond, so that the beacon that has started in Garstang can spread like wildfire through the whole of the country.
>
> FTF (2002: 11)

Although this grassroots movement had not been led by the FTF, given the opportunity it offered them to expand their supporter base, they embraced it and launched the Fairtrade Towns Initiative nationwide in 2001.

A Fairtrade Town is 'any community in which people and organisations use their everyday choices to increase sales of Fairtrade products' (International Fairtrade Towns Network, 2011a). Importantly, a Fairtrade Town is 'a shared achievement and an opportunity for local government, schools, businesses, community organisations and activists to work together' (ibid.). The Fairtrade Town movement has grown dramatically since its inception and, at the time of writing, there are now over 500 Fairtrade Towns in the UK, with 200 more campaigning for the status, as well as 500 other Fairtrade Town campaigns in 23 countries around the world inspired by the UK example (see Table 4.1).[1] Fairtrade Towns in all countries follow a similar set of criteria based upon the five key goals established in the UK system (see Box 4.1). In the Swedish and Belgian systems, there is an additional sixth goal – in Sweden this includes the need for continuous improvement by the towns, and in Belgium there is a provision for the support of local farmers. In the USA, towns must recognise both Fair Trade-certified products and those organisations that are certified by the Fair Trade Federation, following a more ATO-driven agenda, within their resolutions. The emergence of Fairtrade Towns in the South reflects a new development in the Fairtrade Towns movement, and because of their unique context the goals here may diverge slightly from the ones used in Fairtrade Towns in the North.[2] Given the size of the Fairtrade Town movement both across the UK and worldwide, it seems important to move beyond the tale of one small town where local support for the scheme has been active and strong, and consider how other towns have managed to achieve the status, paying particular attention to the distinct cultural contexts and

*Table 4.1*   Fairtrade Towns listed by country

| Country | When first Fairtrade Town was established | No. of 'Towns' |
|---|---|---|
| UK | 2001 | 526 |
| Ireland | 2003 | 48 |
| Belgium (Flanders) | 2005 | 115 |
| Italy | 2005 | 42 |
| Sweden | 2006 | 46 |
| USA | 2006 | 23 |
| Norway | 2006 | 30 |
| Canada | 2007 | 15 |
| Austria | 2007 | 69 |
| Spain | 2008 | 5 |
| Denmark | 2008 | 5 |
| Belgium (Wallonia + Brussels) | 2008 | 3 |
| Brazil | 2008 | 1 |
| Netherlands | 2009 | 16 |
| Germany | 2009 | 53 |
| Australia | 2009 | 6 |
| Finland | 2009 | 6 |
| Costa Rica | 2009 | 1 |
| France | 2009 | 23 |
| New Zealand | 2009 | 2 |
| Luxembourg | 2011 | 10 |
| Japan | 2011 | 1 |
| Ghana | 2011 | 1 |
| Czech Republic | 2011 | 2 |
| | Total | 1049 |

*Source*: International Fairtrade Towns Network (2011b).

coalition of actors that are likely to have influenced the form of these local campaigns.

Malpass et al. (2007a) did just this in their examination of the Bristol Fairtrade City campaign. The campaign in Bristol was driven by individuals within the local authority (who were responsible for procurement policy) who then recruited a range of interested activists and businesses from within the city – from Christian Aid, Traidcraft, Oxfam, fair-trade

## Box 4.1  Five goals to become a Fairtrade Town

1. The local council must pass a resolution supporting Fairtrade and agree to serve fair-trade tea and coffee at its meetings and in its offices and canteens.
2. A range of Fairtrade products must be readily available in the area's shops and local cafes/catering establishments.
3. Fairtrade products must be used by a number of local work places and community organisations.
4. Attract media coverage and popular support for the campaign.
5. A local Fairtrade steering group is convened to ensure continued commitment to its Fairtrade Town status.

FTF (2002: i).

coffee and clothing stores, the Co-op and school and university groups. The Bristol campaign drew on existing coalitions and interests in order to recruit supporters, as well as engaging in the reimagination of Bristol's place-based identity as the second largest slave trading port. The authors argue that Fairtrade Towns have the potential to create 'ethical land-scapes of consumption' when they switch systems of collective provision within council buildings and public spaces to Fairtrade, transforming them into 'ethical places embodying a global sense of place' (Malpass et al., 2007a: 634).

This section expands upon the limited existing research on Fairtrade Towns by exploring three campaigns across different countries. Beginning with Chelmsford, Essex (UK), where the majority of empirical data for this volume was gathered in 2008, I give a full overview of its establish-ment as a Fairtrade Town and the key actors involved in the campaign. I then go on to examples gathered from research in Lund, Skåne (Sweden) and Berkeley, California (USA) in 2011, in order to highlight how the organisation of fair-trade on the national and local level shapes the formation of coalitions around fair-trade and the activities they engage in, as well as to demonstrate the differences in strategy according to the cultural/market differences set out in Chapter 3. The reader will learn that Fairtrade Towns are a very useful tool to galvanise like-minded peo-ple more closely, as well as to publicly sustain the image of the active citizen-consumer. However, at the same time as they generate collective cultures of consumption among diverse organisations within the local community, they enrol those without an explicit interest in the fair-trade movement into the regular consumption of fair-trade goods.

## Chelmsford

Situated in the East of England in the county of Essex, Chelmsford was once a market town and a centre for industry but is now largely a commercial town that is served by a Conservative majority council. In 2008 (the year the empirical research was conducted), Chelmsford had a population of around 167,000.[3] Home to a large number of city-commuters, Chelmsford has a relatively affluent population with gross weekly earnings that are around 14 per cent higher than the national average. Of the economically active population, 83 per cent are in work and over half of these can be classified in SOC 2000 classification groups 1–3 (Managers and Senior Officials, Professional Occupations, Associate Professional and Technical Occupations). Chelmsford has a low unemployment rate among its economically active population, which is 1.5 percentage points below the national average. It has a well-educated workforce, with 30 per cent of working-age residents holding a degree-level qualification, or equivalent. Walking down the high street, one can find the same chain-retail stores that appear in the majority of towns across the UK, as well as some unique features. A small river runs through the town, and following its course, we could expect to pass a family feeding bread to the ducks, a large Tesco's, a Starbuck's coffee store, a shopping mall home to famous UK brands like Bhs, Waterstones and Dorothy Perkins, a bridge where workers are seated on the benches enjoying their lunch-break with Marks & Spencer's sandwiches or McDonalds burgers, and a Poundland diagonally opposite to the Co-operative department store. At the edge of the town next to the library, there is a covered marketplace where local butchers, greengrocers and market-traders sell their goods on selected days throughout the week. The main supermarkets – Asda, Sainsbury's, Tesco and Lidl – can be found on the outskirts of the town.

With its predictable selection of high-street stores, office buildings, rail and bus stations, university campus, and council-run leisure centre and theatres, Chelmsford is a pretty unremarkable town, but it does have a large network of Co-operative stores, which makes it somewhat distinct. The Chelmsford Star Co-operative is one the many independent co-operative retail societies within the UK, operating within Chelmsford and the surrounding districts, with 36 convenience stores and two department stores (as well as travel and funeral services), and over 50,000 members. They have been an important supporter of the Chelmsford Fairtrade Town campaign.

The campaign for Chelmsford to become a Fairtrade Town began in 2002 (and was achieved in 2005), when Alfred,[4] secretary of the local

Trades Union Council (TUC) and active Co-operator, wrote to the local newspaper suggesting that Chelmsford should do more to support fair-trade.[5] This article generated some initial interest, and Alfred, in collaboration with Marcus, the chair of the local Oxfam group, decided to contact existing groups in Chelmsford who might be interested in working towards Fairtrade Town status. Local organisations and faith groups (Amnesty International, CAFOD, the Cathedral group, Christian Aid, Churches Together, Friends of the Earth, Justice and Peace, Oxfam, Society of Friends, UNICEF, Youth Council), as well as political parties and representatives from the local business community, met on several occasions, and the Chelmsford Fairtrade Action Group (CFAG) was established. Seven people formed the first steering group, with Marcus as the chairperson and Alfred as the secretary, and representatives from the Co-op Party and Co-op Society, Youth Council, Christian Aid, and Justice and Peace. It is important to note the key role played by the Trades Union Congress (TUC) in the development of the fair-trade coalition in Chelmsford because trade union involvement has been uncommon in Fairtrade Town campaigns across the UK (Malpass et al., 2007a). The TUC has been active in Chelmsford for over a century, engaged in a number of local campaigns from supporting the miners' strike in the 1980s, to forming an anti-Apartheid group and fighting to save a ward at a local hospital. Alfred has been involved with the TUC for over 30 years, and actually learnt about fair-trade through his attendance at the annual May Day Rally run by the TUC. In fact, given that Alfred also sits on the board of the Chelmsford Star Co-operative Society, it is possible to suggest that he was a key situational factor behind the development of the Chelmsford group. Indeed, one member of the CFAG reflected upon this very fact:

> I don't think it's a coincidence that Chelmsford was the first in Essex. Because it had a group, and it had all party support is crucial, community support from the churches and other organisations which is also crucial, but also, and I'll say this without fear of embarrassing him because he's not here, someone like Alfred, who everyone knows he's quite a strong-willed individual who actually is one of those do-ers and those sort of individuals are not everywhere frankly and they're quite unique in some respects, and I think you know individuals in action are quite important for things.[6]

As Coleman has argued, when individuals are linked in more than one context, a multiplex relationship, 'it allows for the resources of one relationship to be appropriated for use in others' (Coleman, 1988: S108).

Following their first public meeting, attended by over 100 people, the motion to make Chelmsford a Fairtrade Town was proposed by the Liberal Democrat party and was seconded by Conservatives, with support from Labour at a local council meeting in November 2003. This cross-party support is believed to have been a crucial element in the success of gaining the support of the local council. By spring 2004, the council had agreed to use fair-trade tea and coffee for internal meetings and in council buildings in Chelmsford. Thus the council offices, the local swimming pool and the theatres in Chelmsford changed their procurement policies, and arguably became 'ethical places' through the removal of the choice of non-fair-trade options. Malpass et al.'s study noted that within Bristol the impetus for the switch to fair-trade came from within the council who used the Fairtrade City Campaign to 'promote the local reputation of the authority and the way it acts within its jurisdiction' (Malpass et al., 2007a: 638). Within Chelmsford, the support of the council was achieved through a bottom-up approach, and the council offered only limited support for the scheme. For example, the CFAG have asked for a banner in the High street to publicise their Fairtrade Town status, and for community funding, and these have not been approved. This situation has improved over time owing to the appointment of a councillor to deal with the group's activities, and an increasing awareness of the activities of neighbouring Fairtrade Towns, which has created friendly rivalry. While in Bristol, the support of the council enabled 'the widening of fair-trade constituencies' beyond primarily faith-based social networks towards membership according to residency within a place (ibid.), the support of fair-trade within Chelmsford still relies heavily on faith-groups and other social and political activists.

Fair-trade events are one of the key ways in which Town groups seek to raise awareness of fair-trade in their area, as well as recruit new supporters. Events often combine the consumption of fair-trade goods with a social or cultural activity, mirroring the approach of the Co-operative movement in the early twentieth century (see Chapter 2 and Gurney, 1996).[7] For example, the pot luck dinner organised by the United Reform Church in Chelmsford encouraged attendees to bring along a dish cooked with fair-trade ingredients to share in the company of others. Similarly, the visit from a Brazil nut producer to the Chelmsford Star Co-op annual gathering during Fairtrade Fortnight offered co-operative members the chance to learn about fair-trade and its impact on the producer, at the same time as hearing about the progress of their retail society while enjoying fair-trade food and drinks. These social events create a feeling of community among like-minded individuals – or, as Jenny said, 'you feel like you're not alone in fighting your cause you know'.[8] By having so many supporters from other local groups,[9] the CFAG is able to utilise these networks to promote fair-trade at events that are already happening and to benefit from the publicity of these other events. However in so doing, knowledge and awareness of fair-trade can become concentrated within niche networks, with the location of these events restricted to particular places – the Church, Co-operative meetings and staff rooms, TUC events, interested schools – rather than community events that everyone is likely to know about. At the time of the fieldwork, CFAG had just 19 members, most of whom have some connection to the range of organisations already indicated, and who paid a yearly subscription fee of £2 as an expression of their commitment to raise awareness of fair-trade within their town. However, the numbers who regularly attend meetings is significantly fewer. The steering committee has remained relatively stable, now including representatives from Traidcraft and a local schoolteacher. In order to maintain their Fairtrade Town status, the group continues to encourage local retail stores, catering outlets, community organisations and businesses to use fair-trade and runs local events to raise awareness of their movement, particularly during Fairtrade Fortnight.

For those not involved with fair-trade in Chelmsford, contact with fair-trade will be either through shopping within retail stores in the town or in local organisations, workplaces and public buildings that make fair-trade goods the default option. Members of CFAG often visit local stores to ask them to stock more fair-trade goods, thus shaping the availability and position of fair-trade within their local area. While the small town of Garstang was able to convince a large proportion of its small number of retail stores to stock fair-trade, and Bristol drew on existing dedicated 'fair-trade spaces', where consumers were 'spoilt for ethical choice' (Barnett et al., 2007), there are few independent retail stores or existing ethical spaces in Chelmsford. So the impact of this local campaigning must be placed into the context of mainstream retail stores' policies on fair-trade; for example, given that Sainsbury's made the decision to stock 100 per cent Fairtrade lines, it is unlikely that local consumers will be aware that their town is any different from neighbouring non-Fairtrade Towns whose mainstream retail stores offer the same selection of fair-trade products. Having said this, the Chelmsford Star Co-operative Group has offered a lot of support to the Chelmsford campaign,[10] where commitment to fair-trade sits alongside other 'ethical' food concerns, such as supporting local farmers and community projects. However, since Co-operative stores already constitute 'alternative' retail spaces, it is difficult to say how far their involvement in fair-trade has transformed people's perception of Chelmsford as a Fairtrade Town.

Indeed, those residents whom I spoke with in Chelmsford, who were not actively involved in the Fairtrade Town group's activities, knew very little about fair-trade and were mostly unaware that any transformation had occurred within their town.[11] The next extract reveals how there was a lack of understanding about what being a Fairtrade Town might mean.

| | |
|---|---|
| **Moderator:** | Are you aware that Chelmsford's a Fairtrade town? |
| **Fran:** | No. [surprised] |
| **Moderator:** | Do you know what it might mean? |
| **Amanda:** | No. [laughs] |
| **Daisy:** | We've been shopping and we haven't seen anything to do with fair-trade, have we? |
| **Kelly:** | Not in Asda's yesterday. |
| **Daisy:** | Nothing at all. |
| **Danielle:** | Does it mean they're giving it away? [laughs] |
| **Fran:** | Does that mean that they are actually paying Chelmsford farmers a fair price? |
| **Moderator:** | No. |
| **Fran:** | No then. |
| **Moderator:** | Would you think that would be ...? |
| **Fran:** | Well just the local farmers, perhaps they're getting a fair price because they are a bit ripped off sometimes, aren't they, especially the agricultural side. No, I have no idea. |
| **Moderator:** | Ok it just means that the town promotes fair-trade, but ... |
| **Fran:** | They're not doing it very well then are they? [laughs] |
| **Ling:** | No, we should have heard.[12] |

This group of women had not heard that Chelmsford was a Fairtrade Town, despite living in the area for some time and regularly visiting the town centre. Fran thought that Chelmsford ought to be supporting local farmers, something that other Fairtrade Towns have addressed given the local nature of a Fairtrade Town campaign.[13] For these women, Fairtrade Town events had not been noticed and, given that this focus group was held during Fairtrade Fortnight 2008, there was increased publicity about fair-trade in local supermarkets and retail outlets, even if they had not attended Fairtrade Town events.

When the concept of the Fairtrade Town was explained to residents who knew little about it, there was mixture of interested surprise ('oh wow, that's good'), cynicism ('that sounds like another tick-box exercise and PR stunt to me') and lack of interest.

| | |
|---|---|
| **Interviewer:** | Are you aware that Chelmsford is a Fairtrade town? |
| **Henry:** | No. |
| **Interviewer:** | And what do you think that might mean? |
| **Henry:** | Well, they must have a lot of fair-trade shops. |
| **Interviewer:** | And what do you think of the idea of fair-trade? |
| **Henry:** | I've not thought about it a lot to be quite honest. I'm not against it, but must admit I do tend to buy whatever looks nicest and what I fancy; the only exception is the free range eggs, even if they didn't look as nice as the battery ones, I'd still get the free range ones. |
| **Interviewer:** | And do you think there's a particular sort of person who's likely to buy fair-trade regularly? |
| **Henry:** | Erm … somebody that's a bit fanatical about that sort of thing, yes I think so. |
| **Interviewer:** | What do you mean by that? |
| **Henry:** | Well, you know people who've got a thing about helping the Third World even if it costs them money, yeah I mean that's the image I've got, I may be wrong. In fact we've got a friend who is very much like that and she will go all over the shop to get organic, fair-trade, this, that and the other and I think well you know good luck to her, it doesn't do anything for me. |

(Henry, 80-year-old, retired building surveyor)

It is important to highlight is that even though they were unaware that their town was a Fairtrade Town, many of the Chelmsford residents whom I spoke with were actually buying fair-trade products. For example, I found that despite Henry's lack of interest in fair-trade, he had been regularly buying Fairtrade bananas because he shopped at Sainsbury's. Similarly, Daisy, Fran and Kelley described how they liked to visit the Marks & Spencer's cafe for coffee (which is 100 per cent Fairtrade) when they went out shopping together, and yet they swore that they never bought fair-trade. As provisioning policies switch to fair-trade, accidental purchases are likely to become increasingly common. In this context, Fairtrade Towns work to symbolically sustain the image of the active citizen-consumer.

## Lund

Home to one of the most prestigious universities in Scandinavia, Lund has a population of 110,488, a high percentage of which are aged 20–9.[14] Located in the south of Sweden in the Skåne region, it is the 12th largest municipality in the country. The town is governed by a Conservative Alliance (comprising of the Conservative, Centre, Liberal and Christian Democrat parties), and has an unemployment rate that is lower than the national average. Fifty-eight per cent of Lund's population, between the ages of 25 and 64, has a university education, compared to 29 per cent within Sweden as a whole. The medieval City, with cobbled streets, hosts a number of cultural events and festivals throughout the year, and there are three fair-trade World Shops within Lund, which is a large number if we remember that there are just 44 across the whole of Sweden (Krier, 2007). Indeed the aid organisation IM was founded in Lund,[15] and the World Shop 'Klotet' is one of the largest in Sweden (Högberg, 2011), suggesting that the town already had a strong history of engagement with social justice in the developing world. The main supermarkets, ICA and Coop, can be found both within the centre of the town and in out-of-town complexes, both of which offer a large variety of fair-trade products.

In Lund, the Fairtrade City campaign started in 2006 after the municipal union, SKTF, recommended that the municipality ought to include fair-trade within its procurement policy.[16] In Sweden, Fairtrade Cities tend to start from within the municipality, reflecting the Swedish social-democratic approach in which people ought to be paid for the work they do and fair-trade ought to be managed in a public way. Lund was already engaged with fair-trade, with three World Shops and an active fair-trade group led by the Red Cross Youth who were asking local politicians to support fair-trade. A vote by the city council on 4 May 2006 agreed to allocate funds for the campaign, which was housed within the Environmental Strategy Unit, in the hope that Lund would become the first Fairtrade City in Sweden. However, of the 13 members who voted, three voted against the campaign: two from the Moderate party and one from the Christian Democrat party, because it was argued that this action was akin to charity and therefore not in keeping with the local government policy on the use of municipal funds. Nevertheless, when the steering committee was formed it had five representatives from the municipality, as well as representatives from local businesses, the World Shops, the Red Cross Youth and the Swedish Church, who formed into six working groups to engage with different sections of the City. In April

2007, the town achieved its Fairtrade City status (the third such City in Sweden) and announced this to coincide with the Fairtrade Fokus celebrations (their two-week Fairtrade-themed promotional period).

The initial working groups in Lund dissolved over time, and the steering committee now comprises a paid member of staff and around 12 other people with representatives from the municipality, a local church, the hotel chain Scandic, the World Shops and the local supermarkets, ICA and Coop, as well as a Fairtrade ambassador. While activists within Chelmsford struggled to get the support of their municipality, in Lund support originated from this source, thus offering the campaign a certain degree of legitimacy and power to get things done. For example, a sign was erected in 2008 to announce to residents that Lund is a Fairtrade City.

However, having someone employed in the municipality to coordinate the fair-trade campaign can have its downsides. As the coordinator explained, 'some people feel that Fairtrade Cities is more the municipality's thing [and] ... I don't feel that they feel that they own it in that sense'. The coordinator described some of the difficulties of getting volunteers to run events and engage different sections of Lund's society from her position within the municipality. Unlike Chelmsford, where the grassroots network developed through interaction between individuals who came into contact with one another on a regular basis through other networks, in Lund the coordinator had less social capital on which to draw to encourage the different groups to work together.

Fair-trade events are an important part of being a Fairtrade City and the coordinator often had to initiate events. Recent events have included fair-trade stalls in the City centre with a colouring competition for children, fair-trade coffee mornings, fair-trade sampling in supermarkets and stores, and fair-trade supporters dressed in fair-trade banana suits to raise awareness in their town. Events often coincide with World Fair Trade Day and Fairtrade Fokus because it is expected that local events will be held at the same time as these national/international campaigns, making them a focal point for the coordinator to work towards.

Public procurement of fair-trade goods is the main focus of the Fairtrade City campaign in Lund and other Fairtrade Cities in Sweden. It has proved tricky to engage local businesses in Lund, beyond those stores that were already active around fair-trade. For example, the ICA Malmsborgs[17] store in the centre of Lund offers over 200 fair-trade products, and when the controversial film *Bananas!*[18] was released they ran the trailer of this film in the store next to the fair-trade bananas to encourage consumers to choose them. This apparently led to a 500 per cent increase in sales of fair-trade bananas during the period the trailer was shown (Gertten, 2011), suggesting that this device was very successful in destabilising consumers from their established routines (Callon, Méadel & Rabeharisoa, 2002). Visiting local visiting stores to encourage them to stock more fair-trade products is a key part of what it means to be a Fairtrade Town supporter in the UK, but members of Lund Fairtrade City are not very active in this regard. The coordinator described using an intern who called all the local businesses to ask them to stock fairtrade, but this had little success. However, for Lund Fairtrade City this has not proved too much of a problem when it comes to meeting their sixth Fairtrade City goal of 'continuous improvement' because the national availability of fair-trade products is always increasing.

> Just a few years ago there were only a few products and now there are so many. It's the same as we said in the beginning, people buy it but they are not even aware that they buy it because there's so much to choose from so people aren't really thinking about it. But in this way, it's very good for us because we have to show that what's available should increase every year and that's been quite easy because it has increased on a national level.[19]

## Berkeley

Berkeley is well known for its liberal and artistic identity and was described to the author as a 'leader in environmental and social justice'.[20] Situated on the east shore of the San Francisco Bay in Northern California, Berkeley has a population of 112,580 people and is home to the renowned public university, the University of California, Berkeley. It has a highly educated population (68 per cent of the population over the age of 25 have a degree-level qualification) and 93 per cent of those who are economically active are employed. There are a number of local supermarkets, like the Berkeley Bowl and Andronico's, within the City, as well as a weekly farmer's market, and residents would need to travel to out-of-town estates to access the bargain basement stores like Wal-Mart and Target. With a strong tradition of civic participation, over 200 arts and cultural organisations, established green transport networks and high participation in recycling schemes, plus a World Shop run by the San Francisco-based social justice organisation, Global Exchange, it seems hardly surprising that Berkeley became a Fair Trade Town in 2010. However, the city did have a history of engagement with Fair Trade prior to the Town campaign that was less positive. A local attorney, Rick Young, attempted to pass a piece of legislation that would make all coffee shops serve only Fair Trade coffee in 2002; but 'Measure O' was rejected by city voters because it was felt to be too draconian (Murrmann & Weir, 2002). The more consensual approach adopted by the Fair Trade Towns group eight years later proved more successful.

The campaign in Berkeley was instigated by a passionate environmentalist and spiritual leader who saw Fair Trade as an opportunity to pursue and extend her existing commitments.[21] Rachel was introduced to the Fair Trade concept by her dad who was working with Fair Trade in Chicago, and after meeting with a member of FTUSA through her father she was inspired to make Berkeley a Fair Trade Town. In the summer of 2009, Rachel contacted the City council who were keen to pass through the resolution because they saw it as 'something that fits within [their] core values'.[22] Indeed, Rachel admitted that she did rest 'on the principles that make up Berkeley' and realised that the city already fulfilled the majority of the criteria without them really needing to mobilise consumers to demand this status. Given their proximity to FTUSA, they have several employees from this organisation represented on the steering committee, along with representatives from local Fair Trade businesses (Ben & Jerry's, Global Exchange, a local Deli and Senda Athletics), a local teacher and a representative from the Buy Local movement. In July 2010, Berkeley became the nineteenth Fair Trade town in the United States, but the number of local residents who know they are a Fair Trade Town is likely to be limited because the campaign did not need to build grassroots support to achieve this status; it was already there.[23] The key difference in the USA, with two competing labels, is the need to promote both Fair Trade-certified products and other fair-trade labels in the town campaign. At present Berkeley supporters are happy to recognise both labels, but it will be interesting to see how the Towns deal with this tension in the months to come, following the departure of FTUSA from the FLO.

The large number of Fair Trade businesses engaged in Berkeley compared to the other two towns seems an important difference to highlight. This is perhaps not surprising if we remember that Fair Trade businesses have played an important role in the development of Fair Trade movement in the USA relative to consumer support (see Chapter 3). Fair Trade businesses tend to join Fair Trade Town campaigns because they are a tool to encourage local people to 'frequent their businesses'.[24] It is likely the Fair Trade/sympathetic businesses can increase the sustainability of the town campaigns because there will be an economic benefit for volunteering their time to the campaign. Fair Trade events in Berkeley often involve businesses, such as a 'wine down' evening at the Hub (a working space for small social enterprises), which served Fair Trade wine and included a visit from Fair Trade artisan producers, or the 'free cone day' at Ben & Jerry's, which is a regular event that has been explicitly linked to Fair Trade through the group's activities, or the tour of shops offering Fair Trade products on World Fair Trade day through a collective bike ride, called the 'tour de fair'.

Another interesting partnership within Berkeley is their engagement with the 'Buy Local' movement because it was quickly realised that Berkeley residents were very committed to this movement and they did not want to be seen as though they were in opposition to it. The independent supermarkets in Berkeley offer lots of local produce, and successful campaigning by the Fair Trade group needed to take account of this fact when asking stores to stock Fair Trade. The group campaigns under the slogan 'Buy local, buy fair' and have a stall at the weekly farmer's markets organised by the Buy Local group. Jaffee, Kloppenburg and Monroy (2007) have suggested that domestic fair trade developments can be seen as a way of mitigating 'the problems associated with the "defensive localism" of concern to some observers of alternative agro-food systems' (Jaffee, Kloppenburg & Monroy, 2007: 193). Therefore the collaborations between local and Fair Trade activities in Berkeley[25] are a clever way of overcoming the competing ideologies within the ethics of different consumerist movements.

## Fair-trade communities

Fairtrade Towns begin in different ways and are shaped by different interests but they share common goals: to increase the availability, sales and awareness of fair-trade within their town. I began this chapter by saying that fair-trade is a powerful market device because it intervenes in the construction of markets and works to qualify the characteristics of fair-trade goods in the marketplace. Fairtrade Towns offer an example of such an intervention where consumers, local authorities, businesses and other local organisations come together to shape the public understandings of fair-trade and its availability within their community. Individuals and organisations support Fairtrade Towns for different reasons,[26] and it is through the interactions between these different actors, with their diverse objectives, that the qualities of fair-trade products are collectively defined. Fairtrade Towns can spark debate and resistance in certain circumstances, such as the initial objection in Lund or the conflict with local produce in Berkeley, but it is because the movement has been successful in generating shared support from diverse members of the community that the institutionalisation of fair-trade purchasing, or fair-trade choice-editing, is framed as a possible and legitimate action.

Fairtrade Towns networks are important vehicles for the development of social capital[27] and community cohesion. Micheletti suggests that political consumerism 'builds bridges across different groups in society and bonds likeminded people more closely' (Micheletti, 2010: 154). Successful political consumerist networks rely upon already established civil society organisations for the promotion of their aims, at the same time as creating new networks and forms of social capital through their actions. Fairtrade Towns bond people and groups together, as well as generate bridges between diverse actors, who come to share a new identity based upon a sense of collective interest and concern. Fairtrade Town events work to create a culture of consumption organised around the active engagement of a community of citizen-consumers in the fight against global poverty. This community, not merely the individual citizen-consumer, makes the choice to support fair-trade, which has implications far beyond the individual level and forces us to re-evaluate the nature of fair-trade consumption acts. It seems hardly surprising, therefore, that the Fairtrade Towns movement features heavily in FTUSA's future strategy to 'ignite' consumer interest in the fair-trade campaign.

Chapter 3 revealed that the national fair-trade movements in the UK, Sweden and USA have been largely driven by grassroots activists, municipalities and sympathetic businesses respectively. The three case studies in this section highlighted the importance of this national context in the shaping of Fairtrade Town activities. The municipal coordination of the campaign in Lund provided a stark contrast to the campaign in Chelmsford, which was headed by individuals engaged in multiple local groups who therefore possessed high levels of exchangeable social capital. The existence of a sympathetic collection of fair-trade and independent businesses in Berkeley had an important impact on the coordination of fair-trade events in the town. However, local context is also particularly important and requires further research to unpack the interactions between local level circumstances and the national systems of fair-trade promotion and provisioning. In other parts of the USA, where there are not the same levels of support or numbers of independent retailers as in Berkeley, the organisation of Fair Trade town campaigns will differ substantially.[28] The case study in Chelmsford reflects this point, with few independent businesses making it harder for their

Fairtrade Town status to be recognised by those with little interest in fair-trade. In this case, the national policies of the large supermarket retailers are particularly important for generating fair-trade sales (and in some cases awareness) within the local population.

Towns are likely to have varying success in raising the awareness of fair-trade among their general population. It has been argued that citizen-led activism, which creates legislated and voluntary fair-trade spaces, has the potential to communicate the political message of global trade justice to the citizen-consumer (Low & Davenport, 2007). However, it seems important to point out that choice-editing within a Fairtrade town makes it unlikely that all fair-trade consumption acts within these towns are motivated through support for, and knowledge of, the aims of the fair-trade movement. Indeed, research with non-fair-trade supporters in Chelmsford revealed the incidence of 'accidental' fair-trade purchasing, where people had bought fair-trade without being aware that they had done so. We are reminded of what Clarke et al. said about the need to create 'acts not identities' when mobilising and representing ethical consumers in the public realm. It is important to show that fair-trade goods are being bought, which can then be represented as indicative of widespread public support for the fair-trade movement. At the same time as these fair-trade acts are generated and counted, Fairtrade Town campaigns are able to stand-in and symbolically provide 'proof' of this widespread public support, thus sustaining the image of the active citizen-consumer identity.

Becoming a Fairtrade Town relies upon the continued engagement of a network of 'self-selecting' supporters. It is a process that may take a number of years to achieve and involves incremental changes to the 'landscapes of consumption' and the policies of local organisations and businesses. It may be for this reason that those not directly engaged in the campaign know little about it. The fair-trade promotional period, on the other hand, provides a concentrated episode of fair-trade 'exposure', which is specifically aimed at raising awareness and sales of fair-trade among the general population, as well as generating media coverage and business/organisational support. It is difficult to separate Fairtrade Towns from the fair-trade promotional period as Fairtrade Town events are often timed to coincide with Fairtrade Fortnight or World Fair Trade Day. However, because the fair-trade promotional period targets institutions and businesses beyond Fairtrade Town networks, and occurs nationwide or even worldwide, it offers us unique insights into the way the movement mobilises support for its aims and the persistence of a very particular construction of the 'fair-trade citizen-consumer'.

## The fair-trade promotional period

It is Fairtrade Fortnight 2008 (25 February to 9 March) and across the UK 12,000 fair-trade events are being held by fair-trade supporters, ranging from the launch event on London's South Bank that attracts 8000 visitors to local coffee mornings, university debates and fashion shows. Twenty-eight communities have announced their achievement of Fairtrade Town status, and Sainsbury's and the Co-op are switching all of their own-brand tea to Fairtrade, at the same time as Tate & Lyle will switch its retail sugar to Fairtrade. In retail stores across the country, there are creative point of sale displays that highlight fair-trade options, often with images of fair-trade producers; there is also 20 per cent off the price of fair-trade products in the Co-op and Morrisons, and Asda has 'rolled back' the cost of fair-trade while Sainsbury's are awarding triple Nectar points for fair-trade purchases.[29] Sir Steve Redgrave[30] launches Fairtrade cotton T-Shirts in Debenhams and cotton fair-trade clothing is also promoted in Topshop and John Lewis. Harriet Lamb, Executive Director of the FTF, releases her book *Fighting the Banana Wars and Other Fairtrade Battles* (2008), which tells of the success of the fair-trade movement and the poverty it is alleviating. On the other hand, the Adam Smith Institute releases a report entitled *Unfair Trade* (Sidwell, 2008), which questions the degree to which fair-trade actually helps producers in the developing world. Seven thousand people send a Trade Justice postcard to Gordon Brown, the then Prime Minister, to ask him to use his influence in G20 meetings to make all trade fair, 87 MPs sign an Early Day Motion in support of launching a 'Fairtrade Schools' programme, and the Department for International Development awards the FTF £1.2 million to support its work. Fairtrade banana and coffee producers are touring the country on the special Fairtrade Tour Bus to tell consumers and community groups about the benefits of fair-trade. There are 5309 fair-trade 'media hits' in national and local newspapers and television programmes, as well as a number of stories in women's magazines because International Women's Day falls within the two-week fair-trade promotional period (see FTF, 2008a).

Campaigning under the slogan 'Change Today, Choose Fairtrade', Fairtrade Fortnight aimed to communicate to consumers that 'through their daily choices, their actions can have a significant impact to benefit producers' lives in developing countries' (ibid.: 6). Involving, local supporters, retail stores and commercial businesses, NGOs, media outlets, local and national government, Fairtrade Fortnight offered something for everyone. However, its key target was the fair-trade citizen-consumer who was provided with various resources to get involved with the campaign and persuaded through different devices to 'choose' fair-trade (for a detailed overview of this campaign, see Wheeler, 2012).

The fair-trade promotional period has become a common feature of fair-trade campaigning across the world. In October, the two-week campaign 'Fairtrade Fokus' occurs in Sweden, in the USA this is 'Fair Trade Month', and in Belgium there is the 'Semaine du Commerce Équitable'. On the second Saturday of May, the 'global Fair Trade Festival', World Fair Trade Day (WFTD), is organised by the WFTO and is described as 'a worldwide celebration supported by the business and consumer community, by policy makers and media as well as by thousands of social movements, NGOs and more than 100,000 volunteers' (WFTD, 2011a). Some national campaigns arrange for their main promotional period to include WFTD, such as the 'Quinzaine du Commerce Équitable' in France and 'Fair Trade Fortnight' in New Zealand and Australia, which both happen in May. Dedicating certain moments of the year to the promotion of a particular issue is something that can be found in other fields – for example, there is a 'Recycle Week' in June in the UK, and in different states of the USA there are various 'Buy Local Weeks'.

Historical precedents can also be found, such as the annual Co-operative Festival in Britain (discussed in Chapter 2) or the 'Empire Weeks' in the 1920s (Trentmann, 2007). The Empire Weeks were organised by Conservative women's movements to promote empire goods, and we find many parallels between this campaign and the fair-trade promotional period, with images of the producers of empire goods used to promote the movement and the rhetoric of caring for distant others through careful purchasing.[31]

So the promotional period is not a novel concept with its expositional marketing techniques, but its persistence across different contexts suggests that it offers a distinct opportunity as a campaigning device. This section will highlight two related aims of fair-trade promotional periods, which mirror Clarke et al.'s (2007a) findings: first that they provide resources for self-selecting audiences to celebrate and extend their commitment to fair-trade, and second that they increase the visibility of the fair-trade citizen-consumer and the fair-trade movement across various locations.

For the fair-trade supporter, the fair-trade promotional period is a chance to bring together people from within their social networks to celebrate their support of fair-trade and hopefully encourage others to support the movement too. For the Fairtrade Towns, who need to generate media coverage and run events as a condition of their status, the fair-trade promotional period offers the perfect moment for them to concentrate their activities. Indeed, the guides that fair-trade organisations provide supporters with to help them to plan and organise events often assume that supporters are already organised in their community (FFTS, 2010c; FTF, 2008b; WFTD, 2011b). For example, campaigners are encouraged to hold fair-trade fashion shows, stalls, concerts, coffee mornings, pub quizzes, sports days and cooking competitions, all of which would require a base of supporters to organise them. In the UK, the FTF offers tailored action guides to faith groups, reflecting the strong support traditionally found in these networks, and in the Swedish guide, consumers are encouraged to work with their local church and municipality to promote fair-trade. The fair-trade promotional period offers fair-trade supporters the chance to extend and deepen their engagement with fair-trade, but this is always contingent on how fair-trade is organised at the national level (see Chapter 3). So in the UK, fair-trade supporters are given the opportunity to lobby their MPs through Trade Justice postcards (FTF, 2008a), whereas in Sweden, supporters are encouraged to persuade their municipality to procure fair-trade (FFTS, 2010d), and in the USA consumers can sign up to receive alerts from fair-trade businesses about events that have been sponsored by these popular Fair Trade brands (FTUSA, 2009b). The fair-trade promotional period generates 'resources of hope' through its creation of real and imagined communities of fair-trade supporters who together think through the 'extended cultural impact' of their own and others' actions, providing them with opportunities to address this (Littler, 2009: 5). Indeed, in honour of WFTD 2011, 13 towns across the world declared their achievement of Fairtrade Town status, bringing the total number of Fairtrade Towns to 1000. This community of self-selecting supporters are offered the occasion to have fun, at the same time as fair-trade is celebrated and promoted across the country/world.

One of the key ways the fair-trade promotional period communicates its message – that the citizen-consumer makes a difference when they buy fair-trade – is through the careful representation of the fair-trade producer. Fairtrade producer tours are a common feature of the fair-trade promotional period, where fair-trade producers visit towns, universities and events and appear in the media to provide a first-hand narrative of the impacts of fair-trade upon their lives. In Sweden during Fairtrade Fokus 2010 Aubrey and Charity, sugar producers from Malawi, launched the two-week campaign and made visits to Stockholm, Örebro, Hallsberg, Jönköping and Nässjö, as well as to the supermarkets where their sugar is sold (FFTS, 2010d). During Fairtrade Fortnight 2008 in the

UK, the FTF wanted their campaign to make 'real connections' between the 'world of the consumer ... [and] the world of the producer' so as to make consumers 'feel good by changing their choices and changing people's lives' (FTF, 2008a: 6). Malpass et al. have suggested that visits from fair-trade producers to Fairtrade Towns provide an occasion when 'local meets global' in which consumers can rethink the global consequences of their local actions (Malpass et al., 2007a: 641–2). Indeed, fair-trade supporters in Chelmsford often spoke of the producer visits that had been organised in their town and revealed how coming face to face with a producer enabled them to imagine the impact of fair-trade on real people:

> One of the things I remember very much about bananas was when they had the meeting in the cathedral and they had that man from, I think it was the Windward Isles, talking about what a difference it made to him and his family and the Island. I think that was quite important really because you suddenly feel you're able to relate it, to something positive that was happening for someone. You know, it's not just a vague thing out in the ether, it was actually people that were being benefited and I thought that was really quite amazing.
>
> (Lyn, WI representative)[32]

> I have met fair-trade producers when they've come over to this country for the fair-trade events in Chelmsford. I met two or three different fair-trade producers, heard their stories, and also you read about lots of different things. You can probably look on the back of one of the teabags, there's probably a story on there about a fair-trade producer I imagine, well there's a face on there, it's a generic story I think. Meeting a cocoa producer or a, what was the one, fair-trade wine producers from South Africa were at one of the fair-trade events in the last year or two. Meeting those people hearing their stories in the flesh if you like, it does make a difference.
>
> (Leon, 34-year-old musician)

By showcasing fair-trade producers at events, fair-trade supporters are provided with 'proof' of the effectiveness of their shopping choices. This helps to motivate and sustain their support of fair-trade, offering them with memories or 'stories in the flesh' that differ from those generic/vague stories placed on the back of fair-trade packaging.

Fair-trade producers are often the subjects of 'romantic commodification' because they add symbolic value to fair-trade products, justifying their higher price not on the basis of product quality but on the basis of the producer's 'identifiable otherness' (Varul, 2008a: 668; see also Wright, 2004). Fair-trade producer visits certainly, if unintentionally, work to construct the producer as a spectacle for the audience to admire and photograph.[33]

> At the Co-op annual meeting we had a guy who harvested Amazon Nuts, which we call Brazil Nuts, but Brazil produces the smallest proportion of Amazon Nuts and this chap, a real native, a really swarthy South American look, he was growing a fair-trade co-operative for these people who grew the Amazon Nuts. And the way you harvest them, because they're naturally produced trees, you can't transplant them, so they've got to come up from seedlings, and it's totally natural in the sense that these things grow to about 80 feet in a great big cluster, and they drop and if one of these things drops on your head it kills you. So they have a lot of illness and they literally go out from their villages, which are very, very basic, and harvest these things, They were being ripped off by the traders so they all got together and they are producing jolly good quality stuff because they got together and they produce their own health service and things like that, in the middle of the Amazon!
>
> (Oliver, 65 years, retired senior civil servant)

For Oliver, the visit from the fair-trade producer brought him close to 'a real native' and revealed a dangerous way of life that he was unaware existed and had helped to improve through his support of fair-trade. Producer visits often reinforce the predictable before/after narratives (i.e. before fair-trade life was bad, after fair-trade life is better) that imbue the majority of fair-trade marketing. Fair-trade consumers are romantically projected into faraway lands as 'empowered actors', alleviating the suffering and hardship of the hard-working producer by merely using a different brand of sugar or nuts (Varul, 2008a: 661). The fair-trade citizen-consumer is thus framed as a powerful figure whose choices have wide ramifications for the livelihoods of workers in the developing world. For Varul, representations such as this highlight the inequality between the consumer and producer because, rather than achieving the recognition of an equal commercial partner (as the fair-trade movement claims), the portrayal of the producer is in the end in the 'position of the servant' – their situation is always dependent upon the continued purchasing and compassion of the consumer (ibid.: 669). For the fair-trade supporters whom I spoke with, fair-trade producer visits offered them an opportunity to relate to these individuals as people rather than as faceless victims of global capitalism, and to feel that they played some part in ensuring their dignity through trade. While this may indeed reflect unequal relations between the two parties, the fact that fair-trade supporters felt pride and hope through engaging with fair-trade producers should not be ignored.

Producer visits for the fair-trade supporters are complemented by creative point of sale displays in supermarkets and retail outlets that place images of the fair-trade producer next to fair-trade products. Supermarkets are generally supportive of the fair-trade promotional period and use various material devices, such as point of sale displays, cleverly designed packaging and promotional discounts, to guide us towards the 'right' choice (Cochoy, 2007). Fair-trade offers an opportunity for market professionals to destabilise consumers from their established routines and to encourage them to re-evaluate the qualities of goods. Retail outlets use the fair-trade promotional period to their advantage to highlight their ethical credentials and to engage with their local community and customers. For example, Whole Foods in the USA ran a series of events during Fair Trade Month 2011, which highlighted their position as a committed retailer of Fair Trade goods. The fair-trade promotional period offers businesses that are committed to fair-trade the opportunity to promote their goods, and provides the platform for those retailers/businesses who want to make a more public, or deeper, commitment to fair-trade to do so – as exemplified by Sainsbury's in the UK who have regularly chosen the fair-trade promotional period to announce their intention to switch to 100 per cent Fairtrade lines.

With so much visibility for the fair-trade movement and high-profile fair-trade switches, it is perhaps not surprising that those with a critique of the fair-trade movement's aims and claims use this period to raise their opinion. Free trade think-tanks, in particular, time the release of their reports to coincide with fair-trade promotional periods, with the week before WFTD seeing a report by Brink Lindsey (2003) from the Cato Institute in the USA and an article from Lydiah Wålsten (2011) from Timbro in Sweden. In 2008, the Adam Smith Institute published their report on fair-trade, which accused Fairtrade Fortnight of being 'a marketing exercise intended to maintain the Fairtrade mark's predominance in an increasingly competitive marketplace for ethically-branded products' (Sidwell, 2008: 3). As Sidwell argues, 'hard questions are not on the programme for Fairtrade Fortnight' and supporters are 'encouraged to join in, quite uncritically, and help sell fair-trade products' (ibid.: 6). These reports have in common a desire to highlight that fair-trade is not a solution to global poverty and, in more recent years, to challenge the monopoly of the fair-trade label over other ethical brands. These challenges force the fair-trade movement to defend their model of trade, and they do this by constructing a very particular image of the fair-trade citizen-consumer. In this way, we can see how the two organisations use the 'real and discursive figure of the ethical consumer' (Clarke et al., 2007a: 238) to engage in a debate about the efficacy of their models of economic development through trade.

It is interesting to look at the way the FTF defends its vision of the consumer:

> Two billion people work extremely hard to earn a living but still earn less than $2 per day and the FAIRTRADE Mark enables British consumers to choose products that help address this injustice. As no-one is forced to join a fair trade producer organisation, or to buy fair-trade products, you would think that free market economists like the Adam Smith Institute would be pleased at the way the British public has taken our voluntary label to its heart – and to the super-market checkout – to the tune of nearly half a billion pounds worth of goods in 2007 alone.
>
> FTF (2008c)

It was important for the FTF to highlight the voluntary nature of the Fairtrade model and to suggest that the fair-trade citizen-consumer actively and reflexively *chooses* fair-trade products. However, in so doing, the FTF conveniently ignores the growing tendency for fair-trade choice-editing (by towns, churches, supermarkets and brands), which make it far from a 'voluntary label'.

In defending the fair-trade citizen-consumer, the fair-trade movement is able to draw on data from market research surveys, which can be represented as indicative of 'coherent trends in consumer preference' (Clarke et al., 2007a: 237). During Fairtrade Fokus 2010, the FFTS was able to show that sales of fair-trade goods increased by 21 per cent (FFTS, 2010d: 7), and in 2008, the Fairtrade Foundation argued that by the end of Fairtrade Fortnight, awareness of fair-trade had increased by 13 per cent compared to the same time the previous year. A Globescan report (2009) was conducted on behalf of the FLO, and its findings were reported just before WFTD; the report argued that 'active ethical con-sumers' make up more than half of the population in 15 countries across the globe, with fair-trade being the label that consumers trust the most (FTUSA, 2009c). The conflation of changed patterns of consumption and attitudes with the behaviours of individual consumers works to suggest that 'the primary agency of changing consumption is that of consumer choice, rather than ... changed policies of collective provisioning' (Clarke et al., 2007a: 239). Although the fair-trade promotional period is really for existing supporters, through their work with corporations, and by having a period of 'exposure' in which to measure change, it makes it seem as if it 'works' on the general public.

Indeed, I conducted focus groups with 30 residents living in Chelmsford who had no connection to the Fairtrade Town network during Fairtrade Fortnight 2008. Although all of those that attended would have recently come into contact with fair-trade promotional displays when visiting their local supermarket and may have in fact made fair-trade purchases in their weekly shopping, they were unaware that any campaign was running or of buying fair-trade goods.[34] This is illustrated in the following exchange.

| | |
|---|---|
| **Moderator:** | And are you aware that we are at the end of Fairtrade fortnight? |
| **Reshmi:** | No. |
| **Several together:** | No. |
| **Moderator:** | Do you know what Fairtrade fortnight's about? |
| **Karl:** | No. |
| **Emma:** | No. |
| **Diane:** | I imagine encouraging people to buy Fairtrade goods, but I've not heard it anywhere. |
| **Emma:** | No, I haven't seen anything. |
| **Reshmi:** | So when does it finish then? |
| **Moderator:** | Today. |
| **Karl:** | There's not been very much publicity about it, has there? |
| **Dave:** | No, there can't have been otherwise we'd have known about it. |
| **Diane:** | It's not been in the paper. |
| **Karl:** | Well, it's not been on telly. |
| **Reshmi:** | Or nothing in the supermarkets which is one way of promoting it. So that should have really helped them if they'd have advertised it when they're selling their products. I never knew.[35] |

The participants in the previous extract mostly did their food shopping at Sainsbury's, where all the bananas and a large number of the teas and coffees are Fairtrade, and where there were large Fairtrade promotional displays during the fortnight at the Chelmsford store. It seems that, like Fairtrade Towns, the fair-trade promotional period will have limited success in raising awareness among those who do not already have an existing engagement with, or sympathy for, fair-trade. This does not mean that these individuals have not purchased fair-trade goods either accidentally or because they are on special offer, but it does mean we ought to be cautious about representing these consumption acts as indicative of fair-trade support. As one respondent pointed out, 'I could have fair-trade stuff in my house and I wouldn't have a clue, 'cos I don't notice it, I don't see it.' This chapter has shown, and the next chapter will demonstrate, that being a fair-trade supporter involves a lot more than merely buying fair-trade goods.

## Fair-trade as a 'market device'

This chapter has explored two promotional campaigns commonly employed by the international fair-trade movement in order to highlight how they work to generate support from different sections of the community, and how this is then used to justify and motivate changes to systems of collective provisioning. Fair-trade campaigning is about fostering a collective culture among a group of self-selecting fair-trade supporters and integrating their consumption and promotion of fair-trade goods into social and cultural activities. Fairtrade Towns, in particular, are working to generate a feeling of collective community among fair-trade supporters across 24 countries within over 1000 separate town campaigns. But, importantly, this feeling is not necessarily generated among the non-fair trade-supporting communities. The social and cultural activities that are enjoyed by fair-trade supporters within their community are crucial for sustaining their commitment to the movement, at the same time as enrolling others, with varying levels of interest in fair-trade, into the consumption of fair-trade goods. Changes to local systems of provision are motivated in the name of this community of self-selecting fair-trade supporters whose activities sustain the image of the active citizen-consumer. Fair-trade organisations do play a crucial role in publicly shaping the representation of this figure – through the provision of action guides, the reporting of fair-trade sales figures and the organisation of national fair-trade events, like the fair-trade promotional period – but this chapter has shown that the fair-trade supporter and a whole host of other actors play an equally important role in sustaining the image of the fair-trade citizen-consumer.

Through an examination of three Fairtrade Town case studies we have seen that they emerge from different locations. The municipalities tend to take the lead on the campaign in Sweden (and other Nordic countries) in order to promote their identity as a responsible town, whereas in the UK and USA, grassroots supporters have been more important in the initial phase of the campaign. Having said this, in the UK it is becoming increasingly common for Fairtrade Town campaigns to start from within the municipality.[36] In the USA, given the levels of variation across this large country, it is difficult to make broad generalisations on the basis of one case study, but there does appear to be strong support for fair-trade among local businesses (such as Ben & Jerry's and fair-trade stores), reflecting the historical development of fair-trade within the USA (see previous chapter). In all countries, there has been strong support for Fairtrade Towns and fair-trade promotional events among religious and sustainability networks. Given the goals that Fairtrade Towns must meet within their community, regardless of where the campaign starts, networks are established among the business, voluntary/community and municipal sectors as the campaign progresses. Of course, the ability of Fairtrade Town organisers to reach out to other sectors of the community is influenced by their levels of social capital (e.g. municipal employees who are paid to run the campaign may have more difficulty persuading volunteers to promote fair-trade than grassroots campaigners with already established connections in the community), as well as by their influence with local decision-makers. Fairtrade Towns build bridges and networks between diverse groups, which generates a feeling of shared support for fair-trade. This then enables the institutionalisation of fair-trade purchasing, or fair-trade choice-editing, to be framed as a legitimate and called-for action. It is therefore hardly surprising that the national fair-trade organisations are very keen to support the development of Fairtrade Towns.

Fair-trade promotional periods and events provide committed fair-trade supporters with a feeling of community and shared purpose in the fight against trade injustices. The fair-trade promotional period provides a concentrated episode of fair-trade 'exposure' during which time various fair-trade-supporting organisations and individuals join in to celebrate and mobilise the movement and the citizen-consumer. They work to connect an international community, with producers in the developing world being linked to 'glocal' communities of consumers and organisations. Unlike the Co-operative movement, which aimed to instigate a social revolution by educating the working classes and offering an alternative culture based on the shared situation of consumers and producers, the fair-trade movement provides an alternative culture for a selected group of consumers whose social situations are very different from the producers they aim to help. While there is an emphasis on creating a partnership based on equal recognition, the consumer and producer are not engaged in an equal exchange. The producer is always in need of the consumer's continued purchasing, which relies on the consumer sustaining motivation and belief in the effectiveness of buying fair-trade goods. Visits from fair-trade producers to local fair-trade events offer committed fair-trade supporters both these resources, as well a sense of hope about the possibility of participating in a fairer world.

The flip side to this discussion is how far these promotional market devices actually succeed in raising the awareness of those who do not have an existing interest in fair-trade. Discussions with residents in Chelmsford revealed very limited awareness of the promotional period or Fairtrade Town status, suggesting that there is a danger that these activities are contained within niche social networks. Of course, Fairtrade Towns will have varying success in promoting their status depending upon the size of the town, the number of independent retail outlets and how active the group is in the local community. Fair-trade events do seem to be organised for the existing supporters, but there is often an increase in fair-trade sales over fair-trade promotional periods, which makes it appear as though people are choosing more fair-trade because they have been persuaded to do so. In the UK, Fairtrade sales figure drop steadily after Fairtrade Fortnight (see FTF, 2008a: 28), suggesting that those who buy fair-trade in this period have not necessarily been converted to fair-trade because of a commitment to the movement, but rather have been destabilised from established routines through various market devices, such as promotional discounts and creative displays. The degree to which consumers are aware that they have bought fair-trade products during this period, as well as at other times throughout the year, is questionable. Nevertheless, the movement uses increasing sales figures to suggest that more people are buying fair-trade because they support the movement's aims.

Littler (2009) has argued that ethical or 'radical' consumption should not be celebrated uncritically as a progressive and positive force for social change, but neither should it be devalued or dismissed without recognising its political potential. Fair-trade is indeed a symbol of hope around which many different organisations coalesce and, given the huge success of the International Fairtrade Towns movement, it should be recognised as such. This chapter has shown how fair-trade promotional tactics can offer *some* consumers, retailers and organisations the opportunity to act as citizens both within the market and as political campaigners to improve the livelihoods of *some* producers in the developing world. However, at the same time as it offers pathways for some into deeper engagement with trade justice issues, it enlists the support of others without them necessarily being aware of it. This is somewhat problematic given that the model is defended by paying attention to the reflexivity and awareness that surrounds fair-trade consumption acts. As various actors come together to qualify fair-trade as the most effective mechanism for helping disadvantaged producers and the market is shaped accordingly, it is important that the debate does not become closed off and that alternative actions for consumers, producers, corporations and governments are explored.[37] The growing number of Fairtrade Town networks may offer the space for this debate, given their location within the state, market and civil society, but actors within this network need to engage critically with fair-trade as a model and movement rather than merely celebrate it.

# 5
# The Practice of Fair-Trade Support

Calls for individuals to change their consumption behaviours in order to tackle social problems like global poverty and climate change have become increasingly prevalent within contemporary society. The last chapter revealed how a diverse array of institutions, from the government to NGOs, the media, educational institutions and grassroots activist movements, are constructing citizens as co-responsible for global trade injustices and encouraging them to take action by altering the ways they consume and handle everyday goods. Although a great deal of these calls to action rest on the assumption that the key to changing consumption behaviour lies in the provision of the 'right' types of information that will enable the 'citizen-consumer' to choose wisely, we have already seen how infrastructures of provision and social conventions are shaping the 'do-ability' of fair-trade consumption acts. One example discussed was Fairtrade Towns where fair-trade options have been made the standard choice because of the actions of committed fair-trade supporters who together are promoting and celebrating the fair-trade movement; another was fair-trade promotional periods where fair-trade options are highlighted with the aid of creative point of sale displays and price reductions that are likely to destabilise consumers from their established routines and encourage them to reflect on the qualities of consumer goods. Indeed, social-scientific consumer research has for a long time demonstrated how consumption is a highly complex, dynamic and multi-relational social phenomenon, which cannot be understood as a matter of purely individual choice (Halkier, 2010; Miller, 1998; Sassatelli, 2006; Shove, 2003; Warde, 2005). These studies have challenged the neoclassical idea of the consumer as a powerful, rational, utility-maximising actor, and have instead highlighted the range of economic, cultural and social processes that can influence everyday consumer behaviour. This chapter builds upon this tradition of social science research by applying tools from a practice-theoretical perspective (Halkier, 2010; Warde, 2005) to the empirical analysis of the experiences of fair-trade supporters living within a British Fairtrade Town.

If we are to understand fair-trade consumption fully we must take account of the situational, institutional and cultural contexts in which this consumption practice occurs. The socio-demographic characteristics of the consumer, the places and spaces in which fair-trade products are promoted and displayed, and the ways in which fair-trade consumption is framed by the institutions responsible for mediating acquisition and use, are all likely to have a significant impact upon the likelihood of an individual/group consuming fair-trade. As we have seen, these factors vary from country to country, as well as at the local level. The material presented in this chapter has been drawn from interviews and ethnographic research in Chelmsford, UK, and it will be important for the reader to have in mind the distinctive features of this context (as presented in the previous two chapters). For example, the mainstream provisioning of fair-trade and strong grassroots networks of support in the UK offer a different environment for the realisation of fair-trade support from that in the USA where mainstream retailer support for Fair Trade and the numbers of Fair Trade Towns lag behind. Equally, the municipal responsibility for the Fairtrade City in Lund offers an important contrast to the coalition of interested organisations engaged in the Fairtrade Town group in Chelmsford whose activities are organised within specific niche social networks within their community. The approach developed in this chapter acknowledges that consumption is a contingent and complex process that varies across space and time and is shaped by different systems of provision, social networks and cultural understandings. It is therefore an approach that is capable of being applied to other contexts beyond its usage here, for example, to fair-trade supporters in other countries or to other forms of ethical consumption (such as recycling and buying local and organic food).

This chapter begins with a review of the analytical positions through which fair-trade/ethical consumption has been studied using Halkier's (2010) recent characterisation of this emerging field. I then discuss the possibilities of applying a practice-theoretical approach, before presenting the 'careers' of four fair-trade supporters. The reader will learn how the paths into fair-trade support are informed by a range of commitments, and how the actions of fair-trade supporters work to reproduce and expand this practice. I will conclude with an examination of the 'career' of a couple who are committed to a yogic-vegetarian lifestyle

in order to demonstrate how engagement in a different set ⟨
practices can lead to different perceptions of, and dispositions ⟨
fair-trade. In this way, the reader will learn why the image of the fair-
trade supporter as an individual and choosy 'citizen-consumer' fails to
provide a convincing basis on which to understand fair-trade support.

## Fair-trade consumption and theories of practice

Halkier (2010) identifies four key analytical positions that have emerged
to account for the incidence of ethical, or what she terms 'challenged',
consumption. The first position refers to attempts to generate knowledge about how best to *steer consumers* towards more socially acceptable
forms of consumption behaviour. Within the fair-trade consumption
literature this rationalistic position finds its followers among those who
measure (and often lament) the gaps between an individual's attitudes
and knowledge of the fair-trade model and their purchasing behaviours
(Basu & Hicks, 2008; De Pelsmacker, Driesen & Rayp, 2005; Dolan, 2008;
Lamb, 2007).

The second and third positions offer a consideration of the possibilities
for consumer agency in the context of these attempts to direct and control consumer behaviour through the provision of information. On the
one hand, there are those who draw from life-politics- inspired accounts
(Beck, 1994; Giddens, 1991) in order to suggest that the conditions of late
modernity are opening up new possibilities for consumers, or *empowering
consumers*, to use their shopping choices to enact their political agency
(Lyon, 2006; Micheletti, 2010; Shaw, Newholm & Dickinson, 2006).
This optimistic position relies upon the intentionality and autonomy of
consumer action, or votes, towards particular political or social ends. On
the other hand, there are those who question whether using the realm
of consumption to enact political agency is *disempowering consumers* by
encouraging individuals to govern and control their own behaviours
rather than challenge or transform the political organisation of society
(Bauman, 1998; Goodman, 2004; Maniates, 2002). This third position
has sparked debates about whether all individuals are equally able to
participate as citizen-consumers given the inequalities in the number
of votes individuals have. Fair-trade goods can be more expensive than
their non-fair-trade counterparts, and this has led some to conclude that
structural factors such as social class and income determine levels of fair-
trade consumption – 'being a reflexive consumer denotes a particular
position in terms of class, education, and/or level of existing knowledge'
(Goodman, 2004: 909).

Halkier argues that these three positions share the same 'blind spot': a limited acknowledgement that 'domestic consumption activities in themselves are highly complex social everyday phenomena' (Halkier, 2010: 14). This leads her to the fourth position, the *everyday complexities of consumption*, which is characterised by an appreciation of the contingent variations in the handlings and understandings of ethical consumer goods among individuals across space and time. Consumption within this position is understood as an everyday practice carried out collectively by groups of individuals who are operating within particular institutional and material contexts, which in turn are stabilised and transformed through their actions. In the field of fair-trade consumption research, Adams and Raisborough's (2008) 'situated understanding of reflexivity', which suggests that individuals are capable of reflecting upon their actions and conditions at the same time as being bound and enabled by those conditions, and Varul's (2009) exploration of how different cultural and institutional contexts can shape the opportunities to participate in fair-trade consumer action, offer two examples of this fourth position. Although a number of everyday life-oriented approaches could be employed under this fourth position to study the sociology of 'challenged' consumption, Halkier suggests that a practice-theoretical approach can most usefully guide empirical analysis in this field. Let us therefore turn to a brief discussion of how practice theory can be applied to the study of fair-trade consumption.

There has been a great deal of interest in practice theory in recent years (Bourdieu, 1990; Giddens, 1984; Reckwitz, 2002; Schatzki, 1996; 2001; 2002; Warde, 2005), and it is not the intention of this chapter to contribute to the development of a coherent theory of practice, nor to defend the principles upon which it is based. Rather, I utilise elements from this analytical approach to provide new insights into the processes through which fair-trade consumption is organised and carried out. Unsurprisingly, practice theory is concerned with the 'bundle of organised activities' known as practices (Schatzki, 2002). A practice is

> a routinised way in which bodies are moved, objects are handled, subjects are treated, things are described and the world is understood. … It is a 'type' of behaving and understanding that appears at different locales, and at different points of time and is carried out by different bodies and minds.
>
> Reckwitz (2002: 250)

A practice forms a 'block' comprising a number of different elements, including bodily and mental activities, background knowledge, technical know-how, material infrastructure, shared understandings, institutional frameworks and cultural conventions, whose existence 'depends on the existence and specific interconnectedness of these elements and which cannot be reduced to any one of these single elements' (ibid.). A practice, therefore, is a co-ordinated entity (such as ways of consuming, cooking, working), which consists of 'doings and sayings' (activity and its representations) that are linked together by understandings (know-how), procedures or rules, and engagements (the normative orientations about what/how to do) (Halkier, 2010: 29; Warde, 2005: 134).

In order for a practice to come into existence, it must be regularly performed, suggesting that actors continually create and stabilise practices through their habituated everyday actions. Because practices are performed phenomena, they are highly dependent upon social interaction – 'practices come into being in the processes of activities carried out in front of, together with, and in relation to others' (Halkier, 2010: 30). Practices must be socially recognisable to other practitioners, implying that social networks are likely to play an important role in the coordination and maintenance of a practice. Indeed, the existence of over 1000 Fairtrade Town networks across the globe highlights this influential role of social networks in the growth of the fair-trade movement and the practice of fair-trade support.

An important starting point when applying a theory of practice approach to consumption is to recognise that consumption 'is not itself a practice but is, rather, a moment in almost every practice' (Warde, 2005: 137). In carrying out a practice, we will often be required to use things/goods in a particular way, and how we understand and actually use these things will be guided by the organisation of the practice rather than any personal decision about consuming. It follows that if we want to understand fair-trade consumption we must look at the wider practice of fair-trade support, which is likely to generate desires for fair-trade goods. While this seems to create a constrained image of consumption, which is wholly determined by the organisation of a social practice, this is not the case because not everyone will engage in a practice with the same degree of competency or commitment. Practices are 'internally differentiated on many dimensions', and once an individual is enrolled within a practice, their 'subsequent immersion ... often has the features of a career' (ibid.: 138, 140). Thus the ability to demonstrate support for fair-trade is likely to depend upon an individual's knowledge of the aims of the fair-trade movement and their opportunities for learning about them, having access to fair-trade products and the available resources (both money and time), previous ethical consumer behaviour, knowing other people who support fair-trade, and so on. While Bourdieu (1984) was also concerned with the differentiation of consumption, he tended to attribute differences to external, transposable dispositions and structural determinants such as social class, rather than paying attention to how the organisation of practices results in their internal differentiation (Sassatelli, 2007: 107).[1] That is not to say that differences between groups or classes of people cease to be of interest within this approach, rather they become important elements within the organisation, or interconnected web, of a practice. However, the internal differentiation within this practice will not be reducible to any one of these elements alone.

In the suggestion that an individual's career within a practice should become of focal concern, we see echoes of the ideas presented in classical ethnographical work on subcultures (Becker, 1963; Willis, 1978). In these accounts, consumption practices were closely tied to social contexts, and immersion within particular subcultures created forms of understanding and provided opportunities for developing dispositions towards specific substances or cultural artefacts. As we saw in the last chapter, it does seem that a collective culture is organised around fair-trade support in fair-trade town networks, but consuming fair-trade products does not seem to be a requirement of entry. While the participants in the alternative subcultures described by Willis and Becker understood their consumption of drugs or particular modes of transport as something that highlighted their exclusivity from mainstream society, the practices of fair-trade support are geared towards encouraging more people to consume fair-trade and campaigning to move fair-trade into mainstream retail sectors. Fair-trade supporters seem to have disconnected the consumption of fair-trade from membership in alternative subcultures, although this is influenced by the cultural context in which fair-trade consumption occurs. For example, Varul (2009) has revealed that in Germany, where fair-trade is distributed through dedicated fair-trade shops, fair-trade supporters are more likely to stress the exclusivity of their fair-trade consumption. Therefore the forms that practices can take are likely to be conditional upon 'time, space and social context', which enables collective learning within practices to develop in a particular way (Warde, 2005: 139).

Applying practice theory to an analysis of consumption forces us to focus upon consumption processes,[2] and ask how practices are learnt, carried out and evolve within the context of everyday life. Interest moves away from the attitudes and behaviours of an active consumer and instead concentrates on the 'do-ability' of practical performances and how these are negotiated and shaped by social and institutional contexts. Unlike the 'steering position', which sees consumer's attitudes as relatively static properties, a practice-theoretical approach allows the researcher to explore how understandings, procedures and engagements might be contingent upon particular circumstances. And rather than unproblematically ascribing or denying agency to consumers for solving societal problems through their exercise of consumption 'choice' (within the empowering and disempowering positions), practice theory acknowledges that consumption is a highly complex social phenomenon in which routines and reflexivity are intimately connected. The proliferation of information and discourses ascribing responsibility to consumers can create an occasion for agents to reflexively monitor and adjust their actions, but it does not mean that the routine or habituated performances within a practice are completely conscious or reflexive processes. Soper has argued that the practice-based approach presents a challenge to those interested in socially responsible forms of consumption because it portrays consumption as a 'relatively unconscious form of life' (Soper, 2009: 12). However, this line of argumentation rests on the flawed assumption 'that routines and reflections can be kept apart' (Halkier, 2010: 73). As we will see in the narratives that follow, reflexivity is always bound, or 'situated' (Adams & Raisborough, 2008), within the organised practices individuals are engaged in.

The remainder of this chapter looks at the narratives of four committed fair-trade supporters and two non-fair-trade supporters in order to demonstrate how a practice-theoretical perspective can enhance our understanding of fair-trade consumption. Exploring fair-trade support at the individual level may seem counterintuitive given our understanding of practices as 'blocks' of interdependent elements. However, Reckwitz suggests that the 'individual' does have a very 'precise place' within practice theory because s/he is 'the unique crossing point of practices' (Reckwitz, 2002: 256). Agents are engaged in a multitude of bodily/mental practical performances, and it is therefore important to understand how moments of consumption 'map onto one another' and how coherent these patterns of consumption are (Warde, 2005: 144).

## Fair-trade supporters' narratives

The data presented in this chapter has been drawn from 19 in-depth, semi-structured household interviews with both fair-trade and non-fair-trade supporters living in Chelmsford in 2008.[3] Fair-trade supporters are defined as committed fair-traders, whereas non-fair-trade supporters are residents in Chelmsford with no connection to the Fairtrade Town group activities. I made no assumptions about whether non-fair-trade supporters actually bought fair-trade (and indeed some of them did), but rather I aimed to examine how understandings and involvement with fair-trade differed between those inside the fair-trade group and related networks and those outside. In this way, the two groups offered the opportunity to look at how differential levels of commitment affect the practice of fair-trade support.

Respondents were asked to discuss a recent shopping visit with the aid of a shopping receipt, which not only provided a record of actual purchases made during a specific shopping trip but also encouraged respondents to reflect upon their shopping routines – the places, spaces, times and products – as well as the types of issues that tended to influence their consumption 'choices'. If a respondent highlighted a particular issue, for example, organic food, vegetarianism or fair-trade, the opportunity was taken to delve deeper into their levels of commitment to these types of consumer good, considering the degree to which their interest spanned beyond shopping into other areas of their life. In addition, because this project involves a selection of research methods, including participant observation of the Fairtrade Town groups' activities and events, it was possible to gain insight into the wider involvement of participants in practices of fair-trade support. The fair-trade supporters who feature as the case studies in this chapter were connected with the local Fairtrade Town group but were chosen because they had differential levels of commitment to this network and the wider practice of fair-trade support. In this way, the cases reveal the diversity and internal differentiation of the practice of being a fair-trade supporter.

### Alfred

Alfred is a 70-year-old[4] retired National Health Service (NHS) catering manager who spent much of his working life as a chef on ocean cruise-liners. From a young age, Alfred became interested in politics; he joined the Communist Party in his 20s, and was subsequently involved with the labour movement. He is an active Trade Union Congress (TUC) member and is presently the secretary for the local group in Chelmsford. He also supports the Co-operative movement and is on the board of the Chelmsford Co-operative Society. Alfred is a very committed fair-trade supporter and was responsible for initiating the campaign for Chelmsford to become a Fairtrade Town. Thinking back to how he learnt about fair-trade, Alfred says:

> I think it first arose when some neighbours up the road offered to do a Traidcraft stall at a May rally of the Trades Council many, many years ago, and they came for two or three years. Then it sort of dropped off the horizon really but then through reading various literature and the 'Ethical Consumer' and a whole number of other things I suppose, the fair-trade concept came into my consciousness. And I knew we should be doing something about it and I suppose I was buying fair-trade for years and then I raised the whole issue at the Trades Council and that's how I really got involved.

That Alfred learnt about fair-trade through his engagement in an existing social network (TUC), and while pursuing other commitments, is an interesting finding that is in keeping with the conclusions from the previous chapter. The Fairtrade Foundation notes that one third of people learn about fair-trade through their social networks, and the FTF is keen to foster this learning through their support of Fairtrade Town (or school, workplace) campaigns (FTF, 2010b). Having become a practitioner, Alfred continues to share his support of fair-trade among his family and friends, although interestingly he does recognise those who are less committed to the practice than he is:

> They [his family] wouldn't necessarily buy the fair-trade products perhaps with the same enthusiasm as I do, but they are certainly aware of it and they do buy fair-trade. ... Most friends, not all friends, but most friends will be in tune with the same ethical sort of places that we're coming from, I think that's probably fair to say.

Being a fair-trade supporter is recognised as consisting of a bundle of 'doing and sayings' that some individuals are more 'in tune with' than others. Alfred shares his commitment to fair-trade in both formal and informal networks, suggesting that this political consumerist activity fulfils a 'bonding function' among like-minded individuals (Micheletti, 2010).

Alfred's involvement in fair-trade stemmed from his engagement in the TUC and local Co-operative movement, which are both traditionally understood as working-class associations. While it has been argued that fair-trade consumption is more prevalent among those in middle-class positions (Littrell & Dickson, 1999; Varul, 2008b), there are a number of studies that have revealed the difficulties of classifying fair-trade consumers according to socio-economic criteria (De Pelsmacker, Driesen & Rayp, 2005; Lamb, 2007; Pirotte, 2007). As a self-defined member of the working class, Alfred was keen to stress that social class is not relevant and that anyone can be a fair-trade consumer as long as they possess a 'social conscience', which for Alfred is developed through engagement in political and social campaigns. Although Alfred claims social class is irrelevant to his engagement with fair-trade, his class identity and personal history have clearly influenced his entry into and understanding of the practice of fair-trade support. Notions of class solidarity and fairness for workers across the world imbue his account of why he supports fair-trade. However, it would be a mistake to assume that his involvement can be explained by his social class alone.

That Alfred denies the importance of social class can perhaps be understood with reference to the wider organisation of fair-trade support, which, in recent years, has aimed to encourage as many people as possible to consume fair-trade. Those involved in Fairtrade Town networks are guided by the national Fairtrade organisation, which, as we saw in the previous chapter, discursively constructs and appeals to the all-inclusive category of the 'consumer' in campaigning material aimed at already-committed fair-trade supporters. Alfred, as a key actor in the Chelmsford campaign group, has access to this material and is engaged in the active promotion of fair-trade in Chelmsford. Therefore, his commitment to this practice is shaping his understanding of fair-trade consumption as something that 'anyone' can do regardless of their social class.

It is fair to say that Alfred is one of the most committed fair-trade supporters in Chelmsford he, and spends much of his free time trying to expand the movement both locally within Chelmsford and beyond. He is widely recognised by other fair-trade supporters as the most committed supporter in Chelmsford, suggesting that this practice does have the capacity to mark social distinctions between practitioners. However, this social and cultural capital is not really exchangeable beyond relatively contained social networks. Coleman has argued that when individuals are linked in more than one context, a multiplex relationship, 'it allows for the resources of one relationship to be appropriated for use in others' (Coleman, 1988: S108). For example, Alfred uses his engagement in fair-trade networks to promote and extend his other commitments, such as regularly sending emails to fair-trade supporters to promote TUC and Co-operative events. In order for him to gain respect and social capital through these interactions, there must be a degree of *closure* across these social networks. Alfred is not only a central figure within the Fairtrade Town group, but in a number of other local groups where like-minded individuals in similar multiplex relationships can also be found.

Alfred clearly understands his involvement in the fair-trade campaign as an extension of an already-existent campaigning identity. He explains:

> You know, it's a direct benefit, I mean, I think I may have said to you before, that we've been involved in many campaigns but every day you have a cup of fair-trade coffee or drink some fair-trade tea or eat a fair-trade banana, you're a winner. So you get a little victory every day and that's got to be good. It's good for me and it's good for the producers. And I think that's very important actually because you know, we do need these little victories, these little boosts to keep us going [laughs]. It's quite simple really.

Alfred has a very long history of campaigning in which he admits he's 'lost more than I've won', but by consuming fair-trade he is able to reimagine this history and have a 'victory every day'. We see elements of what Soper (2009) calls 'alternative hedonism' as Alfred professes a sense of moral pleasure in knowing his consumption is making a difference. Indeed, a number of fair-trade supporters described how consuming fair-trade gave them a 'warm glow' or a sense of pride in knowing that their shopping was 'doing good'. These kinds of statements have been read as examples of intentional choice and ethical reflection (within the empowering consumer position), although care should be taken to acknowledge the degree to which these 'choices' are made in the context of embodied routines and tacit knowledge that are contingent upon a range of practical, everyday circumstances. Alfred does all of his food shopping at the Co-op as 'a matter of principle'. Given that Co-operative stores have made a commitment to fair-trade and offer a wide range of fair-trade goods, Alfred's routinised use of this store enables him to perform his weekly shop without having to actively reflect upon every item. A practice-informed approach encourages us to explore how this 'routinisation of reflexivity' is practically accomplished (Halkier, 2010) and pay attention to the complex nature of this performance – for example, although Alfred likes to buy fair-trade whenever he can he does note that when his grandchildren visit he does not buy fair-trade fruit juice because the children do not like it. Rather than understanding consumer attitudes as static properties or the citizen-consumer as someone who votes with every purchase, perhaps we ought

to be thinking about the 'do-ability' of fair-trade consumption performances and their conditionings (ibid.: 74).

## Phillipa

Phillipa is a 60-year-old administrator who works for a Christian charity
that organises social events for youth groups. She has three grown-up
children and her husband is a vicar at a local church. She is not heavily involved in the Chelmsford Fairtrade Town group but occasionally
attends meetings and pays subscriptions as a member. Phillipa found it
hard to remember exactly how she learnt about fair-trade but places her
first interest in the 1960s. She describes this political-cultural moment
as one where she was involved in different protest movements because
'all those sort of things were terribly important at the time'. Her interest in fair-trade increased when her local church asked her to run a
Traidcraft stall,[5] which she did as a hobby while her children were
young, nearly 30 years ago.

> When we lived in [name of town] I was a Traidcraft rep. And so then
> I was selling fair-trade stuff. It was when Traidcraft, they didn't do
> food then, they only did completely useless things like jewellery
> and little boxes and erm, I can't think of anything useful they did.
> But they did do Traidcraft coffee, which was disgusting. And which
> I religiously bought and most people simply wouldn't drink it. Yes so
> that was nearly 30 years ago, long time ago. Now of course, because
> Oxfam do that, it's huge. There wouldn't be people like me pottering
> about with their stall.

After giving up her Traidcraft stall, Phillipa did not continue to be
actively engaged in the fair-trade movement, partly because she was
aware that fair-trade products were now widely available through alternative systems of provision (such as in Oxfam shops and supermarkets).
This highlights an important point about the trajectory of this practice, which has evolved over time, as new generations of practitioners
have replaced 'current orthodoxies with new prescriptions' (Warde,
2005: 141). As the fair-trade movement has organised itself into the
mainstream, what it means to be a fair-trade supporter has changed for
Phillipa. Unlike Alfred, a relative newcomer to the practice, Phillipa does
not spend a great deal of her spare time trying to expand the fair-trade
movement. While she occasionally asks local supermarkets to stock
more fair-trade, she sees herself as 'an armchair supporter' who buys
fair-trade as 'a pain-free way of doing one's bit'. The shifting cultural

and economic context of fair-trade, as well as Phillipa's only limited involvement in fair-trade networks in recent years, has gradually altered how she understands and performs this practice.

Just as Alfred understood his involvement as closely linked to his personal history of engagement in social and political campaigns, Phillipa related her support for fair-trade to her Christian background. Indeed a number of fair-trade supporters had come across fair-trade at their church, and understood their decision to purchase fair-trade as intimately connected with their faith – so for Grace, for example, choosing fair-trade was just one part of living a 'personally acceptable Quakerly life', and for Sue, consuming fair-trade and holding a Traidcraft stall at her local church was 'a practical extension of her religious faith'. It seems that past experiences and commitments orient people towards fair-trade options and ethical lifestyles, rather than it being the case that individuals suddenly choose to consume fair-trade because they have been educated about its benefits. While religious motivations are personally important to Phillipa, she is also keen to stress that you do not have to be a Christian to be a fair-trade supporter, thus attempting to construct fair-trade consumption as a non-exclusive activity. She argues that to support fair-trade you just need an 'ethical stance', which instead draws a moral boundary between fair-trade supporters and non-fair-trade supporters. The drawing of boundaries around fair-trade consumption will be explored in depth in the next chapter.

Although Phillipa rejects the necessary association between faith and fair-trade, she was unique among fair-traders in Chelmsford in representing her ability to consume fair-trade in class terms:

> I think there is a sort of middle-classness about it, and I think that it's more expensive, so you also have to be able to say I can afford to do that. And I've got this friend who doesn't buy fair-trade and only has £20 for her food bill and she was very poor in her childhood and so she's never lost that habit in her shopping, so she would never buy organic and she certainly wouldn't buy fair-trade and she absolutely gets hot and bothered when people talk about the planet; she couldn't give a blah about the planet because her concern is about just keeping her head above water and so she can get quite cross about fair-trade. She sees it as a sort of gloss on the cake of middle-class morality, and one has to be quite cautious about it. So I think that there is a sense in which it's fine for people like me now, when, we're both in work and our children are grown up and we may not, we're obviously not earning a lot of money, but we can afford to

choose what we buy … so I think there's bound to be a sort of middle-class element to it. But … of course there's an element also where it's easier to buy fair-trade, if you're not actually hugely rich. I mean, if I were hugely rich I might have a four wheel drive car and drive to the supermarket, I don't know [laughs]. It's just that I can have a concern because it all fits in quite easily, but you know, if in fact, my husband went everywhere by helicopter, I don't know if I'd still feel the same, perhaps I wouldn't. I'd hate to, I wouldn't like to say you know, whatever happened I'd always have the same concern, because I don't know that I would. I'd probably be thinking about my next Dior outfit and going to a spa or something [laughs]. It's a bit inevitable that people like me will be able to be erm …

Phillipa seems acutely aware that fair-trade consumption may not be open to everyone, and suggests that there are clear class/income and lifestyle limits to the practice. In drawing a distinction between her own lifestyle and consumption practices, she imagines how those with greater or lesser incomes and different lifestyle concerns would behave. The exclusivity of fair-trade is established in her statement, with those in higher status groups, in particular, slightly denigrated for their engagement in conspicuous and environmentally damaging forms of consumption. She describes her own involvement as 'inevitable', and reveals how fair-trade 'fits in quite easily'. While social class and stage in the life-course are viewed as crucial to her likelihood of consuming fair-trade, just as important are her previous experiences, which reveal a long career of involvement in, and commitment to, fair-trade and similar practices. That Phillipa was unique in highlighting the relevance of social class can perhaps also be understood with reference to her level of involvement in the fair-trade movement in recent years. The contemporary fair-trade movement has worked hard to stress the non-exclusivity of fair-trade consumption through the fair-trade promotional period and Fairtrade Towns. However, Phillipa's most active involvement with fair-trade occurred 30 years ago, when fair-trade consumption was most commonly associated with middle-class, female, and often religious, individuals (Littrell & Dickson, 1999). It is likely she is drawing on these 'doings and sayings' when she describes the 'fair-trade consumer', whereas other fair-trade supporters draw on the understanding of fair-trade consumption as non-exclusive. That is not to deny the relevance of social class but rather to explore how differential understandings of this practice can emerge, as well as change over time, and the importance of paying attention to the role that shared structures of knowledge, institutional frameworks and infrastructures of provision play in shaping the forms that practices may take. Indeed, it is likely that in other countries where fair-trade remains concentrated in specialist stores (such as Germany) or is associated with an 'alternative' character (such as in the ATO-model in the USA), the practice of fair-trade support will be differentially associated with notions of exclusivity.

Phillipa is also interested in environmental consumption; she regularly looks for organic goods and has chosen not to own a car. When talking about fair-trade she says:

> I think that it's very difficult to say which bit is to do with being ecologically sound and which bit is to do with being fair-trade. Or whether being fair-trade isn't just part of the whole thing of living ethically.

We are reminded that individuals are the 'unique crossing point of practices', who engage in a multiplicity of practices at any one time, each of which are likely to influence one another. Supporting fair-trade 'fits in quite easily' with ecological concerns for Phillipa because they are both about addressing how to deal with consumer goods in everyday life. We see again how reflexivity becomes routinised so that supporting fair-trade becomes part of how Phillipa goes about her daily life without her having to continuously reflect upon every purchase made. However, she does reveal that organic goods are more important to her, and says she 'wouldn't restrict [her] shopping because of fair-trade'. This is an important point to highlight because, despite counting herself as a fair-trade supporter, she does not always consume fair-trade goods. Indeed, just as Alfred made occasional allowances when his grandchildren visited, so too did other fair-trade supporters adopt a more flexible approach to their fair-trade shopping. As we perform different social practices, we are guided by different 'understandings, procedures and engagements'. This makes a consistent performance over time and space difficult to maintain.

### Claire and John

Claire and John are in their mid-thirties and have been married for 12 years. They have two young children, a girl aged four and a boy aged seven. Claire is currently taking a break from work to raise their children and was formerly a teacher at a local secondary school, and John works full-time for an IT firm. They have been fair-trade supporters for the last nine years after coming into contact with fair-trade through John's involvement with the local Oxfam group. The two are not involved in the Chelmsford Fairtrade Town campaign because with young children they do not feel they have enough time; but they always make a point of asking for fair-trade when shopping and have handed in 'stock-it' postcards to local stores to ask them to make fair-trade products available.

It is interesting to note that Claire and John have diverging understandings of, and motivations for, supporting fair-trade. While they both learnt about fair-trade through the same organisation, they have pursued their interest in differing organisations and through different practices, which have provided distinctive contexts they have drawn upon to realise their fair-trade support. John has continued to pursue his support for fair-trade through his involvement with the local Oxfam group. He is also a member of the World Development Movement (WDM), from which he receives information and calls to action about fair-trade and wider development issues. On the other hand, for Claire, contact with fair-trade has mostly come through her involvement with her church and related social networks, which are engaged in a number of charitable outreach programmes, and through doing the weekly shopping where fair-trade purchases are made. This interesting exchange between the couple reveals their different takes on the purpose of supporting fair-trade and draws on wider political debates and ideologies about fair-trade.

**Claire:** It's a charity, isn't it? I'd see it as giving weekly money to charity.

**John:** I wouldn't say it's a charity.

**Claire:** Wouldn't you?

**John:** No. If I buy a fish from the fishmonger's it's not charity. It's business.

**Claire:** But it's not fair-trade. We're talking about fair-trade.

**John:** It's business.

**Claire:** When I buy vegetables or whatever I see it as I give the money to charity each week, in effect you're giving it to the producer, aren't you?

**John:** If it wasn't fair-trade the producer would still get the money.

**Claire:** Yeah, but it's getting a fair price for a producer.

**John:** So you think that's charity that they should … get the fair price? [bemused laughter]

**Claire:** Yeah, because it's a charity as in helping someone.
**John:** But they should be getting it anyway. Shouldn't they get a fair price anyway?
**Claire:** They should, yeah.
**John:** So it's not charity.
**Claire:** No, well, that's how I see it, yeah, a way of helping.

For Claire, who purchases the majority of the fair-trade food for the household, the extra cost of fair-trade products is thought of as a form of charitable giving. While she acknowledges that she is aiming to help producers get a 'fair price' she sees this as an extension of the other activities she's involved with that 'help others'. This financial exchange involves her using her relative privilege rather than participating in an equal trading relationship. However, John appears to be drawing on the discursive resources of the trade justice organisations, Oxfam and WDM, which stress the concepts of 'trade not aid' and producer empowerment through 'fair exchange', in order to construct his understanding of, and reasons for supporting, fair-trade. As a member and supporter of these organisations, he adapts the established forms of knowledge, the 'doings and sayings', within these practices and applies them to fair-trade support. The rather heated exchange between the couple reveals the internal differentiation of being a fair-trade supporter and how individuals can have and develop different motivations for, and understandings of, engaging in the practice.[6]

As Coleman (1988) notes, social networks can provide the structure for information-flow between individuals and can establish particular social norms or expectations around what constitutes appropriate behaviour. Paying attention to the networks and experiences through which Claire and John have pursued their support of fair-trade highlights points of commonality as well as conflict in the understandings, procedures and engagements of different practitioners. Indeed, while John imagined he would always buy fair-trade if he were to have the responsibility for the household shopping, Claire pointed to the difficulties of always choosing fair-trade:

> We always get fair-trade bananas but when they are really yellow, I will go for the other ones because the yellow ones aren't going to last the week and you have one a day. So then I will go for the non-fair-trade ones. Usually I tend to get, what did I do today? [looks at receipt] I got one fair-trade and then a small bunch of the others, non-fair-trade.

Although the life-politics-inspired accounts of consumption behaviour tend to assume that consumers have the power to vote with their purchases, what is often not considered is how this performance relies upon infrastructures of provision. So while Claire would like to buy fair-trade bananas all the time, in some weeks this is not possible. Equally, she describes how the extra cost of fair-trade options sometimes steers her towards non-fair-trade alternatives. A number of practical considerations come into play so that the actual purchase of fair-trade goods is heavily shaped by Claire's need to provide affordable, good-quality food for her family and the variable availability of fair-trade options that meet these requirements within her regular supermarket each week. John's only occasional experiences of carrying out the weekly shopping mean that he is less aware of these constraints and is thus able to imagine different procedures around how to 'do' fair-trade shopping. A practice-theoretical perspective allows us to acknowledge that inconsistent performances (or attitude/behaviour gaps) are less to do with a lack of information, and more to do with the practical 'do-abilities' within daily life.

Claire and John provide just one illustration of the difficulties felt by all respondents (fair-traders and non-fair-traders) of negotiating competing demands and balancing ethical, practical and family preferences when shopping. Debates around new forms of consumer-citizenship and discourses promoting fair-trade suggest that consumers are increasingly using their individual consumption to 'vote' for fairer trade; but in many ways I found just as many votes for 'unfair' trading relations. Because fair-trade supporters admitted that they did not always buy fair-trade and instead prioritised other concerns such as price, quality and competing ethical consumer products like organic and local food, we are encouraged to question the importance, or *not*, of consuming fair-trade products for being a fair-trade supporter.

For most fair-trade supporters what it means to be a fair-trade supporter extends beyond individual shopping choices. Often the actions of fair-trade supporters in Fairtrade Town networks work to encourage others to learn about fair-trade – like organising events such as fair-trade fashion shows and fair-trade coffee mornings, etc., and giving gifts that are fair-trade to promote awareness; or work to remove the choice of non-fair-trade products from the shelves through campaigns to shift systems of collective provision – like 'stock it' postcards requesting that local stores and spaces provide fair-trade options. For Claire and John and Alfred and Phillipa, buying fair-trade products is an important part of the practice of fair-trade support, but through looking at the range of other activities they engage in, we can see that consumption is not the only, or even the main, way to 'do' fair-trade support.

## Resisting recruitment

Having examined the narratives of some committed fair-trade supporters, it will be useful to consider how individuals who are not committed to fair-trade respond to this practice. While the alternative culture built around fair-trade in the Chelmsford Fairtrade Town network aims to encourage more people to use fair-trade, it is not necessarily the case that non-fair-traders are aware of this culture (see previous chapter) or perceive it similarly to the fair-traders. Warde suggests that gauging the different levels of commitment to a practice can help us to understand its differentiation, and that in particular it is important to consider how individuals resist 'being recruited in the first place' (Warde, 2005: 145). The case study presented below demonstrates how engagement in a very different set of social practices can lead to very different understandings of, and commitments towards, fair-trade. The reader should be aware that this particular case study has been chosen because the couple had a passionate commitment to an alternative social practice, that of yogic-vegetarianism – the majority of non-fair-traders did not exhibit this level of commitment when discussing their shopping routines, although they did often reveal strong commitments towards family members (like the fair-traders above).

Helen and Mark are in their forties and work in local government roles – although not for Chelmsford council (so they may not be consuming fair-trade at work). They have been living in Chelmsford for four years, and do the majority of their food shopping online at Sainsbury's, which means they are less likely to come in contact with fair-trade advertising at the point of sale. Mark decided to become a vegetarian after the UK foot and mouth crisis (2001), when he got 'a real realisation that big companies were cutting corners to maximise profits and therefore taking advantage of me'. However, Helen reflects that it was their attendance at a meditation course at around the same time that really made them embrace vegetarianism. They were told at this course that they would get more from their meditation if they followed a traditional Indian yogic diet.[7] This diet is supposed to promote positive self-being by reducing the ingestion of particular substances (such as meat, eggs, garlic, onions, caffeine, chemicals), which have a negative effect upon the body and mind. Their consumption of foodstuffs and toiletries is guided by their understandings and performance of yogic principles and teachings. They like to buy organic products wherever they can afford to, and Helen tries to cook everything from scratch because most ready-made vegetarian foods tend to contain onions and garlic. Of course, this is sometimes not possible as the couple negotiate competing demands[8] and available provision of foodstuffs. Mark and Helen believe that pursuing this lifestyle has enabled them to experience 'clarity and lightness of mind'.

Like the practice of fair-trade support, being a yogic-vegetarian seems to extend beyond merely consuming differently – as Mark says 'since we've changed our diet we have changed so much'. As the couple have become immersed in the yogi lifestyle, they have become more committed to this practice. They regularly attend a local meditation centre and have visited a spiritual meditation university in India on a number of occasions, where they meet with other like-minded individuals and collectively experience the power of meditation and share cooking ideas. Unlike fair-trade supporters, they do not spend their free time trying to recruit more people to the practice; rather, they prefer to spend their free time walking in the countryside and generating greater self-awareness and positive energy. Once they have generated enough positive energy, they feel they are able to share this with others, for example, inviting friends to dinner, or creating a relaxing environment for Helen to conduct sports massage in.

When I asked them about fair-trade consumption and the concept of helping others through their shopping, they had slightly different views on this consumer label. Helen admits that when she first heard about fair-trade through an article on the news, she thought it was 'a brilliant idea'. But after seeing some negative news coverage detailing how the money does not get back to the farmers, she is now unsure whether fair-trade is not just 'a loss leader' used by supermarkets to get you to shop with them. On looking at their receipt, because they shop at Sainsbury's they had bought fair-trade bananas, but this was by default rather than because she had picked fair-trade especially. She says:

> I mean, I wouldn't deliberately not buy something fair-trade, you know, if it was what I wanted and that was all there was, I'd buy it, and I'd probably feel that oh you know I've bought fair-trade, but it wouldn't be a conscious choice to actually go and get it.

While Helen is rather ambivalent towards fair-trade, Mark suggests that fair-trade is not particularly relevant to his understanding of yogic principles. Because yogis do not like traces of violence to be attached to the food that they eat, I was curious whether this would mean they would be drawn towards fair-trade. However, Mark explained why this was not the case:

> I know that you've got some child slave who's beaten up or whatever to pick the coffee beans and stuff, but I'm not consuming that kid, whereas that animal that was one minute eating the grass and then gets this funny feeling that all his mates are disappearing, and they say they start sweating before they even get the bolt in their head and that adrenaline has entered all those molecules and then people consume that. So even if that kid is being beaten, or maybe even killed or whatever, I'm not going to consume that act. But if I eat a dead animal that's been murdered, I'm consuming that act, aren't I? It's becoming part of me. That's the kind of the difference.

Because fair-trade is not about ingesting violence in the same way that the consumption of meat is, Mark is not interested in this consumer label.[9] Using fair-trade products does not make sense in the context of his practices, which concern principles of self-preservation.

While the practice of fair-trade support encourages individuals to engage in activities that promote the consumption of fair-trade goods among like-minded individuals and the wider population, for Helen and Mark being a yogic-vegetarian is about engaging in activities that enable them to develop into positive selves. Helen and Mark were unaware that Chelmsford was a Fairtrade Town and were not aware of any promotional events in their town because the principles around which they organised their lives were very different from fair-trade supporters. They do not belong to any local campaigning or Christian faith-based networks, and their consumption is oriented by their concern for their own bodies and minds rather than a concern for Third World producers. That is not to say that Helen and Mark are unethical or selfish consumers, but rather that their approach to achieving social change is based first and foremost on practices that begin with the self. I want to end this section with a quotation from Mark, which was in response to a question about how individuals can make a difference to global poverty or environmental destruction, because it reveals their alternative political ideology.

> Get to know the self – if everyone spent time doing that then, we mentioned and agreed earlier, that you can change the atmosphere of a room through your moods, your thoughts; so if everyone tried

to focus on happiness and peace, not flowery things but solid vibrations, then you change the whole world.

## Returning to a theory of practice

> I wouldn't say I woke up one morning and decided to be involved [with fair-trade].
>
> (Jenny, age 42, youth worker)

The case studies presented in this chapter and the previous quotation from a committed fair-trade supporter highlight the opportunities that a practice-theoretical approach can offer us when exploring how fair-trade consumption/support is organised and carried out. Rather than assuming that the provision of information is alone enough to motivate behavioural change or ascribing/denying power to the 'citizen-consumer' without exploring the processes through which consumption is achieved in daily life, a practice-theoretical approach can provide insights into how people learn about and pursue their everyday commitment to this issue. By moving attention away from a narrow focus upon the act of consuming fair-trade, it becomes possible to acknowledge that being a fair-trade supporter involves a lot more than merely choosing one product over another. This concluding section will reflect upon three important issues that this chapter has highlighted – the role of social networks in motivating and sustaining fair-trade support, the differentiation of fair-trade support, and the do-ability of fair-trade consumption – and will comment upon how a practice-theoretical approach can enhance our understanding of everyday fair-trade consumption/support.

We have seen that awareness of, and engagement with, fair-trade often emerges, and is sustained, through individuals' involvement in social networks. For example, after meeting fair-trade at their local church, through a friendship group, or through the Co-operative or Oxfam group, the fair-trade supporters described in this chapter went on to pursue their involvement through these and other organisations. Knowledge about fair-trade (or its lack) seems to be heavily shaped by the social capacity of groups who seek to extend existing interests into the arena of fair-trade support, as well as generating expectations and norms around how to 'do' fair-trade support. It is interesting to note how fair-trade supporters were active in different kinds of networks (both formal and informal), and how they were able to create bonds and social capital between these diverse groups by drawing on multiplex relationships.

Micheletti has argued that political consumerism is unique because its focus on everyday concerns (about what and where to shop) encourages individuals and groups to build new coalitions and communities around a new identity – that of the consumer who cares about fair-trade (Micheletti, 2010: 156). There is thus 'a bonding function' in practising fair-trade support, which generates trust among like-minded people and 'people who differ from one another on a number of characteristics' (ibid.: 9). For this practice to come into existence, it must be regularly performed by multiple bodies/minds and recognised as constituting a specific bundle of 'doings and sayings' by others. Social networks like Fairtrade Towns, therefore, play an important role in generating this awareness and the 'social recognisability' of fair-trade support as a unique practice, as well as providing individuals with a sense of belonging to a wider movement. Echoing the conclusions of the study by Clarke et al. (2007b), this suggests that attempts to motivate behavioural change ought to move away from addressing people as individual consumers and rather appeal to people as members of communities of practice.

Not everyone engages with fair-trade with the same degree of commitment, and nor do they perform the same procedures or attach the same understandings to their actions across space and time. While much existing literature seeks to explain fair-trade consumption with reference to socio-demographic characteristics (Adams & Raisborough, 2008; Goodman, 2004; Littrell & Dickson, 1999) or by devising attitude profiles of individuals (De Pelsmacker, Driesen & Rayp, 2005; Dolan, 2008), little attention is paid to how these elements are coordinated within this practice or how the internal organisation of the practice might itself generate desires for fair-trade goods. If we take social class as an example, we can acknowledge that this external characteristic has some influence upon the differentiation of fair-trade support, given that fair-trade goods often cost more than non-fair-trade goods and the historical association of fair-trade with middle-class groups (see next chapter). However, its influence is not fixed across space and time, and nor is it the only element upon which entry into, and activity within, the practice is based – for example, how and why people engage with fair-trade is also influenced by infrastructures of provision, involvement with social networks, institutional frameworks, cultural conventions, individual biographies and so on. Paying attention to the trajectory of a practice, and the careers of individuals within a practice, offers us the opportunity to explore how these coordinated elements interact to generate particular 'understandings, procedures and engagements', without privileging any one element over another. The result is an account that reveals the complexity of fair-trade consumption and its embedded nature within social and institutional contexts.

Adopting a practice-theoretical approach enables us to account for the differentiation of fair-trade consumption behaviours and encourages us to explore the dimensions upon which the practice might vary in different countries where there are different systems of provision, public discourses and levels of state involvement. It is likely that in countries where there is less mainstream availability of fair-trade, being a fair-trade supporter will involve different 'procedures', such as visiting specialised stores to source fair-trade goods. So, for example, Roger from Minnesota (USA) described how in his town there was very limited availability of fair-trade, with just one coffee shop that served fair-trade and Wal-Mart offering fair-trade coffee. This meant that he had to spent a lot of his time talking to local stores and his congregation to encourage them to stock/buy fair-trade, as well as source some fair-trade products from online retailers. It is also likely that the 'engagements' of a supporter will vary in a context where there are competing 'understandings' of what constitutes fair-trade – such as in the USA where the choice of an ATO model sits alongside the Fair Trade Certified model, or in Sweden where consuming fair-trade is more about securing human rights for workers than lobbying one's government for change. Rachel from Berkeley recognised both FTUSA- and FTrF-labelled goods but was aware of and could discuss the differences and potential conflicts between the two, suggesting that this is a debate that can influence the practice of fair-trade support in the USA. And Ulla from Lund did not engage in the same sorts of campaigning activity that we found in the UK, such as visiting local stores or organisations to ask them to stock more fair-trade, because this was seen as the job of the municipality. However, she did volunteer at a local World Shop and encouraged friends and family to support fair-trade.

This chapter has demonstrated that consuming fair-trade goods is not the only, or even the main, way to 'do' fair-trade support. The actions of fair-trade supporters in Fairtrade Town networks often work to encourage others to use and learn about fair-trade or work to remove the choice of non-fair-trade products through campaigns to shift systems of collective provision. All these actions extend the practice of fair-trade support to other interested individuals and create a *collective* practice of which individual consumption is merely one part. Indeed, we are forced to question the importance of consuming fair-trade products for being a fair-trade supporter. An individual can consume fair-trade without being a fair-trade supporter, for example, when fair-trade becomes the standard option in particular places and retail outlets (like Helen and Mark), and an individual can count herself or himself as a fair-trade supporter without always consuming fair-trade. A narrow focus on the conscious act of fair-trade consumption in existing literature has meant that the contingent nature of fair-trade consumption performances is often overlooked. While individuals may believe that fair-trade is a worthy cause, they may be constrained from always acting upon this belief because of a number of practical constraints, such as needing bananas that will last the whole week. Many of the fair-trade and non-fair-trade supporters were oriented by a number of different social practices, which made always shopping for fair-trade impractical or irrelevant. Competing ethical labels, family concerns, price and quality were all factors that made fair-trade options less appealing. This chapter has revealed that people are often not consistent – or at least they struggle hard to be so.

By viewing fair-trade support through the lens of practice theory, we are able to deal with inconsistencies between people's attitudes and behaviour and acknowledge that people behave in practical ways when they consume. The empowering and disempowering positions that discuss the possibilities for consumer-citizenship through consumption choices fail to recognise that consumption is neither fully reflexive nor constrained because reflexivity is always bound within the organised practices individuals are engaged in. It might therefore be better to focus upon the everyday social flow and 'do-ability' of fair-trade consumer practices and performances and consider the conditions under which these performances are made possible (Halkier, 2010). It follows that strategies for changing patterns of consumption must act on the collective level and seek to transform social practices rather than focusing on the individual level of consumer choice. Recent moves towards collective fair-trade provisioning policies in retail outlets and public spaces (many of which are led by the Fairtrade Towns movement) can be seen as a step in the right direction towards this objective. However, changing systems of provision alone will not be enough for there is more to fair-trade support than merely buying fair-trade goods.

It is important to remember that outsiders to the practice may have very different understandings of, and dispositions towards, fair-trade goods. Indeed those who engage in a very different set of social practices can be oriented away from fair-trade because the established conventions, or 'doings and sayings', of these practices clash with the conventions of fair-trade support. While most fair-trade supporters were keen to stress the non-exclusivity of fair-trade consumption, we have seen that there are clear differences between fair-trade supporters and those who are less committed or uncommitted to fair-trade. The tendency to stress the non-exclusivity of fair-trade consumption reflects the organisation of fair-trade support, which seeks to expand the movement by bringing it into mainstream markets. However, we saw in the rejection of any necessary relationship between social–demographic characteristics or religion and fair-trade consumption how Alfred and Phillipa both constructed a moral boundary – the possession of a 'social conscience' or 'ethical stance' – between fair-trade supporters and non-fair-trade supporters, thus constructing it as a different kind of exclusive activity. The next chapter takes up this point and explores how fair-trade and non-fair-trade supporters understand the distinctiveness of fair-trade consumption, and the extent to which it is conceived as exclusive or universal.

# 6
# The Normalisation and Exclusivity of Fair-Trade Consumption

Fair-trade consumption is represented by some of the most powerful institutions in UK society as a moral duty and a form of global citizenship (see Chapters 3 and 4). Local and national government support fair-trade; schools teach about fair-trade consumption as part of the National Curriculum for Key Stage 4 citizenship and geography; both print and television media feature a high proportion of positive stories about fair-trade, especially during Fairtrade Fortnight; business and retailers promote fair-trade options; and a number of churches (and other sites of worship) are encouraging their congregations to switch to fair-trade. Fair-trade organisations, like the FTF, FFTS and FTUSA, appeal to the all-inclusive figure of the 'consumer' in their campaigning material in order to suggest that every person in society has the capacity and responsibility to influence trading relations through their purchasing activity. Fair-trade consumption 'deems itself to be based upon morally objective grounds', calling upon all individuals to recognise and act upon universal understandings of the avoidance of harm to humans (Fagan, 2006: 125). Indeed, George Alagiah (a former patron of the FTF) famously branded Alex Singleton (a free trade advocate) 'immoral' in a debate about fair-trade because Alex offered a critique of the fair-trade model (Waitrose, 2007).

However, it is important to remember that fair-trade consumption is a moral duty that comes at a price. Despite the switches to fair-trade-only lines by a number of chain-retail outlets and manufacturers (such as Sainsbury's, Starbucks and Ben & Jerry's), there remains a perception that fair-trade goods are more expensive than non-fair-trade lines – a perception that is well-founded if we look at the price of fair-trade products beyond the handful of commodities (such as coffee, tea, bananas and chocolate) that have successfully penetrated the market.

At the same time as fair-trade consumption is represented as something that we all ought to be doing, it is also the case that fair-trade goods cost more money. It will therefore be interesting to explore how those who do not organise their consumption along fair-trade lines react to the suggestion that they ought to change their ways.

This chapter considers how fair-trade and non-fair-trade supporters in the UK draw socio-economic, cultural and moral boundaries around fair-trade consumption and the 'fair-trade consumer' in order to justify why they do or do not buy fair-trade. It explores the complex relationship between fair-trade consumption and social class, considering the degree to which this consumption practice is evaluated as exclusive or ordinary. It is worth highlighting that in other countries, where social class divisions are less pronounced (like Sweden), or where other structural divisions like 'race' are just as important (like the USA), the drawing of boundaries is likely to vary. However, this chapter argues that there is no simple relation between fair-trade consumption and social divisions because we are dealing with individuals' 'lay normativities' – that is, those everyday rationales that matter greatly to actors concerning 'what is of value, how to live, what is worth striving for and what is not' (Sayer, 2005a: 6).

## Examining social class and fair-trade consumption

Informed by the reflexivity thesis, much existing research has tended to draw on an abstract image of the fair-trade citizen-consumer who, regardless of material, cultural and affective circumstances, constructs their self-identity through their everyday lifestyle choices (Bennett, 2004; Goodman, 2004; Lyon, 2006; Micheletti, 2003; Murray & Raynolds, 2007; Scammell, 2003). However, it has been found that ethical and fair-trade consumers do tend to fall into higher socio-economic categories, be better educated, have higher incomes, be slightly older and are usually women (Co-op, 2007; Dickson, 2005; European Commission, 1997; Littrell & Dickson, 1999; Tallontire, Rentsendorj & Blowfield, 2001). In this research, discussions of social class were never too far away from discussions of fair-trade consumption, whether its relevance was denied or affirmed. This finding moved me to consider the applicability of Bourdieu's (1984) thesis that people's tastes for cultural products are markers of their social class. Bourdieu argued that people's tastes for consumer goods were intimately connected to their social position so that those in higher social groups, with high levels of cultural capital, appreciated 'high' (or 'legitimate') culture whereas those in lower social groups enjoyed 'popular' culture. He suggested that individuals perform their distinction from class others when evaluating other's tastes, and thus consumer goods and practices become the site for displaying cultural capital and asserting ones position in the social space.

Varul (2008b) detected the performance of distinction among fair-trade consumers who compared their own morally worthy behaviour with the lack of care displayed by class others. Varul conducted a series of in-depth interviews with fair-trade consumers and found that consumers construct themselves as ethical subjects through their engagement with fair-trade consumption. This 'ethical self' was then compared to the attitudes and behaviours of other people whose shopping habits exhibited 'moral indifference' (Varul, 2008b: 8). These evaluative judgements were often aimed at competing sections of the middle classes (with references to 4x4 drivers or businessmen), but those on low incomes were not immune. 'Often stereotyped under-class consumption behaviour (expensive branded track suits, game consoles etc.) was contrasted with [consumers'] own behaviours during past spots of low income (e.g. as students)' (ibid.), and this 'under-class' consumer behaviour was importantly used as a stark contrast to 'the more authentic poverty' of fair-trade farmers (ibid.). Fair-trade goods were appreciated by his participants because of both their aesthetic qualities (i.e. they taste and look better than alternatives) and because the search for an ethically best-buy reveals one's superior knowledge. However, because Varul did not speak with non-fair-trade supporters, he was unable to comment upon how far those without a 'taste' for fair-trade regarded this activity as distinctive.

My research reveals that it is problematic to assume that fair-trade consumption only attracts middle-class consumers who use these goods in order to display their distinction. Fair-trade supporters tended to stress the non-exclusivity or ordinariness of fair-trade consumption and, although on closer inspection these claims to ordinariness were inflected with judgements about social class, fair-trade consumption was valued regardless of its association with any social group. Non-fair-trade supporters, on the other hand, identified a recognisable type of person who they thought bought fair-trade regularly, and yet many of them had in fact bought fair-trade products (on examination of their shopping receipts or through discussions about their shopping habits), making this distinctive characterisation puzzling. Although non-fair-trade supporters provided a number of reasons why they did not identify with the fair-trade movement, there was more going on here than simply 'refusing what they are refused' (Bourdieu, 1984: 471).

The previous chapter highlighted the importance of internally differentiating a practice on the basis of an individual's recruitment and commitment to it rather than on the basis of structural determinants like an individual's social class. However, it also drew attention to the importance of the trajectory within a practice and how 'doings and sayings' evolve and change over time and space. The fair-trade movement has undergone a major transition in the past ten and more years, as it has pursued mainstream outlets for the distribution of its products. As fair-trade products have moved into the mainstream, they have become both more affordable and prevalent. While fair-trade supporters used to have to visit specialist stores to source fair-trade products, they can now, at least in the UK, access an array of fair-trade offerings at their local supermarket. The Fairtrade-certified logo has been attached to supermarket-own product lines as well as everyday brands, such as Cadbury's and Dunkin Donuts, suggesting that fair-trade is increasingly characterised not by its rarity but by its ordinariness. Fair-trade consumer goods do not appear to fulfil the requirements for being 'highbrow' cultural objects and, as more and more big brands and supermarkets embrace the Fairtrade label, the boundary between the 'ordinariness' and 'exclusivity' of fair-trade has become blurry.

Alongside the concerted efforts of the fair-trade movement to stress the non-exclusivity of fair-trade and expand the market availability of fair-trade goods, we are also witnessing a growing trend towards omnivorousness (Bennett et al., 2009; Chan & Goldthorpe, 2007; Peterson & Kern, 1996). In an extensive survey of consumer tastes in modern Britain, Bennett et al. (2009) found that it was hard to detect a distinctive lower- or middle-class culture because the middle classes actively engaged in popular culture.[1] Importantly, they found that there was 'little sense of overt cultural superiority or condescension on the part of the middle classes' and that respondents tended to deny a 'cultural hierarchy of value' (ibid.: 252, 255). They suggested that this was because 'almost no one publicly defends traditional standards, or legitimate culture, for its own sake' (ibid.). Therefore, the fair-trade supporters claim that fair-trade consumption is a non-exclusive activity may reflect this omnivoric orientation and the difficulties felt by these respondents of characterising cultural activities according to social class. However, it does not account for why non-fair-trade supporters associated fair-trade consumption with particular social status groups, nor can it account for their felt need to justify why they did not use fair-trade. To address these questions, it becomes important to explore the moral economy of fair-trade.

## Uncovering the normative dimension

In their comparison of the imagery used to promote fair-trade (of deserving, yet distant fair-trade farmers) and the representations of the undeserving, yet proximate, white working class in the UK, Adams and Raisborough argue that fair-trade offers 'an expansion of the space for middle class compassion, but for a different and distant "deserving" poor' (Adams & Raisborough, 2008: 1175).[2] Although the authors concede that fair-trade consumers tend to be found in the middle class, they are 'reluctant to simply graft "the middle-class consumer" into the moral economy of FairTrade' (ibid.: 1176). They draw on Sayer's (2005a) concept of 'lay morality' in order to argue that fair-trade consumers are likely to be found in all social classes. Sayer's work criticises Bourdieu for ignoring the normative dimension of the struggles of the social field. He argues that 'moral judgements are likely to be less sensitive [than aesthetic ones] to the social position of the valuer and the valued' (Sayer, 2005b: 951), because ethical sentiments and norms have a 'universalising tendency/generalising moment' deriving from 'the reciprocal character of social relations', as well as an awareness that we can be treated poorly (or well) by people regardless of their social class (Sayer, 2005a: 136). Sayer suggests that people are embarrassed (as well as resentful, guilty, defensive and shamed) by the existence of class inequalities, and they tend to search for alternative ways to justify their distinctiveness. Moral boundary-drawing offers individuals the opportunity to value and differentiate themselves from others without having to resort to social class. However, these justifications are always made in the context of, and often in response to, class inequalities. But moral boundary-drawing has a 'crucial ambivalence at its heart' because, although it gives us reasons to differentiate ourselves from others, 'it also treats the merits claimed for our own group as universally valid' (ibid.: 184).

In Chapter 5, we saw how Alfred identified the fair-trade consumer with reference to his/her moral characteristics – someone who possesses a 'social conscience'. In denying the relevance of social class, Alfred erected a moral boundary between himself and others who do not buy fair-trade. Thus, the various symbolic boundaries that people draw to differentiate themselves from others may not always operate in alignment with one another. Lamont (1992) reached similar conclusions in her study of middle-class working men in France and America, and proposed that individuals draw boundaries along three separate axes – socio-economic, cultural and moral – with individuals in the two countries placing more value on some boundaries than others.

Socio-economic boundaries are drawn on the basis of judgements concerning someone's social position as indicated by their wealth, power and professional success; cultural boundaries are drawn on the basis of education, intelligence, taste and command of high culture; and moral boundaries are drawn on the basis of evaluations of moral character and can refer to things like honestly, integrity and care for others (Lamont, 1992: 4). Unlike Bourdieu, Sayer and Lamont suggest that moral boundaries are unlikely *always* to be indicative of class position because people can pursue particular commitments even if they do not bring them any external rewards (but do bring them internal rewards). Sayer calls for us to pay more attention to people's 'lay normativities', which go beyond issues of the unequal distribution of goods and recognition and move to questions of 'what is good or bad, how we or others should behave' because these are the things that matter greatly to actors concerning their 'commitments, identities and ways of life' (Sayer, 2005a: 5, 6).

Of course definitions of 'good' or 'bad' behaviour will be heavily influenced by existing 'cultural repertoires', which introduces questions of power into individuals' evaluations of supposedly universal moral qualities (Lamont, 1992: 7). Within any given culture, there will inevitably be 'a hierarchy of moral discourses' through which individuals are governed via various 'modes of subjection' to alter their practices and think about ethics and morality in particular ways (Heckman, 1995: 40). Individuals do not necessarily alter their practices in line with hegemonic moral discourses, but rather draw on alternative moral understandings (which have emerged through engagement in a different set of practices or collective traditions) in order to justify why these 'modes of subjection' do not apply to their local and particular situations. Heckman terms this process of justification 'local resistance' – something that non-fair-trade supporters regularly employed in order to account for their lack of interest in fair-trade.

Fair-trade consumption is represented as an explicitly ethical activity, which is publicly defended by a range of actors across a number of important institutions, such as schools, churches, municipalities, retailers, the media and so on (unlike the objects of legitimate culture as identified by Bennett et al.'s (2009) survey). Until quite recently, its regular performance relied on individuals being able to pay the often higher price for fair-trade goods in order to achieve a 'degree of moral goodness' (Fagan, 2006: 123). This has complicated evaluations of the morality of fair-trade consumption and the socio-economic characteristics of the fair-trade consumer, given that not everyone has equal capacity to afford these products. By listening to how individuals in Chelmsford articulated socio-economic, cultural and moral boundaries between themselves and the fair-trade consumer, it is possible to learn a great deal about the relationship between fair-trade, social class and morality.

## Researching moral boundaries and the fair-trade consumer

The data presented in this chapter is based on eight focus group discussions in Chelmsford – four with fair-trade supporters that took place between January and April 2008, and four with non-fair-trade supporters that were conducted during Fairtrade Fortnight 2008 (a time of the year when awareness of fair-trade should be at its highest).[3] Fair-trade supporters were recruited through the Chelmsford Fairtrade Town networks, whereas non-fair-trade supporters were recruited through adverts (in local supermarkets and in the village hall where the groups were to be conducted), which asked people to attend chocolate- and coffee-tasting sessions. It is difficult to identify people negatively by characteristics they lack, and I was concerned, given the representation of fair-trade as a morally worthy form of consumption, that if focus group participants were aware of my interest in fair-trade this might affect the types of people who attended the interview. That is, only individuals who had already thought about or were interested in fair-trade or people who held strong opinions on the subject would turn up; and it would increase the likelihood of socially desirable responses in favour of fair-trade. I therefore used the chocolate- and coffee-tasting as a 'focusing exercise' (Bloor et al., 2001), before moving to a discussion of the factors that influenced people when shopping for these commodities.[4] While there were some drawbacks to recruiting the focus groups on this basis, the majority of those who attended did not think of themselves as fair-trade supporters and none were involved in the Chelmsford Fairtrade Town network.

Focus groups are a great tool for accessing group meanings, processes and norms, which has made them popular among academic researchers in recent years (Bloor et al., 2001; Finch & Lewis, 2003; Stewart, Shamdasani & Rook, 2007). The focus group provides a unique opportunity for a group of individuals, who may or may not be known to each other, to come together to examine, and in some cases challenge, the normative and collective understandings that underpin our taken-for-granted assumptions (Bloor et al., 2001). Because the morality of fair-trade consumption tends to be taken for granted by a variety of organisations and actors, and because discourses surrounding fair-trade consumption act as a possible 'mode of subjection' in their calls for individuals to act, it could be argued that these representations provide a normative frame upon which consumers can draw in order to evaluate their own and others' consumption practices. Importantly, we must remember that because 'the cut-off line between "good" commodities and "bad" ones is the object of an ongoing social and political conflict', it is unlikely that everyone will accept the normative demands placed upon them by fair-trade organisations and other institutions (Sassatelli, 2007: 159). In this way, the focus group methodology gave individuals the opportunity to discuss and reflect upon their moral responsibility for distant others through their consumption choices.

It is generally accepted that members of focus groups will search for consensus, in a process known as 'norming', when discussing and reflecting upon issues collectively, in order to create a sense of group cohesion (Finch & Lewis, 2003). Given that this chapter is concerned with whether people perceive fair-trade consumption as a distinctive activity and how they draw symbolic boundaries, it is important for the reader to be aware how the two sets of focus groups formed a consensus around a different set of issues. In the non-fair-trade groups, where most participants agreed that the things that mattered to them were taste, price and familiarity, the consensus tended to form around the idea that the fair-trade consumer 'was not like us', and in this way members may have exaggerated the characteristic differences of fair-trade consumers. Similarly, in the fair-trade groups, where participants recognised one another as committed fair-trade supporters, the consensus formed around the identification with the fair-trade consumer, which in some cases resulted in groups stressing the non-exclusivity of fair-trade consumption and performing its ordinariness. However, we have seen that responses in individual interviews do demonstrate that fair-trade and non-fair-trade consumers continue to hold these understandings of the exclusivity of fair-trade, even if they are present to a lesser degree.[5] Nevertheless, it is interesting to observe how the claims of non-exclusivity made in the last chapter compare with those given by focus group participants.

## The fair-trade consumer is not like us, but ...

Participants in the non-fair-trade focus groups classified both fair-trade consumers and the practice of fair-trade consumption/support using different symbolic boundaries around fair-trade consumption. The boundaries were regularly used in varying ways, with moral boundaries often being valued in and of themselves. But equally, there were examples of 'local resistance' to the notion that fair-trade consumption is the only way to be a moral/ethical consumer.

The following exchange took place between a group of mothers (aged 32–45) who were all taking a break from employment to bring up their children.[6]

| | |
|---|---|
| **Moderator:** | So what sort of person do you think buys fair-trade? |
| **Fran:** | Someone with a conscience, someone ... social status I think is a contribution. |
| **Lindsey:** | Yes, it comes into it. |
| **Fran:** | It does, like the organic social status, people like to be seen. |
| **Ling and Amanda:** | Hmm [nods]. |
| **Fran:** | Like recycling, it's very trendy to be seen recycling now, erm I mean Carla told me off 'cos obviously I'm driving the car around all the time with the kids and she was saying about the carbon and I said, 'But you sit there and chain smoke', if you're worried about the ... she just went all quiet and I said well ok then. But it is a conscience thing I think. And if you can then it's great, if you can afford to do it. |

The group argues that fair-trade consumers are those who can afford to spend more on their shopping and who do so in order to project an image of their social status through their 'conspicuous consumption'. If we apply Bourdieu's ideas to their characterisation of fair-trade consumers, it is possible to suggest that this group of women were making a distinction between their own approach to consumption, which they claim operates according to a logic of necessity, and the consumption of those with higher economic and cultural capital who make shopping choices according to their 'distance from necessity'. In this way, Fran's criticism of those 'trendy' shoppers who recycle lots and buy organic food – earlier discussed by this group as something that only 'people with money to waste' will buy – can be partly understood as a judgement that reflects this different level of cultural capital. However, Fran's agreement that fair-trade consumption is 'great if you can afford to do it' suggests that there is more going on here than simply 'refusing what she is refused' (Bourdieu, 1984: 471).

We could read Fran's statement as an example of the potential autonomy of moral judgements from aesthetic and socio-economic judgements, so that certain goods and practices can be understood as 'valuable regardless of whether the dominant happen to value them' (Sayer, 2005a: 121). Because fair-trade has made Fran, in her own words, 'aware of other people's suffering', it could be suggested that she can see the value of fair-trade as a moral good in its own right. Having said this, her description of her friend's attempt to make her more aware of the environmental impact of her consumption hints at a challenge, or 'local resistance', to the attempts of various ethical consumption discourses to encourage people to alter their practices in line with their campaigns. Even if Fran recognises the value of fair-trade and low-carbon consumption, she uses her own circumstances – which include being a single parent on a tight budget who has to feed and chauffeur five children – to defend her reasons for not using fair-trade and to construct herself as a different kind of 'respectable' subject through the prioritisation of the moral care for her children.

Sayer, drawing from Skeggs (1997), has argued that when individuals are denied access to certain goods because of their position in society, this inequality can cause them great distress and encourage them to search for alternative ways to gain respectability. In the hierarchy of moral discourses, Fran's caring for her family takes priority and reduces the relevance of those discourses which stress the care for distant others. Like the Bourdieuian approach, we can see that the moral boundary in this case (possessing a 'conscience') does operate in accordance with socio-economic and cultural boundaries, but importantly, the second reading allows for the expression of lay normativities, revealing the possibility that certain actions can be understood as 'good' regardless of their association with hegemonic discourses and particular social status groups.

The problems of assuming that the moral boundaries drawn around fair-trade consumption necessarily operate in the same way as aesthetic and socio-economic boundaries can be seen in the discussion among a group of Sainsbury's shoppers.

**Moderator:**    So do you think there's a particular sort of person that buys fair-trade?
**Dave:**    Rich [small laugh].
**Emma:**    Middle class.
**Karl:**    Stupid [laughs] … I'm only joking.
**Diana:**    No I would think, despite the little bit of cynicism.

Karl:        Naive rather.

Diana:       I would still think that it's a thinking person that buys it, I still think that if you go for fair-trade you have got some morals about things, I mean even though I am cynical and I might not always buy it myself, a better me would buy it. I always think that if I had more money I would possibly buy that.

Nicole:      Yeah, yeah I agree with Diana on that.

Emma:        I don't think it's all about money, I think you know even if you've got plenty of money you still would make, you could still make discerning decisions about how you spend it and rich people don't waste their money.

Diana:       No, I think that's my excuse to myself if I don't buy it, but when I've got more money I will.[7]

Although it is initially suggested that the 'fair-trade consumer' is someone who occupies an affluent middle-class position, this is discussed by the group who come to a different understanding of the relationship between income and fair-trade consumption. Diana characterises the 'fair-trade consumer' as a 'thinking person' and someone who has 'some morals about things' in a similar way to how Fran discussed the fair-trade consumer in the previous extract. Interestingly, although Diana seems to identify with both of these statements, she distances herself from consuming fair-trade because she believes it to be too expensive. She can imagine that 'a better me would buy it', but this is countered by her own acknowledgement that using socio-economic boundaries are only 'an excuse to herself'. As Emma confirms to her, an individual's income does not automatically determine their decision to buy fair-trade goods, and they also need to possess certain forms of cultural capital and moral dispositions that allow them to make 'discerning decisions'. Unlike the first extract, where Fran sees income as a real obstacle preventing her from engaging in fair-trade consumption, we see in this extract how income becomes an illusory barrier. Socio-economic and moral judgements do not necessarily operate in alignment with one another because it is possible to be 'rich' and not engage in ethical purchasing behaviour.

Karl's assertion that the 'fair-trade consumer' is naive, which is later expanded upon and discussed further by the group, is worth considering because it reveals a defensive challenge to the fair-trade movement's attempt to encourage individuals to alter their consumption behaviour. Rather than revealing one's 'superior knowledge', as Varul found in fair-trade consumers' own accounts of their consumption, Karl describes the fair-trade consumer as an individual who lacks certain forms of knowledge because of their inability to see through the marketing messages and gather 'real' facts about the effects of this label upon farmers in the Third World – as he says, 'they're sold on the label and sold on this whole premise that this is going to help a better world ... with no obvious evidence'.

Karl feels that it is important to justify why he does not consume fair-trade, which suggests that he is aware that fair-trade is generally represented as a morally sound consumer choice. His cynicism and defensiveness towards this consumer label are based upon his belief that fair-trade does not help to alleviate poverty in the developing world. This will be a particular focus of the next chapter when we will examine how respondents rated the effectiveness of fair-trade consumption as an individual political action. For now, it is important to draw attention to how Karl draws a cultural boundary (rather than a socio-economic or moral boundary) between himself and fair-trade consumers in order to defend himself from those hegemonic discourses that are attempting to govern him in a particular way and in the process constructs himself as a more 'savvy' consumer – while fair-trade consumers are 'sucked into buying things based on what the packaging says', he is not!

To this point, we have seen that the morality of fair-trade consumption has generally remained unquestioned. It has been accepted that those who buy fair-trade are doing so because they believe (even if misguidedly) that they are helping people in the Third World. However, it was not always the case that participants agreed that those who consume fair-trade are necessarily morally superior individuals. It is interesting to look at the ways in which the morality of the 'fair-trade consumer' is challenged with reference to socio-economic and cultural judgements, as well as to alternative moral boundaries, in the following extract. The discussion between Joe, a Black-British[8] gas engineer, and Michael, a White-British carpenter, who were both in their thirties, takes place following my request for Joe to expand upon his earlier claim that fair-trade consumers, just like supermarkets who refuse to give you a plastic bag while leaving the lights on during the day themselves, have 'double standards'.

| **Moderator:** | Ok, you said there that you think fair-trade shoppers have double standards, can you tell me a bit more about that? |
| **Joe:** | Well, they drive 4x4s. |

| Michael: | I was gonna say that, they think they're doing some good to another country by buying that sort of product and helping out, but it comes to some sort of famine relief or something like that, like a natural disaster, I don't think they're first to put their hands in their pocket. |
|---|---|
| Joe: | No! |
| Michael: | But they think they're doing a good by buying something like that because they're not actually seeing no end result you know, as you say they're still going out in their 4x4s or sort of E-type Jags. |
| Joe: | 'Course they are ... going on aeroplanes. |
| Michael: | And still living it up. You know that's probably how they make themselves feel good. |
| Joe: | That's it, they make themselves feel better first by saying 'Well, I've done my bit' and then that's enough. But they don't advertise the fact that they've got this other stuff going on in their house. |
| Michael: | 'Cos they've done their little bit by buying a packet of coffee which is fair-trade. |

It is clear in this exchange that socio-economic and moral boundaries are being heavily drawn around those who consume fair-trade. Those that buy fair-trade are people with high disposable incomes who consume fair-trade in order to 'make themselves feel better' while also engaging in a selection of environmentally damaging forms of consumption. Joe and Michael are drawing attention to the contradictions that they see in those people who are trying to make them change their practices in line with the normative demands of ethical consumption campaigns. Articulating the recent public debates surrounding irresponsible consumption in the UK, in particular the 4x4 drivers who have been increasingly blamed for climate change, the men seem to be questioning why they ought to buy fair-trade when those that they imagine are encouraging them to buy it are 'living it up'. At a time when practices of individual consumption were being placed under increased scrutiny and hegemonic discourses framed certain actions as unethical,[9] we see how 'local resistance' to these 'modes of subjection' are made on the basis that these changes have made life difficult or more expensive for the 'ordinary' consumer.

As we saw in the first focus group extract, Fran's dismissal of her friend's attempts to encourage her to think about the environmental impact of her consumption reveals that not all individuals are equally convinced of the applicability of these moral discourses to their own personal situations. For Joe and Michael, we could argue that a protest is articulated against those members of society, which later included supermarkets and local councils, who wanted to stop them from doing what they enjoy while at the same time being responsible for the same 'bad' practices. At the heart of this protest is a real sense of inequality in that while people like them will be losing out because of these changes, those who can afford to drive 'E-type Jags' will be relatively unaffected and are able to buy fair-trade coffee in order to appear to the world as morally superior.

Focus group participants were aware that those who buy fair-trade are automatically assumed to be good people, and their responses to this often revealed a struggle for equal recognition. They demonstrated their awareness that there is more than one way for an individual to consti-tute him/herself as a moral subject through involvement in different social practices, but because of the existence of a 'hierarchy of moral discourses' they felt they were not always recognised for their efforts. For example, Michael drew attention to the fact that he will often give money to famine relief and natural disaster charities, confirming himself as a moral subject in a different (and in his opinion superior) way. By paying attention to his 'lay normativities', we find that it is not that Michael does not care about people in the Third World, but that he believes that fair-trade consumption is not necessarily the only, or indeed the best, way to achieve this aim. For Michael it is important to evaluate the ethics of an action in the context of the range of prac-tices an individual is engaged in, and because he imagines, rightly or wrongly, that fair-trade consumers only buy fair-trade in order to make themselves feel better after driving around in their 4x4 cars, he rejects the automatically assigned moral status of the fair-trade consumer.

It was, however, quite unusual for groups to reject the morality of fair-trade consumption outright; instead what tended to happen was that people offered reasons why they were not concerned with fair-trade. This tended to involve placing their consumption choices into the con-text of the range of practices they were engaged in before agreeing that they might consider fair-trade in the future.

**Lisa:**   See when I buy for my baby I buy organic. Fair-trade does not help my baby and her digestive system so I'm sorry, nah ...

**Hazel:**   So it is the benefit to us, it's not the benefit to them we're look-ing at.

| | |
|---|---|
| **Lisa:** | Yes. |
| **Hazel:** | I think what we're doing is about us, not about ... |
| **Lisa:** | Yes, like vitamins and minerals I look at, I don't look to paying somebody to pick my tea-leaves. However, there may be the odd product that I will buy.[10] |

In this exchange Lisa reveals how the care for her child is at the forefront of her mind when she is shopping. We are reminded of Miller's ethnographic account of everyday consumption behaviours and the importance of paying attention to how the pursuit of and commitment to particular social practices (like parenthood) will cultivate individuals' orientations and dispositions towards consumer goods. Importantly, Lisa does not dismiss fair-trade consumption completely because she acknowledges that 'there may be the odd product that I will buy'. It is possible that she makes this statement in order to appease herself to her fellow participants and, using the dominant representation of fair-trade consumption as a medium for moral action, demonstrates that she is not unethical because she still buys fair-trade occasionally. However, it is also possible that Lisa makes this statement because she can see the value of fair-trade consumption as a moral action even if it rarely enters her field of concern. Later when the group were discussing the effectiveness of different individual actions, Lisa demonstrates this. She admits that she would prefer to give to charity but reveals how she feels it is important for everybody to try to do something to help other people and says 'if you only ever buy fair-trade bananas then great, you're doing something'.

Another good example of an alternative understanding of ethical consumption, which ends in an agreement of the moral value of fair-trade as a concept, is demonstrated in the following extract. In order to set the context for this, Amanda was very concerned for the welfare of animals (particularly following a recent TV documentary showing the mistreatment of chickens), and the group had had a long discussion about caring for animals before the following exchange took place.

| | |
|---|---|
| **Moderator:** | Ok, so we're obviously quite concerned about animals and the way that they've been treated. Fair-trade's about helping people, so I was just wondering what you think about it in terms of that. 'Cos if you're concerned about animals ... |
| **Danielle:** | Why aren't we concerned about people? |

| | |
|---|---|
| **Amanda:** | I think I'm more concerned about animals than I am people, because I mean people could consciously do things themselves or they're put into it, whereas animals they haven't got a choice, have they. |
| **Danielle:** | But what about those children that are working for 5p a day. |
| **Fran:** | Yeah ... if they're lucky. I mean they are forced into that situation. |
| **Amanda:** | But then is that our fault? |
| **Fran:** | Well, the thing is you're supposed to help other people, aren't you? |
| **Danielle:** | So are we thinking, should we go more for the fair-trade stuff, to buy more fair-trade is that to help those children? |
| **Amanda:** | I think I'll be more aware, yeah.[11] |

Amanda began talking about animal welfare after she had admitted that she was unlikely to buy fair-trade because she generally used her shopping choices to care for her son who had ADHD and who needed particular sorts of food in order to manage his medical condition. So perhaps like Lisa, in order to appease herself to the group for rejecting fair-trade, she offered an alternative understanding of ethical consumption – based on care for animals – to construct herself, and gain recognition as, an alternative moral subject. However, what is interesting about this exchange is how Amanda was persuaded to rethink her position on fair-trade after Danielle raises the issue of child labour, and Fran says that we 'ought to help other people'. Of course we could say that Amanda's agreement that she would be 'more aware' of these issues was a product of the process of the group discussion where members search for consensus.

However, I would argue that, because Amanda was not afraid of voicing her opinion even when it differed from the majority of the group and because she did not really change her position on fair-trade when she later argued that she was unlikely to be able to fit fair-trade shopping choices into her tight budget, we are witnessing at this point in the focus group a 'generalising moment' where lay understandings of what constitutes morality are guided by a duty of care for other people (compassion) and an awareness of the reciprocity of social life (Sayer, 2005a). In particular, once the issue of fair-trade was related to child labour, this group of mothers could relate to and supported the value of fair-trade, which connected to their wider moral practices surrounding parenthood. We saw a similar situation in Michael's dismissal of fair-trade consumers and the practice of fair-trade consumption as a false morality pursued only by those who want to hide their 'bad' behaviour, which was countered by Michael's agreement that it is important to give money to charity to help people who are suffering in the Third World.

It seems that while fair-trade as a consumption practice is often understood as the preserve of people with high economic and (sometimes) cultural capital, the concept that fair-trade provokes – understood as a duty to care for other people – does not necessarily interact with these economic and cultural judgements. Focus group participants tended to agree with and could see the value of helping people in the Third World even if they found ways to justify why they did not, or could not, organise their consumption along these lines. As Sayer has argued, morality has a 'universalising character' because we can recognise that we ought to treat people with respect and dignity regardless of social divisions. Of course participants were likely to have been heavily influenced by the prevalence of liberal-humanist discourses within our society, which will have constrained how they were able to evaluate the morality of fair-trade consumption.

Although Sayer and Heckman both warn against characterising morality as 'mere internalised and memorised bits of social scripts' (Sayer, 2005a: 7), our moral beliefs are central to who we are; they are not arbitrary or subject to the 'vagaries of preferences that characterise other choices that subjects make' (Heckman, 1995: 113). We are able to challenge or resist hegemonic moral discourses, and the fact that the non-fair-traders did not challenge the suggestion that we ought to treat others with respect, reveals a shared understanding of morality when engaging in arguments about fair-trade. However, the 'modes of subjection', which attempted to govern them to act upon this shared understanding of morality in a particular way – by consuming what are perceived to be more expensive consumer goods – did often meet with resistance and encouraged respondents to assert socio-economic, cultural and alternative moral boundaries around their own and others' practices in order to justify their inaction or gain recognition for engaging in different moral actions.

The paradox of this section is that despite their characterisation of the fair-trade consumer as someone who was 'not like us', many of the participants in these focus groups had bought fair-trade on a regular basis. We spent some time discussing shopping routines in general, and it emerged that they regularly visited places where fair-trade coffee, for example, was the standard option.[12] Bananas were a popular topic of discussion within the groups, being easily recognisable as a fair-trade product, and just under half of respondents shopped at supermarkets with 100 per cent fair-trade banana policies. Although, systems of provision were switching to fair-trade, making fair-trade options the norm, these participants did not recognise themselves as fair-trade consumers. The boundary between the exclusivity and normalisation of fair-trade consumption has become blurry, as those without a taste for fair-trade continue to imagine that the fair-trade consumer has distinctive characteristics, at the same time as they themselves consume fair-trade. The rapid transformation and increasing availability of fair-trade in the UK does not appear to have caught up with people's understandings and evaluations of the fair-trade movement, highlighting the importance of paying attention to the trajectory of practices of fair-trade support.

## Anyone can be a fair-trade consumer, but ...

Fair-trade supporters tended to stress the non-exclusivity of fair-trade consumption. Unlike the non-fair-trade supporters, there was an awareness of the mainstream availability of fair-trade in the UK. In addition, many of the fair-trade supporters were actively engaged, through the Fairtrade Town network, in promoting fair-trade and appealing to the all-inclusive figure of the 'consumer'. However, when we examine fair-trade supporters' claims of non-exclusivity more closely, we find that they are not quite as simple as they first appear. Just as Savage, Bagnall and Longhurst found that individuals' claims to 'ordinariness' were 'defined relationally', so that comparisons between the 'ordinary' and the 'non-ordinary' were polluted with references to class (Savage, Bagnall & Longhurst, 2001: 876), we too find that fair-trade supporters' classifications of fair-trade consumption draw on a number of symbolic boundaries – some of which can be read along class lines.

Let us begin with an extract from a focus group conducted with a fair-trade group at the local university.[13]

| Moderator: | What sort of person do you think buys fair-trade? |
|---|---|
| **Jackie:** | People like us, normal people really ... might be a bit, I don't know sometimes you just get a bit more aware, don't you, but I don't think we're rushing out to buy it because we think we're ... I dunno! |
| **Keith:** | It's interesting, a few years ago we did a town collection for a Chaplaincy-inspired and led project ... and the |

|            | extraordinary thing was that the most generous givers were old people and people who obviously hadn't … |
|------------|--------|
| Jackie:    | Hadn't got much. |
| Keith:     | … who hadn't got much. Now whether one could translate that to the purchase of fair-trade goods I don't know because fair-trade goods are much more widely disseminated and everyone needs coffee and tea, you know; but I have a feeling that it's people whose consciences have already been pricked or who knows what it is actually to try and live on a budget and you know who may have more sympathy with the campaign. |
| Jackie:    | Yeah, fairly normal people that might have read something and it just kind of gets stuck in their minds, doesn't it. |

The fair-trade consumer can be anybody, but it is generally someone who is more aware and has 'read something' about the subject. Jackie constructs a cultural boundary between the fair-trade and the non-fair-trade consumer, but obviously feels a bit uncomfortable classifying the practice as something that is superior to how others organise their shopping. Her statement with its telling pause, 'I don't think we're rushing out to buy it because we think we're … I dunno', suggests that she is aware and cautious about the fact that fair-trade consumption may be associated with the display of distinction. Bennett et al. (2009) found that middle-class respondents tended to be open to diversity and shied away from snobbish remarks about other people's tastes. However, they also detected the continued existence of subtle boundaries that respondents used when assessing their own cultural participation. Jackie's hesitant characterisation of the fair-trade consumer reveals this complex and subtle superiority – she is aware that fair-trade is a 'good taste' and may therefore appeal to a particular sort of person, but she doesn't want to (at this point) invoke a 'hierarchy of value'.

Interestingly, one of the ways in which the non-exclusivity of fair-trade consumption was achieved in the focus group was through identifying the practice with people in lower-class positions. Keith speculates that the people who might buy fair-trade are those 'who haven't got much', and suggests that these people are more likely to have sympathy with the movement's aims. Keith tries to claim the ordinariness of fair-trade consumption, but in so doing reveals his own distance from those 'who haven't got much'. He offers a romantic characterisation of the experience of poverty among people living within the UK, and suggests that these people will be able to identify with the aims of the fair-trade movement because they, like the fair-trade farmers, will have had the experience of living on a budget and will want to help. The experience of poverty is imagined to create certain moral dispositions and an automatic sympathy towards others who are struggling under 'similar' conditions. We are reminded of Adams and Raisborough's (2008) suggestion that fair-trade farmers are represented as the 'deserving poor', which is likely to evoke feelings of compassion and sympathy among relatively affluent consumers. The moral status attached to the struggling yet noble fair-trade farmer is projected by Keith onto those who 'haven't got much' in the UK. Keith eschews the general assumption that the fair-trade consumer occupies a middle-class position, but at the same time he draws a moral boundary that relies upon the imagined experience of poverty, from which he is disassociated. In distancing himself from 'the poor', he reveals the classed underpinnings of his perspective.

It is interesting to note that, later in the focus group, Keith and Jackie's description of those who are unlikely to be interested in fair-trade seems to offer quite a different understanding of the morality of those in lower-class positions.

Keith:   But you see if we're looking at, why do we buy this product ... we buy this product because by buying that product that directly benefits Mr X or Miss Y in country Z. Now why can't that actually also feed into why do we need to buy this foodstuff and not that foodstuff to ensure that our children don't grow up obese, you know in one sense we're talking about the same kind of lifestyle choices we're talking about food which saves lives, you know and on the broadest possible canvas not making our kids eat turkey twisters should be seen as important as buying this coffee or this flour or whatever it is because the choice of that foodstuff means that it will save lives. So I think potentially if we can see fair-trade as interlinked with so many other things ... sorry.

Jackie:  No, I agree with that, I think there's always gonna be so many people that you kind of see walking down smoking cigarettes and flicking their butts, and having turkey twizzlers in their bags who just really don't care do they, no ... what's it got to do with me kind of thing.

Keith:   It's very hard to see how you could ever get past the hard core where nothing is going to influence them ... not even war and natural disaster.

**Jackie:** I know [small laugh] ... no, to me I'm like really anti-smoking and you hear some people saying 'I ain't got enough money to feed the kids', but bugger me they manage to find a packet of cigarettes every day and you think come on, you know.

Their classification of those who don't buy fair-trade is here much more in keeping with Varul's suggestion that fair-trade consumers use fair-trade in order to display their ethical distinction. In keeping with his earlier romanticisation of 'the poor', Keith suggests that the issues are the same whether it is the welfare of your own child or of a distant child. However, in this extract he uses the existence of shared concerns and priorities to condemn on a common basis rather than to praise. Keith suggests that we ought to take a more holistic approach towards the ethical consumption of foodstuffs, paying particular attention to the 'turkey twizzlers' that caused such debate around issues of nutrition and social class. 'Turkey twizzlers' became the focus of a campaign to improve school dinners led by the chef Jamie Oliver; but it has been pointed out that this was a 'deeply moralistic campaign', which did not hide a 'snobbish disdain for people's behaviour and values' (O'Neill, 2008).

Jackie quickly associates those who feed their children turkey twizzlers with the type of person who is unlikely to consider fair-trade. Whereas she earlier seemed quite cautious about suggesting that those who buy fair-trade come from a particular class position, she here classifies the non-fair-trade consumer as someone engaged in a whole range of what we might consider 'underclass' behaviour. She draws socio-economic, cultural and moral boundaries around those irresponsible and uncaring mothers who claim to be unable to feed their children but then smoke a packet of cigarettes every day. We can see that those 'normal people' who buy fair-trade are, after all, quite distinctive along class lines.

We find a similarly ambiguous challenge to the assumption that fair-trade consumption is a middle-class activity in the discussion between Val, a retired executive officer in the civil service and Patrick, a university lecturer (both of whom are committed Christians) in the Chelmsford Fairtrade Town focus group.

**Val:** I mean, what I notice having come from a much poorer area, in [name of town], what is very moving is that sometimes you see quite poor people struggling to buy fair-trade because they can identify so much with the cause, and they'll often be very responsive, and I'm always a

|                | little surprised that Chelmsford isn't more responsive because it is more affluent. |
| :--- | :--- |
| **Moderator:** | Do you think affluence is important then? |
| **Patrick:** | Well, if you're affluent you can buy more, you can also buy dearer, can't you, you don't have to buy the cheapest. |
| **Val:** | I mean, I always say in talks that you know one of the obstacles to fair-trade, people often assume that the primary obstacle is price, I think that's a little bit misleading but obviously you're not gonna get the rock bottom cheapest because if you've got that, then you've squeezed everyone in the chain and obviously the producer is the easiest to squeeze. Quality for quality, fair-trade as food often stands up in price to similar products. |

We will notice how Val, like Keith, attempts to challenge the general assumption that fair-trade consumption is exclusively a middle-class activity by associating this activity with 'poor people'. Again there is a romantic characterisation (or speculation) that the experience of poverty creates particular moral dispositions that make those in lower-class positions more likely to support fair-trade. Although she describes how she has witnessed 'quite poor people struggling to buy fair-trade', I would suspect that Val could only have witnessed this at her then-local church where she ran a fair-trade stall, suggesting that those 'poor people's' commitment to fair-trade may have been part of their wider commitment to their Christian faith rather than solely a product of their class position.

What is particularly interesting about the exchange is how on the one hand Val believes that 'poor people' will often struggle to buy fair-trade because they understand that it is important to help others, and yet on the other she believes that greater wealth ought to make it easier to pay the premium for fair-trade goods and states that 'obviously you're not gonna get the rock bottom cheapest'. She seems to both deny and then acknowledge the importance of price in her attempt to match her proselytising with the fact that fair-trade items have to guarantee a particular price. Val sustains the romantic image of the poor yet moral consumer, but also reveals her distance from this position because she ignores the reality that a number of 'poor people' are very likely to have to buy the cheapest range of goods in order to feed their families even if that does 'squeeze' the producer. However, Val's characterisation of the struggling, Christian fair-trade consumer raises an important connection to the arguments put forward in the previous chapter.

Through the application of a theory of practice it was demonstrated that the fair-trade supporter is often an individual who becomes aware of fair-trade through their engagement in existing networks and activities. The focus group data supports this position, with the majority of focus group participants recognising that the fair-trade consumer has particular moral and cultural dispositions towards fair-trade that are developed through their involvement in existing commitments. In the following extract – which takes place in the focus group with fair-trade supporters who are not heavily involved in the town group activities – someone in the group (Sandra) had suggested that fair-trade was a 'very middle-class thing, *Guardian* readers', but this was challenged by another member of the group (Linda) who counted herself as 'working class'; the discussion that followed is very illuminating.

| | |
|---|---|
| **Moderator:** | So do you think that affluence is important then? |
| **Linda:** | Hmm … once you get to a certain amount of money … erm you are always looking for the best deal, well no the people that erm, erm … |
| **Kathy:** | [laughs] You're tryin' to word it in a certain way. |
| **Linda:** | The people that acquire a lot of money usually do so at the expense of other people, the people that give a lot of money away usually remain poor, but they are more kind of socially aware. |
| **Moderator:** | What does everybody else think of that? |
| **Sandra:** | Well, I, I, to … in my mind sort of classes, the middle class and working class is not just about money, it's about an attitude I think, and I think there's always been a left wing ethically conscious section of the working class and I hope that that's where I fit in. |
| **Linda:** | Yes! |
| **Sandra:** | Yes, but … I've got to admit that my lifestyle now is, I live in a middle-class area surrounded by middle-class people, I've come away from my roots, then again back to the [gestures to another member, Milena], I had a very evangelical Christian upbringing so I suppose that's part of it, I think. There's always people that have ethics as an important part of the way they live their lives. |
| **Tim:** | Hmm, I mean money isn't always going to come down to it, I mean if you are literally on the breadline, yes you won't be buying fair-trade 'cos it is more expensive, but I guess I started buying it when I was buying for myself |

as a student and at that point, I didn't have the money, I lived on overdraft but ... because you're always buying things that you wouldn't say, wasn't literally just bread and water, you could afford to spend an extra 20p on a jar of coffee so you know it's getting that balance.

**Peter:**   I think people that buy fair-trade tend to be people who are more socially conscious, more, maybe Christian, maybe political, maybe liberal or some reason like that, that they're perhaps a bit more thinking about things, but there's also the financial thing as well. I think if you really are in a difficult financial position, you're gonna look for what's cheapest not necessarily what's fair-trade, but once you have a, once the financial side isn't the key thing then I tend to think it tends to be people who've got a more progressive or Christian, or humanist, or something like that, even though not how much money you've got 'cos just because you're rich, you probably might not buy fair-trade.[14]

In many ways, we can recognise the position that is put forward here in the discussion among non-fair-trade consumers in the Sainsbury's focus group. The fair-trade consumer is someone who has some 'morals about things' or, in this case, the fair-trade consumer is more 'socially conscious'. What this discussion seems to add is a consideration of where those moral dispositions are likely to have originated.

Because of the rejection of the association between social class and fair-trade consumption put forward by Linda, Sandra reflects upon what it is about her that makes her consume fair-trade apart from her social class. She picks up on something that another participant had already mentioned, and reveals that her 'evangelical Christian upbringing' is likely to be a significant factor. Importantly, those people who have always had 'ethics as an important part of the way they live their lives' are likely to be fair-trade consumers. MacIntyre (2007) and Heckman (1995) have argued that it is important to understand virtue/moral beliefs in the context of the practices and longer traditions they are embedded within as well as in the context of the narrative of an individual's life. Sandra seems to be suggesting that her upbringing instilled certain values in her with regard to how she ought to behave towards others, which have had an impact upon the ways she orients herself in the world. The practice of fair-trade support makes sense in the context of both her life narrative and the longer traditions and values associated with Quakerism.

The suggestion that fair-trade consumers are people who have certain moral dispositions, which have been developed through involvement in adjacent practices, is also supported by Peter, who implies that the 'socially conscious' are not only those with religious backgrounds but can be those who are more liberal or progressive in outlook possibly as a result of engagement in political activity. However, Peter is also very aware that those without sufficient economic capital are likely to be constrained from using fair-trade in order to express their duties towards others.

Despite the fact that the group deny the relevance of social class through paying attention to social practices, it is important to note that Linda initially (hesitantly) distances fair-trade consumption from social class by arguing that those who are rich are unlikely to consider fair-trade because they have 'acquired their money at the expense of others'. It is interesting how the possession of large amounts of money is often understood, by both non-fair-trade and fair-trade participants (including Phillipa in Chapter 5), to limit the likelihood and credibility of consuming fair-trade. Rather than adopting a snobbish orientation towards the practices of those in lower-class positions, the socio-economic and moral boundaries work together to differentiate and establish the moral worth of the fair-trade consumer from those who conspicuously and irresponsibly consume goods regardless of the financial or moral cost.

Varul (2008b) has argued that fair-trade supporters often distinguished their own morally worthy behaviour from the moral indifference exhibited by competing sections of the middle classes. Drawing from Bourdieu, who suggested that those fractions of the middle class who were closest together competed with one another over the valuation of cultural practices and the related advantages these practices brought, it seems important to probe a little further into what these 'competing' fractions are struggling for. While Bourdieu suggested that there was a need to maintain the rarity of consumer practices to ensure that the advantages were only accessible to those from particular social positions, we ought to remember that fair-trade consumption is not characterised by its rarity but is rather widely available and is expanding into mainstream markets partly *because* of the practices of the fair-trade supporters. Fair-trade consumers do not seem to be able to use their support of fair-trade to ensure capital advantages for themselves – they may achieve 'sub-cultural capital' in which they are able to gain respect and reputation, but this is not really exchangeable beyond relatively contained social networks (see Bennett et al., 2009: 255). Following Sayer, it seems possible to suggest that fair-trade consumption is pursued because it is seen as valuable in its own right regardless of its association with any social status group and regardless of whether it brings any external rewards to fair-trade supporters. The struggles of the social field in this case seem to be about which ways of life and whose definitions of morality ought to be most valued.

The relationship between social class and fair-trade consumption tended to be a very thorny issue in the focus groups, with the majority of participants seeking to distance the practice of fair-trade consumption away from any class group. However, as we have seen, despite their claims of non-exclusivity, further inspection reveals how the fair-trade consumer is often constructed as distinctive on the basis of socio-economic, cultural and moral boundaries. One of the rare overt classifications of the fair-trade consumer along these boundaries demonstrates this.

**Matt:**  I think you, far be it from me to tell you how to conduct your own research but my sense is that essentially fair-trade is being driven by middle-class, liberal, left-leaning for the most part people. And they're, they're only a relatively small segment of the population, and really if fair-trade is going to take off then it has to penetrate much more forcefully other large segments and notably 'Joe Soap' out there, or 'Mrs Joe Soap' who really doesn't know anything about fair-trade, and I hope that therefore perhaps in your focus groups you might include some of those. Otherwise I think you'd get a skewed picture.[15]

Matt's classification occurred at the very end of the Co-op member focus group, and associates the fair-trade consumer with the liberal middle classes while suggesting that the non-fair-trade consumer is someone who lacks the knowledge to choose fair-trade and who watches 'lowbrow' daytime television. Despite the potentially denigrating nature of the characterisation of the non-fair-trade consumer as 'Mrs Joe Soap', Matt's statement also reveals a desire to understand this figure. He wants to know why 'Mrs Joe Soap' is not interested in fair-trade in order for fair-trade to 'penetrate' the market more successfully. As a committed fair-trade supporter whose practices are organised around expanding the market for fair-trade goods, Matt suspects that fair-trade consumption is currently carried out by those with particular characteristics, but he clearly wants to imagine a time when it will not be, when it will be non-exclusive.

In this way, even the most overt characterisation of the fair-trade consumer as exclusive is tempered by a desire for non-exclusivity.

We can see that the situation is a little more complex than using fair-trade consumption as a form of class distinction (Varul, 2008b). To be sure there is an element of this, but to understand it solely as this is to ignore the claims of and calls for non-exclusivity. Fair-trade consumption is promoted by fair-trade supporters who are pursuing this practice because they believe in its moral value. It is fair to say that all the fair-trade participants agreed that fair-trade consumption had moral value regardless of who did it. So Matt would be quite happy if 'Mrs Joe Soap' starting buying fair-trade because this would mean that there would be greater benefits to the producers. Like the non-fair-trade supporters who could recognise the moral value of fair-trade regardless of whether they actually bought it, Matt is suggesting that consuming fair-trade has a moral value in and of itself regardless of its association with any social group. However, we should not neglect to consider how questions of power are introduced into his statement: Mrs Joe Soap ought to buy fair-trade regardless of whether she is interested in fair-trade because both fair-trade supporters and the institutions that promote fair-trade believe that it is the right thing to do.

## Lay normativity and the fair-trade consumer

It is important to begin this summarising discussion by noting that the drawing of symbolic boundaries is a culturally variable phenomenon, with individuals in different countries valuing some boundaries more than others – for example, Lamont found that in America, socio-economic boundaries were valued over cultural boundaries, whereas in France, cultural boundaries were more important than socio-economic ones. In both contexts, moral boundaries were drawn, but it is likely that the 'cultural repertoires' available to respondents to judge what constitutes decent behaviour will vary in different countries.

The examples in this chapter are drawn from participants living within the UK, and we therefore ought to be cautious about extrapolating the findings to other countries without conducting additional research. Because of the mainstreamed nature of fair-trade provision in the UK, it is possible to suggest that there may actually be a diminishing relevance to the classifications of the 'fair-trade consumer' utilised by respondents in this chapter. Yet in spite of the fact that more and more people are likely to be consuming fair-trade in the UK without being aware of it or without expressing a strong commitment to the aims of the fair-trade movement, we have seen that the 'fair-trade consumer' continues to be constructed as an individual with distinctive characteristics.

This arguably makes the conclusions of this chapter particularly relevant to contexts where fair-trade products remain concentrated in specialist stores and associated with distinctive groups (such as in Germany, as argued by Varul, 2009). On the other hand, in Sweden, where social class divisions are less pronounced than in other parts of the world, the drawing of socio-economic boundaries around the fair-trade consumer is likely to be less prevalent than in the UK and USA where there remain significant inequalities between social groups. Given that similar promotional tactics and messages are employed across the international fair-trade movement with an appeal to the morality of helping distant others, the arguments presented here ought to be recognisable to audiences in other countries, even if not directly comparable.

This chapter has focused principally on the ways in which British fair-trade and non-fair-trade supporters have characterised the 'fair-trade consumer' and how they used different symbolic boundaries and drew upon their lay normativities in order to justify or defend their level of support for fair-trade. I sought to understand the degree to which social class is used within individuals' characterisations of the fair-trade consumer, and found that social class remains an important factor in the differentiation of this practice. However, I argued that, because the boundary between the exclusivity and ordinariness of fair-trade consumption is being eroded as the practice of fair-trade support is evolving, and because we are dealing with people's lay morality, there is no simple relationship between social class and fair-trade.

Fair-trade supporters and non-fair-trade supporters differed with regard to the strength of the symbolic boundaries they employed to define the 'fair-trade consumer'. But both groups understood this figure to occupy a particular socio-economic position and to hold (or lack) particular forms of knowledge and moral dispositions that predisposed them to choose (or not choose) fair-trade. While Varul argued that those who consume fair-trade do so in order to display their ethical and cultural distinction over class-others, I have shown that it is problematic to assume that ethical and cultural judgements always operate in alignment with one another or to assume that fair-trade is necessarily used as a form of class-display. To be sure, we have found some support for Varul's claim, with both fair-trade and non-fair-trade participants recognising that fair-trade consumption can be used by individuals as a way of demonstrating their social status. However, to understand fair-trade consumption purely as a form of class-display is to ignore how fair-trade as a form of moral action might be valued regardless of its association with any group. Judgements of morality were very often inflected with judgements about social class and cultural capital, but moral boundaries did operate independently of these judgements. So although non-fair-trade participants did understand the fair-trade consumer as exclusive on the basis of social class and interest in other 'ethical' consumption practices (like organic food and not using plastic bags), and described how they often felt excluded from engaging in fair-trade consumption because they lacked economic capital, there was also some agreement in the moral value of fair-trade consumption regardless of these factors. The non-fair-traders tended to acknowledge the worthiness of helping people in the Third World, even if they did not follow these judgements through to the actual purchase of fair-trade goods. On the other hand, although fair-trade participants' stereotyped accounts of the lack of care shown by those in lower-class positions effectively demonstrated the continuing existence of moralising discourses that stigmatise the consumption behaviours and ways of life of the working classes (Horowitz, 1985), their claims that the fair-trade consumer could be anyone revealed how the moral value of fair-trade consumption is recognised regardless of who carries it out. If 'Mrs Joe Soap' started buying fair-trade tomorrow this would be understood as something positive – by fair-trade supporters, if not by 'Mrs Joe Soap' – rather than a threat to the exclusivity of the practice.

The trajectory of the fair-trade movement towards greater mainstream availability of fair-trade products, at comparable or equivalent prices to everyday brands (and indeed the use of the Fairtrade-certified logo by everyday brand), and the shifting of systems of public fair-trade provision, are changing the face of the fair-trade consumer. Yet it was striking to note that, in spite of these shifts, the fair-trade consumer continues to be characterised as a distinctive figure. There remains a perception that fair-trade is more expensive than everyday brands – which is certainly the case for some fair-trade products, even if coffee, tea, sugar, bananas and chocolate are broadly comparable in price to non-fair-trade alternatives. Because fair-trade consumption is widely represented by powerful institutions within British society as a desirable moral action and because it is morality that comes at a price, it was unsurprising that participants highlighted the unequal access to these consumer goods. When access to moral goods is denied on the basis of an individual's capacity to pay for it, questions of power are inevitably raised as people compete over whose definition of morality is most valid. The struggles for equal recognition that were found in the non-fair-trade-supporter extracts revealed the complexity of the relationship between fair-trade consumption, social class and morality. The historical trajectory of fair-trade in the market has left an unclear boundary between the ordinariness and exclusivity of fair-trade. And rather than simply 'graft the middle-class consumer into the moral economy of fair-trade', this chapter has suggested that the socio-economic status of fair-trade consumer is the subject of ongoing debate and active intervention. Social class is but one factor in the organisation of the practice of fair-trade support, and only time will tell whether differential understandings of this factor will develop and thus change the form the practice takes.

Despite detecting a consensus around the moral value of the concept that fair-trade provokes, those who did not knowingly organise their consumption along fair-trade lines did offer a number of normative and practical justifications for why they do not use fair-trade. In this chapter, I have mainly focused upon how individuals have explained their reasons for not consuming fair-trade on the basis of social class and their involvement in different social practices, which have generated alternative moral priorities and understandings. I have not paid much attention to the resistance from non-fair-trade supporters, which dealt with their evaluations of the effectiveness of the mechanism of fair-trade consumption as a tool for alleviating poverty in the developing world. Respondents raised important questions about the legitimacy of those discourses that were attempting to govern them to consume fair-trade products on the basis that this action was able to bring real benefits to Third World farmers. These questions will be examined in the next chapter using both quantitative and qualitative data sources.

# 7
# The Politics of Fair-Trade Consumption

The fair-trade citizen-consumer is frequently mobilised by various actors to use his/her purchasing power to alleviate poverty in the developing world. Unlike government aid and charitable donations, it is claimed that the trading partnership between the fair-trade consumer and the fair-trade producer has a unique power to reach the people who need it most and make a difference – the frequently invoked 'Trade is better than Aid' slogan. Indeed, recent growth in fair-trade sales in the USA have been linked to the declining prevalence of charitable giving in order to suggest that consumers are seeking alternative ways to make a difference (FTUSA, 2010). Yet almost no academic attention has been paid to how individuals evaluate the effectiveness of fair-trade consumption as an individual action relative to other individual actions, such as paying taxes, donating to charity and campaigning for change. This is quite surprising given the claims that consumers in a late-modern, risk-society are looking beyond 'traditional' politics in order to enact their citizenly duties.

This chapter explores how individuals in the UK evaluated the effectiveness of fair-trade consumption as a 'political' action relative to the other actions open to them that aim to achieve a similar end-result (i.e. the reduction of poverty in developing countries). It begins by highlighting why this is a relevant question for exploration, and then uses data from the UK National Omnibus Survey (conducted between 2002 and 2005), Module 236, 'Public Attitudes to Development', commissioned by the government department DFID (ONS, 2002; 2003; 2004; 2005), to demonstrate who is most likely to believe that buying fair-trade is an effective action. Supporting the conclusions of previous chapters, we will see that those who prioritise fair-trade over other actions tend to have high levels of concern for poverty in the developing world, as well as distinctive socio-economic and demographic characteristics. Returning to the residents of Chelmsford, I then examine how fair-trade supporters and non-fair-trade supporters responded to a similar question to that asked in the Omnibus Survey, providing insights into how those with differing levels of commitment to fair-trade evaluated the effectiveness of individual consumer power.

## Individual consumer activism

It has been argued that 'new' forms of ethical consumerism, such as fair-trade, can be understood as forms of individual political participation (Dickinson & Carsky, 2005; Follesdal, 2006; Goodman, 2004; Lyon, 2006; Micheletti, 2003; Murray & Raynolds, 2007; Scammell, 2003; Shaw, Newholm & Dickinson, 2006). As we saw in Chapter 2, the writings of Giddens (1991) and Beck (1994) have been employed to suggest that people's decisions to consume ethically ought to be understood as arising from the conditions of late modernity in which everyday life decisions take on political significance. As citizens lose faith in the power of national governments to pass laws that will improve the situation of global workers, it has been suggested that they search for alternative ways to challenge global inequalities; they 'take politics into their own hands' when they recognise that their role as consumers can offer a 'new arena for responsibility-taking' (Micheletti, 2003: 5). However, a study of Danish consumers found that those who boycott or 'buycott' consumer goods do not generally distrust political institutions and politicians, but instead regard all forms of political participation as more efficient than individuals who do not engage in political consumerism (Andersen & Tobiasen, 2006: 213–14). Similarly, we have seen that committed fair-trade supporters, particularly in the UK, are often engaged in a whole range of 'political' activities through their membership in Fairtrade Town groups and related social networks. So it is not necessarily the case, as life-politics-inspired accounts would have it, that those who consume fair-trade products do so because they are disillusioned and distrustful of traditional political modes of engagements or political institutions.

Indeed, it is likely that conceptualisations of consumer power will vary between different countries given their different institutional configurations of responsibility between state and market actors. While much of the scholarship on political consumerism is drawn from the Scandinavian context (Follesdal, 2006; Micheletti, 2010), comparative studies reveal that this phenomenon varies greatly between countries, especially given the distinctive nature of political society within Scandinavia. In their study of consumer trust in food across six European countries, Kjærnes, Harvey and Warde (2007) found that respondents from Britain, Italy and Portugal were more likely to believe that their consumer voice matters than respondents in Norway, Denmark and Germany. In social-democratic Norway, consumers exhibited high levels of trust in public authorities to manage food safety issues, and were the least likely to assert 'their prerogatives as sovereign consumers in the market place' owing to their 'confidence as a citizen in the Norwegian state' (Kjærnes, Harvey & Warde, 2007: 182). By contrast, consumers in Britain were more active over food issues, and seemed to have powerfully 'incorporated the ideology of the active consumer' in comparison to respondents in the other five countries (ibid.). The data presented in this chapter comes from respondents in the UK, and it is therefore likely that the analysis would differ in other contexts, particularly in Sweden where there is a more consensual relationship between state and civil society (similar to Norway) – although research in Sweden has suggested that Swedes are very active political consumers, albeit around environmental forms of consumer activism, such as recycling (Stolle, Hooghe & Micheletti, 2005).

The evaluation of fair-trade consumption compared to donating to charity is also likely to be subject to significant variations between countries. For example, if we look at the World Giving Index (CAF, 2010), we learn that Sweden sits in 45th place out of 153 countries, with 52 per cent of the population donating money to charity and just 12 per cent of people volunteering their time to an organisation. This compares to 73 per cent of people donating to charity in the UK and 29 per cent of people volunteering their time, and 60 per cent of people donating to charity in the USA and 39 per cent of people volunteering – the UK sits in eighth place whereas the USA is in fifth place. Of course this data refers to general charitable actions and does not distinguish between overseas and domestic giving, with the former attracting distinctive socio-economic groups (Micklewright & Schnepf, 2009). But it does highlight how countries differ in terms of their repertoire of available or acceptable individual actions. Comparative quantitative data ought to collected in order to discover the applicability of the findings in this chapter to other countries.

Although it appears that UK consumers are the most likely to take on the role of the active consumer, it is important to examine whether they believe that fair-trade consumption is a more effective way that they can contribute to the alleviation of poverty in developing countries than donating to charity, paying taxes or putting pressure on politicians. This is a relevant and important question, as we will remember in the previous chapter how Michael argued that donating to charity was a more effective way of helping people in the developing world than buying fair-trade goods, and in Chapter 5, Claire and John debated about whether buying fair-trade was akin to a charitable donation. Since fair-trade organisations tend to portray trade as a better solution to global development than government or charitable aid, and stress the power of the individual consumer over national and international governmental organisations, we might suspect that fair-trade supporters would prioritise fair-trade over other individual actions. However, given that many fair-trade supporters in the UK do not always consume fair-trade goods, and instead put their energies into encouraging members of the public, local businesses, organisations and council buildings to use or stock fair-trade, their evaluations of the effectiveness of individual consumer power might not coincide with fair-trade organisations' representation of it.

Little academic attention has been given to how those who do not engage in 'political' consumerism evaluate the effectiveness of their consumer power relative to other individual actions. We saw in Chapter 6 how, despite the fact that they recognised the moral value of fair-trade, non-fair-trade supporters offered a number of practical and normative reasons why they could not or did not alter their consumption in line with the aims of fair-trade campaigns. Some have described this as the 'attitude–behaviour' gap where people profess to care about issues like fair wages and conditions for farmers, but then their actual behaviour does not reflect this concern. Jackson (2005) suggests that the reasons for consumers' inaction arise from the fact that they are 'locked-in' to unsustainable consumption patterns because of both the infrastructure of modern urban living and because of their deeply held emotional commitments to certain practices of consumption.

However, this tends to assume that the 'problem when it comes to changing patterns of consumption is the *consumer*' (Malpass et al., 2007b: 244). It is the consumer who is responsible for solving the world's problems and therefore it is the consumer who must be worked upon in order to achieve various social and political goals. Malpass et al. offer a 'scandalous suggestion' in order to deal with the persistent findings that consumers reject or make excuses for the fact they do not organise their consumption in a sustainable way (ibid.: 245). They suggest that rather than hear these rejections as excuses from *consumers*, we should listen to them as statements from *citizens* who are 'asserting finite limits to how much they, as individuals, can be expected to be responsible for' (ibid.: 247). In keeping with this suggestion, this chapter will be considering whether the alleviation of global poverty through consumption 'choices' is something that non-fair-trade supporters in the UK (a context that celebrates the active consumer) felt was within their power or responsibility to achieve.

## The National Omnibus Survey

The Omnibus Survey is carried out monthly by the UK Centre for National Statistics, and usually achieves a sample of around 1800 adults per survey month (although in 2005 a sample of 1250 adults was achieved), with one adult selected per household. While the Omnibus Survey has been carried out in more recent years, in 2006 the question of interest for the purposes of this analysis was altered, and in 2007 and 2008, the research was conducted by a private agency and the data was therefore unavailable.[1] Using a conventional multi-stage random probability design, the Omnibus Survey selects one adult (defined as age 16 or over) at random in each sampled household. All interviews are conducted face to face, and the response rate is typically around 65 per cent. I have pooled the data for the four survey rounds, providing a sample size of 6581 individuals. The data is weighted to correct for the higher probability of being sampled in small households.

The question of interest asked respondents to choose the three most effective ways they could contribute to reducing poverty in developing countries. It read:

**In which ways, if any, do you think you as an individual can most effectively contribute to reducing poverty in developing countries? Please choose up to three ways. Starting with the most important and then the next most important and so on. (Show card)**

1. Paying taxes – a proportion of which is spent on International Aid by the Government
2. Donating to charities or other appeals on behalf of developing countries
3. Supporting socially responsible business and investment
4. Buying fair-trade goods
5. Working in a developing country to promote development
6. Being involved in church or campaign groups working on behalf of developing countries
7. Putting pressure on politicians to increase the assistance which the Government gives to developing countries

8. Travelling to a developing country as a tourist
9. Other (please specify)
10. Do not think can contribute effectively as an individual to reducing poverty in developing countries (Spontaneous only)

Office for National Statistics
(2005 [Technical Report: 105])

This question offers us the opportunity to discover how effective individual consumers believe 'Buying fair-trade goods' is at alleviating poverty in developing countries relative to other individual and political solutions, and because it asks respondents to rate their answers according to importance, we can explore whether people believe that consumer power is more important than other individual actions. This question also minimises the possibility of socially desirable responses that favour fair-trade because rather than situating fair-trade consumption as 'the' desirable response, it instead asks the respondent to choose from an array of other individual actions that are all given equal weight.

Module 236 also asked a range of questions about respondents' attitudes towards poverty in developing countries and the role of governments, charities and international organisations in its reduction, two of which (level of concern about poverty, and opinions on the role the UK government ought to be playing in the reduction of poverty) are used to gauge the likelihood of individuals prioritising fair-trade over other actions.[2] In addition, the core questionnaire of the Omnibus Survey collects a range of demographic and socio-economic information (e.g. age, sex, education, occupation and personal income), and these are used to examine the correlates of prioritising fair-trade.

## Selection of relevant variables to include in the analysis

There were two main questions that I wanted to address using the Omnibus Survey data. First, what are the characteristics of those people who have prioritised the category 'buying fair-trade goods' (i.e. people who have identified this as the most important or second most important way they can contribute)? Second, what are the characteristics of those people who prioritise 'buying fair-trade goods' relative to other individual actions, such as donating to charity, paying taxes and putting pressure on politicians? And has the likelihood of choosing fair-trade over other individual actions changed over the four years of the Omnibus Survey? The first question provides an important addition to the existing research on the profiling of fair-trade supporters, while the second can go some way to helping us understand how individuals evaluate the effectiveness of consumer action versus other actions and whether their evaluations have changed as awareness-raising campaigns for fair-trade have increased over the four years (such as Fairtrade Fortnight and the growing numbers of Fairtrade Towns).

From existing research, I identified socio-economic and demographic measures (sex, age, income,[3] socio-economic classification, level of education), as well as levels of concern about poverty, as variables that were likely to have an impact on the likelihood of choosing fair-trade. After conducting the fieldwork, I thought it would be important to include an independent variable that measured an individual's opinions about the role the UK government ought to be playing in the alleviation of global poverty. As the discussions in Chapters 5 and 6 have demonstrated, those who support fair-trade are often involved in a range of individual and collective forms of activism and are not, as a life-politics-inspired understanding of ethical consumption might suggest, engaging in fair-trade consumption because they are distrustful of the traditional political system. This variable (which asked whether individuals thought the government ought to be strengthening world trade or providing more aid) proved to have significant effects on the likelihood of prioritising fair-trade.

To tackle the first question, I used a binary logistic regression in order to examine the associations between my selected variables of interest and my dependent variable (the likelihood of prioritising fair-trade). In this way, I was able to determine the effect of each independent variable while holding the other variables in the model constant. For the second question, I used a multinomial logistic regression in order to examine whether those who prioritised fair-trade were significantly different in terms of their socio-demographic profile and their attitudes towards poverty in developing countries from those who had prioritised other individual actions. In order to construct a dependent variable for this second question, I had to convert the three-answer responses given by respondents to the Omnibus Survey question into a single 'profile' variable. In creating the profile variable, it was important to ensure that those who had prioritised fair-trade were not placed into any of the other categories. The ordering of the variable had to be carefully considered because each category was overwritten by the one that followed. Therefore, the 'other' category was defined first because I was less interested in those who specified these individual actions than I was in those who prioritised 'paying taxes'. The 'paying taxes' option, unlike the other options in the Omnibus Survey question, is something the majority of individuals

Table 7.1 The profile variable

| Categories of the profile variable | Answer 1 | Answer 2 | Answer 3 | Number | Percentage |
|---|---|---|---|---|---|
| **Other** | If none of the other categories | If none of the other categories | If none of the other categories | 323 | 4.91 |
| **Fair-trade** | If 'Buying fair-trade' or 'Supporting socially responsible businesses'[a] | If 'Buying fair-trade' and answer 1 is 'supporting socially responsible businesses' | | 1156 | 18.57 |
| **No impact** | If they don't think they can have an impact | | | 545 | 8.28 |
| **Charity** | If 'Donating to Charity' | If 'Donating to Charity' and if answer 1 is not fair-trade | If 'Donating to Charity' and answer 1 or 2 is not fair-trade | 1363 | 20.71 |
| **Campaigning for change**[b] | If 'Pressure on politicians' or 'campaign groups' | If 'Pressure on politicians' or 'campaign groups' and if answer 1 is not fair-trade | If 'Pressure on politicians' or 'campaign groups' and if answer 1 or 2 is not fair-trade | 1342 | 20.39 |
| **Tax** | If 'Paying taxes' | If 'Paying taxes' and if answer 1 is not fair-trade | If 'Paying taxes' and if answer 1 or 2 not fair-trade | 1852 | 28.14 |
| | | | | 6581 | 100.00 |

*Notes:* [a] I felt that those who had placed 'supporting socially responsible businesses and investment' first followed by those who prioritised fair-trade ought to be considered in the same category as those who prioritised fair-trade, because both responses involve using consumer choices.
[b] Before I conducted the fieldwork, I had placed those who prioritised 'paying taxes' and 'putting pressure on politicians' into the same category as 'traditional' political solutions in the same category. After conducting the fieldwork however, I felt that, because fair-trade supporters did not seem to be any less likely to put pressure on politicians than those who did not buy fair-trade, I ought to separate the two actions. Equally, I had originally placed those who prioritised joining 'church or campaign groups' into the 'other' category and given that the majority of fair-trade supporters in Chelmsford were attached to either a church or campaign group, I felt that they should be included in one of the main categories. I therefore placed those who prioritised putting pressure onto politicians and joining campaign groups into the same category (Campaigning for change) while I placed those who prioritised paying taxes into another.

were likely to be compulsorily doing already. Although recognised as one of the key obligations of citizenship (Marshall, 1950), paying one's taxes does not require an individual to devote their time or money (above and beyond this obligation) to contribute to the alleviation of poverty on a daily basis in the same way that fair-trade consumption, or campaigning, individually or collectively, might. The organisation and ordering of this profile variable is illustrated in Table 7.1.

## Individual contributions to the alleviation of poverty: The National Omnibus Survey

### Prioritising fair-trade

Let us begin by addressing the first main question using the Omnibus Survey data: what are the characteristics of those who have identified 'buying fair-trade goods' as the most important or second most important way they can contribute? Graph 7.1 reveals the probability of individuals prioritising fair-trade according to a range of individual factors. Overall, the probability of placing fair-trade first or second is 35 per cent, and this varies according to socio-economic status, level of education, sex and age as well as by the level of concern shown for poverty in developing countries and one's opinions about the role the UK government ought to be playing. Those in managerial/professional positions, women and those in older age categories are more likely to choose fair-trade than those in semi-routine/routine occupations, men and those in younger age categories. It is interesting that income has little effect on the probability of choosing fair-trade given the discussions among fair-trade and non-fair-trade supporters in the previous chapter, who suggested that income alone was insufficient to explain why someone might buy fair-trade.

Attitudes of concern towards poverty in developing countries increase the probability of choosing fair-trade, with those who display high levels of concern more likely to prioritise fair-trade. By contrast, those who are unconcerned about poverty in developing countries and those who do not have an opinion about the role the UK government ought to be playing are up to three times less likely to choose fair-trade. Those who think that the government ought to be working towards creating a fairer world trading system are, unsurprisingly, more likely to prioritise fair-trade. Interestingly, those who think the government ought to provide more financial aid or help strengthen the role of international organisations are more likely to choose fair-trade than those who are unconcerned about poverty. This suggests that people who prioritise fair-trade

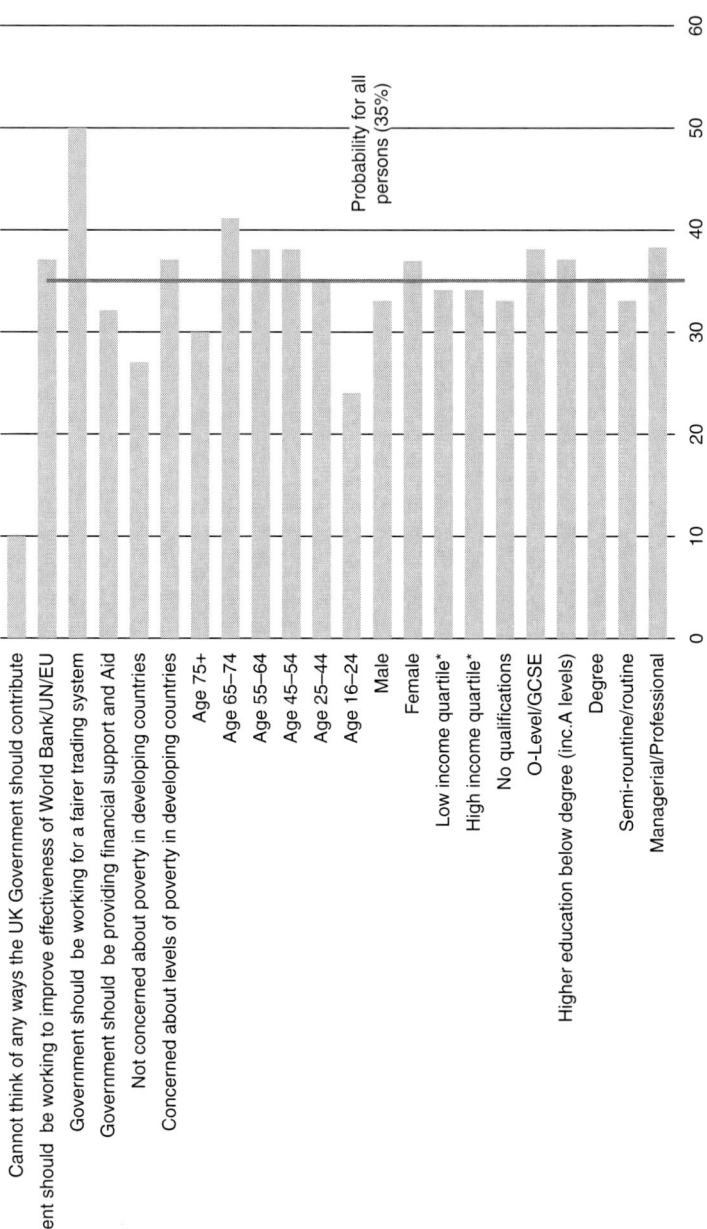

*Graph 7.1* The probability of prioritising 'buying fair-trade goods'
*Note:* * For information on the income variable, see note 3.

may not see fair-trade as a superior alternative to governmental aid and the work of international organisations in the alleviation of poverty, but rather as an important supplement to these other activities.

While Graph 7.1 provides us with insight into the probability of prioritising fair-trade, it cannot tell us the effect of individual characteristics/ attitudes when controlling for other factors. Table 7.2 provides the results of several binary logistic regression models, which reveal the direction of effect of each independent variable on the likelihood of choosing fair-trade while controlling for all the other variables; Models 1 and 2 use socio-economic and demographic characteristics,[4] while Models 3 and 4 introduce the attitude variables. The regression models provide us with a similar picture to that provided in Graph 7.1, with the additional information that the likelihood of choosing fair-trade has increased yearly, which may reflect increased awareness or belief in the effectiveness of fair-trade over this time period. However, it reveals that, even when controlling for attitudes of concern for poverty and opinions on the role that the UK government ought to be playing, other things being equal, women, older people and those in higher socio-economic groups were still more likely to prioritise fair-trade than the average individual. This supports Pirotte's (2007) study, which found that both attitudes towards development and socio-economic characteristics are important if we are to understand the likelihood of an individual supporting fair-trade.

In order to illustrate the strength of the effect of the independent variables upon the likelihood of prioritising fair-trade, it is useful to use predicted probabilities. I have selected a particular set of 'optimal' fixed characteristics (of a woman aged 55 with below degree-level qualifications, in a professional occupation, who is concerned about poverty and thinks the government ought to be working towards a fairer world trading system, responding in 2005) and have discovered that her probability of prioritising fair-trade is 62 per cent compared to an average probability of only 36 per cent in the sample as whole (see Table 7.3). By changing individual characteristics, we learn that men are less likely to prioritise fair-trade than otherwise similar women to the tune of five percentage points, which may reflect the fact that women 'remain the gender which bear the mantle of responsibility' for shopping (Miller, 1998: 96). Despite fair-trade supporters' tendency to stress the classless nature of fair-trade consumption (see Chapters 5 and 6), it appears that an individual's socio-economic status does have an important impact on the likelihood of prioritising fair-trade. Those who hold identical demographic profiles and attitudes but come from socio-economic groups at the opposite ends of the spectrum differ in their probability

*Table 7.2* Binary logistic regression, dependent variable 'prioritises buying fair-trade goods'

| | Model 1 (SE) | Model 2 (SE) | Model 2 (SE) | Model 4 (SE) |
|---|---|---|---|---|
| Female | 0.214** (0.065) | 0.219*** (0.060) | 0.186** (0.060) | 0.233*** (0.061) |
| Age in years (16+)[a] | 0.005** (0.002) | 0.004* (0.002) | 0.004* (0.002) | 0.004* (0.002) |
| Year (2002–5)[b] | 0.096** (0.028) | 0.103*** (0.026) | 0.109*** (0.027) | 0.101*** (0.027) |
| **NS Socio-economic classification** | | | | |
| – Managerial/Professional (Ref) | 0 | 0 | 0 | 0 |
| – Intermediate | −0.202* (0.101) | −0.164 (0.095) | −0.160 (0.095) | −0.144 (0.097) |
| – Small employers | −0.085 (0.126) | −0.116 (0.118) | −0.116 (0.118) | −0.072 (0.118) |
| – Lower supervisory | −0.036 (0.118) | −0.029 (0.111) | −0.016 (0.111) | −0.012 (0.112) |
| – Semi routine/routine | −0.245** (0.091) | −0.245** (0.083) | −0.224** (0.083) | −0.189* (0.085) |
| – Not classified | −0.588*** (0.156) | −0.657*** (0.143) | −0.611*** (0.114) | −0.584*** (0.146) |
| **Education level** | | | | |
| – Degree | 0.022 (−0.117) | −0.004 (−0.109) | −0.074 (−0.111) | −0.181 (−0.112) |
| – Below degree | 0.118 (−0.081) | 0.138 (−0.077) | 0.093 (−0.078) | 0.044 (−0.079) |
| – Other[c] | 0.265 (−0.305) | 0.332 (−0.278) | 0.306 (−0.276) | 0.354 (−0.280) |
| – No qualifications (Ref) | 0 | 0 | 0 | 0 |
| Income* | | −2.28$^{e-06}$ (−2.28$^{e-06}$) | | |
| **Concern about poverty** | | | | |
| – Concerned (Ref) | | | 0 | 0 |
| – No strong feelings | | | −0.148* (0.074) | −0.109 (0.075) |
| – Not concerned | | | −0.419*** (0.112) | −0.171 (0.118) |
| – Don't know if concerned | | | −2.363*** (0.588) | −1.272* (0.589) |

(*continued*)

*Table 7.2* Continued

| | Model 1 (SE) | Model 2 (SE) | Model 2 (SE) | Model 4 (SE) |
|---|---|---|---|---|
| Opinions of UK Gov action | | | | |
| – Working towards a fairer trading system (Ref) | | | | 0 |
| – Provide aid | | | | –0.785*** (0.094) |
| – Strengthen int. org. | | | | –0.512** (0.163) |
| – Can't think of any ways | | | | –2.141*** (0.227) |
| – Other[d] | | | | –0.569*** (0.085) |
| Constant | –1.036*** (0.165) | –1.112*** (0.130) | –1.071*** (0.131) | –0.593*** (0.151) |
| Number of observations | 5998 | 6572 | 6553 | 6241 |
| Degrees of freedom | (12/5986) | (11/6561) | (14/6539) | (18/6403) |
| F | 4.53 | 6.07 | 6.61 | 11.40 |
| Probability > F | 0.0000 | 0.0000 | 0.0000 | 0.0000 |

*Notes:*
*** $p < 0.001$; ** $p < 0.01$; * $p < 0.05$.
[a] Age was also entered using dummies, which revealed a small non-linear effect so that those over the ages of 75 were statistically no more likely to choose fair-trade than those aged 16–25.
[b] Dummies for year were also tried but the effect of year was linear.
[c] Full-time students, those who have never worked or are long-term unemployed, and those whose occupation is not stated or is inadequately described.
[d] Encouraging increased private sector investment, reducing conflict and war, cancelling debts owed by developing countries, specified 'other'.

of prioritising fair-trade by up to 14 percentage points. Those who do not have an opinion on the role the UK government ought to be playing in the alleviation of global poverty are more than three times less likely to prioritise fair-trade than an individual with exactly the same profile who believes that government ought to be working towards a fairer world trading system. This is particularly interesting because it tends to suggest that those who choose fair-trade do not do so because they distrust traditional political institutions and want to enact their citizenly duties in an alternative sphere as consumers, but rather that they believe there is a role for both consumers and governments to play in the alleviation of global poverty.

*Table 7.3* Predicted probability of prioritising 'buying fair-trade'

The case of a 55-year-old woman with below degree-level qualifications, in a professional occupation, who is concerned about poverty and thinks the government ought to be working towards a fairer world trading system, responding in 2005. All probabilities have been rounded to the nearest whole number using the regression estimates from Table 7.2 (model 4). The mean probability in the sample, of prioritising fair-trade, was 36 per cent

| Fixed characteristics | Probability of prioritising 'buying fair-trade' (%) | Variable that changes | Probability (%) (change) |
|---|---|---|---|
| Age = 55 | 62 | Age = 18 | 59 (−3) |
| Female | 62 | Male | 57 (−5) |
| Professional occupation | 62 | Unclassified socio-economic group | 48 (−14) |
| Government should be working for fairer trading system | 62 | Government should be providing more aid | 43 (−19) |
| Government should be working for fairer trading system | 62 | Cannot think of any ways the UK government should contribute | 16 (−46) |

Believing that the government ought to be providing more financial aid makes an individual less likely to choose 'buying fair-trade' than if they had felt that the government ought to be doing more to work towards a fairer world trading system. It seems likely that those who think the UK government ought to be providing more financial aid will have prioritised the option 'paying taxes which will be spent on International Aid' rather than 'buying fair-trade goods'. Those who think the government ought to be working for a fairer world trade system seem to subscribe to the dominant discourses surrounding the effectiveness of trade over aid, and are therefore likely to place 'buying fair-trade goods' over 'paying taxes'. In order to explore this further, it will be necessary to turn to the second stage of the analysis, which looks at the characteristics of those who prioritise other individual actions over consuming fair-trade.

## Buying fair-trade relative to other actions

This section will examine (a) whether those who prioritise other individual actions over fair-trade are significantly different (in terms of socio-demographic and attitude profile) from those who prioritise fair-trade, and (b) whether the likelihood of prioritising fair-trade over other actions has increased as awareness-raising campaigns for fair-trade have become more prevalent. To begin, let us first look at how individuals rated the effectiveness of all the different individual actions offered in the Omnibus Survey question. Graph 7.2 shows the percentage of people who placed their chosen action as the most effective or second most effective way they could contribute. We can see that donating to charity is the most popular response, followed by buying fair-trade, paying taxes and putting pressure on politicians. Given that 'buying fair-trade' is the second most popular response and the percentage of people choosing fair-trade has increased on a yearly basis, as fair-trade has grown in popularity, it seems possible to argue that an increasing number of individuals – like those identified in the binary regression model – do believe that consumption is an effective way of tackling social problems such as poverty. Indeed, in 2007 and 2008 when the survey question was repeated, the buying fair-trade category overtook 'donating to charity' as the most popular response (TNS, 2008). It is interesting to note that the number of people who prioritised paying taxes, working in a developing country and being involved in campaign groups has, on the whole, steadily decreased over our four year period, while the number of people who feel they cannot have an impact has increased. Although this seems to lend some support to the suggestion that fair-trade consumption is offering some individuals the opportunity to participate in political action in alternative spheres, it also appears that fair-trade is not offering those who do not believe they can have an impact (such as those who are uninterested in or distrustful of the political system) a new opportunity to participate.

Having examined the basic trends across the answers to the Omnibus Survey question, we now want to find out whether those who prioritised one of the other individual actions over fair-trade are different from those who have not. In order to achieve this, I have constructed a multinomial logistic regression model using the derived 'profile' variable (described in the methodology section) as the dependent variable (assigning 'buying fair-trade goods' to the base category). This will allow us to compare the effects of the independent variables on the likelihood of prioritising another action over fair-trade. The results of this regression analysis are presented in Table 7.4. While in the binary

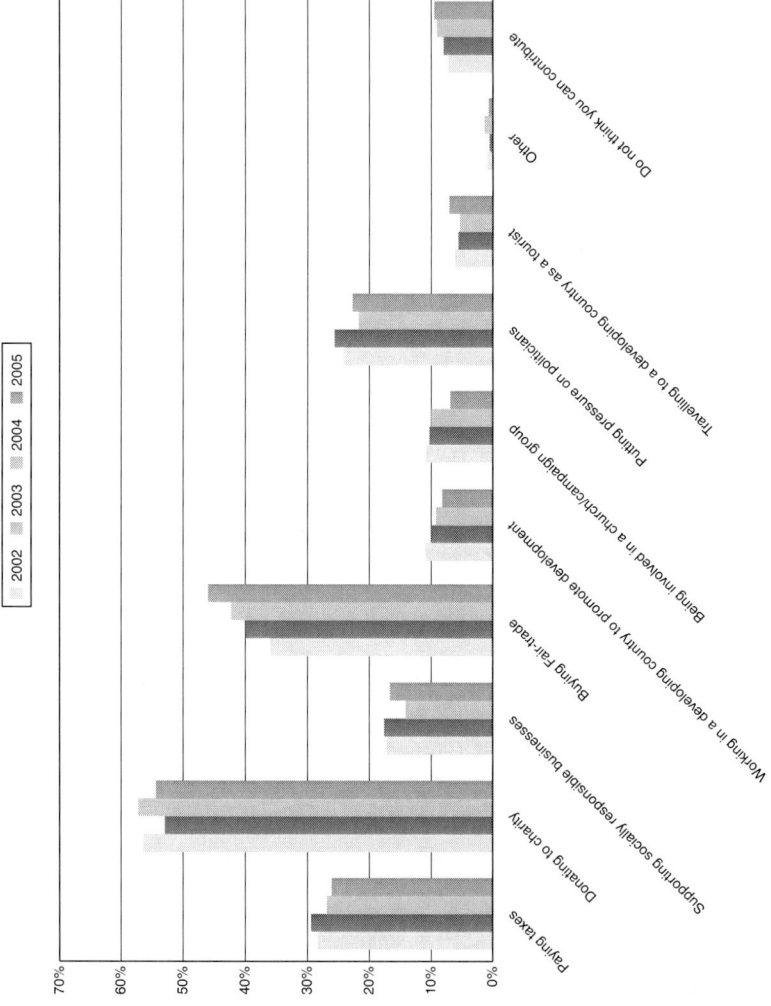

*Graph 7.2*  The most effective ways of alleviating poverty, 2002–5

*Table 7.4* Multinomial logistic regression, likelihood of prioritising 'buying fair-trade' relative to other individual actions

| | Coefficient for 'Other' (SE) | Coefficient for 'No Impact' (SE) | Coefficient for 'Donating' (SE) | Coefficient for 'Campaigning for change' (SE) | Coefficient for 'Paying taxes' (SE) |
|---|---|---|---|---|---|
| Female | -0.139 (0.188) | -0.107 (0.153) | 0.237* (0.102) | -0.016 (0.101) | -0.308** (0.096) |
| Age in years (16+) | -0.003 (0.006) | 0.015*** (0.004) | -0.010** (0.003) | -0.009** (0.003) | -0.010*** (0.003) |
| NS Socio-economic classification | | | | | |
| – Managerial/Professional (Ref) | 0 | 0 | 0 | 0 | 0 |
| – Intermediate | -0.015 (0.305) | 0.433 (0.255) | 0.147 (0.160) | 0.327* (0.159) | 0.156 (0.148) |
| – Small employers | -0.235 (0.340) | 0.228 (0.288) | 0.082 (0.188) | 0.115 (0.190) | -0.330 (0.185) |
| – Lower supervisory | -0.037 (0.328) | 0.147 (0.277) | 0.114 (0.178) | 0.071 (0.178) | -0.156 (0.171) |
| – Semi routine/routine | 0.013 (0.257) | 0.313 (0.221) | 0.266 (0.137) | 0.236 (0.138) | 0.055 (0.137) |
| – Not classified | 0.191 (0.497) | 1.041** (0.356) | 0.525* (0.247) | 0.733** (0.243) | 0.307 (0.239) |

(continued)

Table 7.4 Continued

| | Coefficient for 'Other' (SE) | Coefficient for 'No Impact' (SE) | Coefficient for 'Donating' (SE) | Coefficient for 'Campaigning for change' (SE) | Coefficient for 'Paying taxes' (SE) |
|---|---|---|---|---|---|
| Education level | | | | | |
| – Degree | -0.054 (0.312) | -1.115** (0.363) | -0.251 (0.180) | 0.083 (0.176) | 0.430* (0.172) |
| – Below degree | -0.170 (0.227) | -0.301 (0.174) | -0.171 (0.122) | -0.087 (0.123) | 0.269* (0.121) |
| – Other[a] | 0.770 (0.717) | -0.037 (0.741) | 0.332 (0.513) | 0.075 (0.544) | 0.905 (0.478) |
| – No qualifications (Ref) | 0 | 0 | 0 | 0 | 0 |
| Income | 1.57$^{E-05}$* (8.86$^{E-06}$) | -1.57$^{E-06}$ (8.07$^{E-06}$) | 2.95$^{E-07}$ (4.67$^{E-06}$) | -3.03$^{E-06}$ (4.63$^{E-06}$) | 1.21$^{E-05}$** (4.06$^{E-06}$) |
| Year (2002–5) | -0.140 (0.083) | 0.109 (0.067) | -0.043 (0.043) | -0.146*** (0.043) | -0.107** (0.041) |
| Concern about poverty | | | | | |
| – Concerned (Ref) | 0 | 0 | 0 | 0 | 0 |
| – No strong feelings | 0.576** (0.202) | 1.016*** (0.164) | 0.044 (0.120) | -0.249* (0.124) | -0.050 (0.113) |
| – Not concerned | 0.836*** (0.247) | 1.526*** (0.198) | -0.268 (0.177) | -0.432* (0.184) | -0.648*** (0.175) |
| – Don't know if concerned | 2.698*** (0.750) | 1.317 (0.818) | 0.477 (0.727) | -1.308 (1.179) | 0.082 (0.829) |

Opinions of UK Gov action

| | | | | | |
|---|---|---|---|---|---|
| – Working towards a fairer trading system (Ref) | 0 | 0 | 0 | 0 | 0 |
| – Provide aid | 0.572* | 0.654** | 0.979*** | 0.774*** | 1.168*** |
| | (0.285) | (0.239) | (0.145) | (0.151) | (0.138) |
| – Strengthen int. org. | -0.010 | 0.220 | 0.157 | 0.587* | 0.478* |
| | (0.445) | (0.388) | (0.267) | (0.251) | (0.235) |
| – Can't think of any ways | 2.215*** | 3.197*** | 1.461*** | 0.190 | 1.009** |
| | (0.432) | (0.382) | (0.363) | (0.482) | (0.391) |
| – Other[b] | 0.558* | 0.478* | 0.495*** | 0.834*** | 0.689*** |
| | (0.247) | (0.214) | (0.131) | (0.132) | (0.123) |
| Constant | -2.074*** | -3.216*** | 0.021 | 0.281 | 0.305 |
| | (0.605) | (0.468) | (0.313) | (0.308) | (0.292) |
| Number of observations | | | 5898 | | |
| Degrees of freedom | | | 95/5803 | | |
| F | | | 10.20 | | |
| Probability > F | | | 0.0000 | | |

*Notes:*

\*\*\* p < 0.001; \*\* p < 0.01; \* p < 0.05.

[a] Full-time students, those who have never worked or are long-term unemployed, and those whose occupation is not stated or is inadequately described.

[b] Encouraging increased private sector investment, reducing conflict and war, cancelling debts owed by developing countries, specified 'other'.

logistic regression education and income were not good predictors of the likelihood of choosing fair-trade, in the multinomial model they become significant variables when we look at the likelihood of an individual prioritising 'paying taxes' over fair-trade or thinking they cannot have an impact on poverty in the developing world. Those who have higher incomes and hold educational qualifications are more likely to believe that the most effective way they can individually contribute to the alleviation of poverty is through paying their taxes, which will then be spent on International Aid.

Table 7.5 illustrates how the likelihood of being in the 'paying taxes' group relative to the 'buying fair-trade' group (of the profile options outlined in the methodology; see Table 7.1) changes with different values of the independent variables. In keeping with earlier findings, an individual's likelihood of choosing fair-trade increases with age whereas their likelihood of choosing 'paying taxes' decreases with age. Women are less likely than men to choose 'paying taxes' but are more likely to choose fair-trade than men. As we can see, a 25-year-old man who has a high income and is in a professional occupation has a probability that is five percentage points higher than a man with the same characteristics who is in the lowest income quartile of prioritising paying taxes. Whereas the likelihood of this man choosing 'buying fair-trade' increases by eight per cent from the highest income quartile to the lowest income quartile. It is interesting that, other things being equal, having a lower income is positively associated with the chances of choosing fair-trade and negatively associated with support for paying taxes. Given that we are controlling for levels of concern about poverty, this suggests that the characterisations of the 'fair-trade consumer' by Keith and Val in the previous chapter – namely that concerned rich people are less likely to support fair-trade than concerned poor people – were reasonably accurate.

Importantly, we can see in Table 7.5 that those who believe that the UK government ought to be providing more financial aid to developing countries are 43 per cent more likely to prioritise paying taxes than those who support working towards a fairer world trading system. This indicates that government action through aid is regarded as more effective by this group than the creation of a fairer global market. However, it should be noted that according to the regression coefficients, those who prioritised paying taxes were more likely to hold any views of UK government action (including the opinion that the government could not make any difference) other than that it should support a fairer trading system, which suggests that they believe there are limits to what the

*Table 7.5* Predicted probability of prioritising 'paying taxes' or 'buying fair-trade'

The case of a 25-year-old man with degree-level qualifications, in a lower supervisory or technical occupation, in the highest income quartile who is concerned about poverty and thinks the government ought to providing more aid, responding in 2005. All probabilities have been rounded to the nearest whole number using the regression estimates from Table 7.3. The mean probability in the sample, of prioritising paying taxes, was 29 per cent and the mean probability of prioritising fair-trade, was 18 per cent

| Fixed characteristics | Probability of prioritising 'paying taxes' (%) | Probability of prioritising 'buying fair-trade' (%) | Variable that changes | Changed Probability of prioritising 'paying taxes' (change) | Changed Probability of prioritising 'buying fair-trade' (change) |
|---|---|---|---|---|---|
| Age = 25 | 47 | 13 | Age = 55 | 44 (−3) | 16 (+3) |
| Male | 47 | 13 | Female | 37 (−10) | 14 (+1) |
| Highest income quartile | 47 | 13 | Lower income quartile | 42 (−5) | 14 (+1) |
| Degree-level qualifications | 47 | 13 | No qualifications | 34 (−13) | 14 (+1) |
| Government ought to be providing more aid | 47 | 13 | Government should be working for fairer trading system | 33 (−14) | 29 (+16) |
| Government ought to be providing more aid | 47 | 13 | Cannot think of any ways the UK government should contribute | 40 (−7) | 11 (−2) |

government can achieve in terms of regulating the world trade arena. This suggests that they do not subscribe to the dominant discourses, which stress the importance of individual citizen-consumer power or the superiority of trade over aid. On the other hand, those who believed that the UK government ought to be working towards a fairer trading system were 125 per cent more likely to prioritise fair-trade than those who supported the provision of financial aid; and those who prioritised fair-trade were less likely to believe that there was nothing the government could do than those who prioritised paying taxes. This suggests that those who are likely to believe that fair-trade consumption is an effective individual action are also likely to believe that there is a continued need for the government, as well as the individual consumer, to support fairer trading relations. It also demonstrates a consistent underlying conviction in the power of trade (whether through individual action or through government regulation) rather than aid to make a difference to world poverty.

The likelihood of choosing 'paying taxes' increased by 38 per cent from an individual with no qualifications to an individual with degree-level qualifications, whereas the likelihood of 'buying fair-trade' decreased by 12 per cent from an individual with no qualifications to an individual with degree-level qualifications. The fact that those who are better educated are more likely to prioritise paying taxes and are less likely to prioritise buying fair-trade than the less well qualified raises doubts over the debates about consumer reflexivity, which assume that the only thing that stands in the way of people becoming responsible citizen-consumers is more information, and instead highlights the importance of paying attention to the ways individuals learn about and integrate fair-trade into their lives. This finding is also very interesting because if we think of paying taxes as a rather passive form of action, it casts doubts on the perspective that (educated) people often like to put forward – that high levels of education leads to more active engagement in the political process.

People who have little interest in poverty in the developing world are more likely to believe that they cannot have an impact, and despite the fact that there have been a number of awareness-raising campaigns in the UK during the period of the Omnibus Survey (such as Fairtrade Fortnight and a growing number of Fairtrade towns), there was no significant change over the four years in the likelihood of an individual choosing fair-trade over 'no impact'. This suggests that fair-trade is not offering new ways for people who are not already interested in, or who do not already have some sympathy for, the movement to engage in 'life-political' action. Conversely, the likelihood of prioritising 'campaigning for change' (putting pressure on politicians, joining a church or campaign group) did decrease relative to choosing fair-trade during the four-year period, which seems to suggest that fair-trade was more appealing to those people who were already engaged in campaigning activity. As we have seen in Chelmsford, committed fair-trade supporters are individuals who are usually involved in a number of adjacent practices (like joining local campaign or church groups) through which they come into contact with fair-trade. It seems likely that fair-trade offers these already-interested campaigners the opportunity to broaden, not substitute, their engagement by using consumer action. Having said this, the likelihood of people prioritising donating to charity over fair-trade has not decreased significantly over the four-year period, which suggests that not everyone with existing sympathies towards development issues understands fair-trade as an effective individual action.[5]

The fact that the likelihood of prioritising 'paying taxes' and 'campaigning for change' over buying fair-trade did decrease over the four years offers some limited support for Micheletti's claims that 'new' forms of political consumerism 'signal[s] that citizens are looking outside traditional politics and civil society' to have an impact on important issues (Micheletti, 2003: 3). However, we should interpret these findings cautiously given the fact that while 46 per cent of respondents in 2005 claimed that 'buying fair-trade goods' was an effective way of alleviating poverty in developing countries, it is unlikely that 46 per cent of the UK population knowingly bought fair-trade on a regular basis given that fair-trade retail sales figures only totalled £195 million in 2005 (FTF, 2009c). It is likely that respondents in the Omnibus Survey have drawn on the hegemonic discourses and promotional strategies of the fair-trade movement, which have suggested that fair-trade consumption is a powerful and effective individual action (see Sassatelli, 2006), and have applied this understanding to their evaluation of the different responses offered in the Omnibus Survey question. However, they have not necessarily taken this evaluation of the effectiveness of fair-trade to the supermarket – suggesting that it might be a good action if others do it.

There has been a tendency to understand individuals' unwillingness to participate in political consumerism as a symptom of their apathy. For example, Hilton has argued that 'consumerism has its tremendous limitations as a social and political movement in the immense gulf between the aims of its leaders and the apathy of its rank and file' (Hilton, 2003: 3). However, Yeo (1974) encourages us not to dismiss low levels of participation under the label of 'apathy' as if this label enables us to put an end to the matter. Rather he points out that the language of apathy tends to conveniently attribute blame and moral failings to individuals or collectivities that are not necessarily inherent to them but are the product of the structures and systems within the society in which they live (Yeo, 1974: 287). As Malpass et al. (2007b) have pointed out, citizens are often justifiably sceptical about the ethical problematisation of consumer practices that place responsibility for global problems in the hands of individuals rather than in the political, economic and legal structures that coordinate global trading relations. Those who believe they have 'no impact' or who choose an alternative solution like 'paying taxes' (which requires very little of them beyond the automatic deduction from their wages), or who agree that fair-trade might be an effective individual action but do not buy it themselves, should perhaps not be understood as apathetic or uninterested but rather as challenging the assumption that their individual consumer action will be effective given the organisation of global trading systems. With this in mind, let us now turn to the views from residents in Chelmsford, starting with those who have high levels of commitment to the fair-trade movement.

## Fair-trade versus other actions: Opinions from the residents in Chelmsford

### Fair-trade supporters

Given the findings from the Omnibus Survey and what we already know about fair-trade supporters' practices, we might have doubts about whether committed fair-traders would evaluate fair-trade consumption as a more effective individual action over other individual and governmental actions. In this section, we see that to a certain extent, fair-trade supporters in Chelmsford do defend fair-trade as an important individual action; although we should remember that as the fair-trade supporters were asked to talk about why they supported fair-trade, it is very unlikely that they would not express the merits of fair-trade over other actions. However, this does not mean that they do not engage in other actions, or that they necessarily believe that consumers can, alone, alleviate global poverty.

As we saw in the Omnibus Survey, those who prioritised fair-trade tended to be more likely to think that the government ought to be working towards a fairer world trading system rather than providing more financial aid. The qualitative data supports this finding, with the majority of fair-traders agreeing with those dominant discourses that frame trade as a more effective solution to poverty than aid.

**Oliver:** I think one of the things that we've learnt is that so much Government Aid is wasted and just money poured down the drain. Because your fair-trade premium goes straight to the people on the ground floor, and the village gets round and decides whether they're going to spend it on new fences for their gardens, which I think one lot did to stop the animals getting in, or that they invest, whatever they do. In the case of the government, we know that an awful lot of governments, not just the black African ones, a lot of governments steal the money and use it for all sorts of graft. I think there's pretty strong evidence that fair-trade is probably a darn sight more effective than sending a few billion pounds over.

**Erica:** I think fair-trade helps them stand on their own two feet.

**Oliver:** Yeah, and they want to, to be fair to them.

**Erica:** Whereas Government Aid, you send it over to these foreign countries and you've got people that are employed over there to distribute it out, so they're taking part of it before it's actually going to where it's supposed to be going. And so, I think fair-trade is far superior I feel.

(Oliver, 65 years, retired senior civil servant;<br>Erica, 63 retired registrar)

For Oliver and Erica, there is a feeling that fair-trade is a more direct, and therefore effective, way of ensuring that their money reaches the people who need it most. Not only do the benefits from fair-trade get to the people on the ground who can decide for themselves how the money is spent, but fair-trade encourages self-sufficiency and encourages producers to 'stand on their own two feet'. While it might seem that Oliver favours individual consumption over governmental action, it is interesting to be aware that he is a member of the Co-op Party and is therefore involved in the wider political movement to encourage a fairer world trading system. So even if on the one hand he believes that governmental aid may be stolen by corrupt governments, he also believes that as part of a larger political movement, it is possible to work with these governments to improve the situation for people living in poverty. As a keen beekeeper, Oliver also regularly donates to the charity 'Bees Abroad' – an organisation that supports beekeeping projects in the developing world – suggesting again that he does not use fair-trade consumption as an alternative to other individual actions.

The understanding of fair-trade as a more direct way of getting money to the people who need it is demonstrated by John, who explains why he would favour buying fair-trade goods over putting pressure on his local MP:

> If I want things to change it's easier to buy a fair-trade pear than to tell my MP that fair-trade is great for everyone. Because then he's got to convince his party; he's got to convince the public; then he's got to go into the European whoever, and then there's the whole, it takes about ten million years, if it is approved, to get approved. Whereas, I suppose, consumerism is my direct action. And it's immediate. And you don't need many consumers to make a difference in the sense that, if everyone, at Easter bought a fair-trade Easter egg, not a big one but a small one, that would be a huge volume of fair-trade Easter eggs that would be sold. But it's a small expense to the consumer. So I think that says a lot more than a long-winded way of going through your MP for anything.

Despite the fact that John understands consumerism as a more direct action, he still regularly fills in campaign cards sent to him by the World Development Movement and Oxfam, and has written to his MP on a number of issues. Although fair-trade is understood as an important individual action, fair-trade supporters use fair-trade as an extension to an already-existing repertoire of behaviours, such as donating to charity and campaigning in groups.

While consumer action is seen as important, there remains an awareness of the limits of consumer power and the vital role that governments and charities must continue to perform.

**Moderator:**  So just talking there about aid, I mean how do you rate the effectiveness of fair-trade as a means of promoting international development then?

**Beth:**  I think it's very effective but I mean, [laughs] I don't have any statistics I don't know if anyone else has?

**Lyn:**  I mean it's difficult because only those people that are producing those sorts of things are getting that aid, and there are a lot of other people who aren't in that world who still need aid, and you know there are other charities which, you know I'm sure we all support in our own way,

|  | hopefully that are getting at those other people ... but there are a lot of others apart from producers of coffee and food and things like that, that need help. |
| --- | --- |
| **Peter:** | From my perspective, fair-trade is important for the reasons I mentioned earlier, but it can never, it would never even try to replace certainly governmental aid. |
| **Lyn:** | Hmm [nods in agreement]. |
| **Peter:** | And obviously the various churches and the charities do a lot of work in developing countries, but it is just, it's an extra, but you could never, I mean as you said, you could never replace government aid and government negotiation on multi-national agreements to support places, I mean we're talking basically places like Africa and South America, and you could never replace those things with fair-trade but it obviously does help individuals and also, we come back to the fact of people doing something personally to help, and handing money over to an organisation that's trying to do something.[6] |

On reading this extract one might wonder why someone like Lyn or Peter continues to buy fair-trade given the fact they are aware that it only helps a small percentage of the people who are living in poverty. Although fair-trade can never hope to replace the efforts of governments and charities to alleviate the huge problem of global poverty, Peter's suggestion that fair-trade supporters choose fair-trade in order to do something 'personally to help' seems particularly illuminating. Consuming fair-trade is seen as a way in which people can express their commitments and feel that they are contributing in their own personal way to the alleviation of the poverty of some of those people who are suffering in the world. In his study of ethical consumers, Newholm argued that often the most important motivation for individuals to use ethical products was a need 'to feel comfortable with themselves' (Newholm, 2000: 114). We can perhaps see the same thing here; despite the fact that they are aware that it will not make a huge difference to global poverty, fair-trade supporters felt a need to express their values through their consumption.

| **Sandra:** | If you feel concerned about something then you must do something about it, and even though you might think well it's only a drop in the ocean, you know the ocean's made up of lots of drops, I think I heard someone say [laughs]. |
| --- | --- |

> I'm a believer in the snowball effect and the fact that you can
> influence other people by talking about it, raising awareness
> and you know spreading that way as well as actually buying
> the products, tell people why you're doing that. I think it's
> important and can work that way.

**Milena:**  You know, instead of saying, you know something is wrong
and you don't do anything about it, it is better to at least …
you know you're doing your bit, and yeah I completely agree
with that you know like you said, many people will do it and
then things will change.[7]

Importantly we find here a recurrent theme in fair-trade supporters'
understanding of the effectiveness of their individual consumption:
a feeling of a community of like-minded individuals who are together
'sending a message' to supermarkets, big businesses and governments of
their desire for a larger political change. Although the Omnibus Survey
asked individuals to rate the effectiveness of their individual actions,
and the literature on the growth of political consumerism suggests that
the power is now in the hands of the *individual* consumer, it was very
rare for fair-trade supporters to discuss the effectiveness of their shopping 'choices' without reference to an imagined community of other
fair-trade consumers. As Milena optimistically makes clear, if lots of people buy fair-trade then things will change. Each individual consumption
act is seen to strengthen a collective movement.

> If it was just me doing it then it wouldn't be effective at all. Erm …
> absolutely zilch, just makes me feel better. I'm an optimist, I think
> that me plus lots of other me's are doing it and it is making a dif-
> ference, just the fact that there are more fair-trade items appearing
> on shelves. Tesco are doing their own fair-trade orange juices, their
> own fair-trade coffee, that sort of thing. … So, yes, I am an eternal
> optimist and me making that choice is making a difference because
> if I'm making a choice then I believe in my head that other people
> are doing it as well. I also believe that if I stop making that choice
> then other people are stopping as well, so, yeah, I really do think it
> makes a difference.
>
> (Leon, 34-year-old musician)

It is interesting that Leon is able to imagine the impact of aggregate
individual acts of consumption because we will see that this concept
was either absent, or treated with great scepticism, by non-fair-trade

supporters. While fair-trade supporters receive 'proof' that their collective purchases can 'make a difference', through, for example, visits from producers to the Fairtrade Town events, information from the FTF and increased fair-trade products on the supermarket shelves, non-fair-traders generally do not have access to, or notice, this. Being involved in the Fairtrade Town network and various other organisations (e.g. Leon is also involved with Oxfam and a youth environmental group in Chelmsford), fair-trade supporters are able to socialise with like-minded individuals, which not only enables them to support fair-trade in ways beyond individual consumption but perhaps also makes it easier for them to imagine the impact of their consumption as part of a collective movement.

As Littler (2009) points out, 'radical' consumption has both possibilities and limitations as a form of political action. Although fair-trade supporters may prioritise buying fair-trade over other individual actions, they do reveal clear limits to the effects of individual consumer power. Indeed, as we have seen, a number of fair-trade supporters do not actually always consume fair-trade and instead are engaged in a collective practice that is organised around awareness-raising campaigns and local promotional activities. Fair-traders seem aware that consumer politics could never replace alternative forms of aid and governmental intervention, but they see it is an important way that both individuals can express their commitments and feel they are making a difference, and groups of individuals can send a message to those in power to make greater political changes. Importantly, however, the majority of the fair-trade supporters in Chelmsford are involved in the wider campaign for trade justice and therefore do not limit their engagement to just shopping differently.

### Non-fair-trade supporters

The Omnibus Survey suggested that those who prioritise another option over fair-trade are those who have different attitudes towards the role of the UK government, or have low levels of interest and relative concern towards issues affecting the developing world. While some non-fair-trade supporters clearly had an interest and concern about poverty in developing countries, the majority of non-fair-trade supporters were either not particularly interested or had not had any experiences that had made them believe that individual consumer power could be very effective. Importantly, none of the non-fair-traders were involved in campaign groups fighting for the alleviation of global poverty, and were therefore presented with fair-trade as an individual consumer action rather than something to supplement a range of already-existing activities.

Because I spoke with a diverse collection of 'ordinary' consumers, I found a number of varied reasons why someone might choose another individual action over fair-trade. However, as with the fair-trade supporters, an individual's evaluations of the effectiveness of their chosen action were closely linked to their experiences and the practices they were involved with. Sarah, a 29-year-old student studying for a degree in social work, had spent eight years working as a tour guide in South America and, while she occasionally bought fair-trade, she was concerned that she did not know whether the money she spent on fair-trade goods actually got back to the producers. She thought that one of the best ways to help those in poverty was through visiting developing countries and supporting their economies through tourism. She highlighted the importance of the money actually getting to the 'local people', so in a sense her argument was quite similar to those offered by fair-trade supporters, because it favoured using consumption – albeit within developing countries rather than through local consumption practices – as a more direct way of reaching those people that needed it most.

By contrast, Maria, an economist in her 30s, argued that fair-trade was an ineffective way to alleviate poverty in the developing world, and suggested that poverty would be more effectively relieved by governmental policy changes such as lifting the ban on genetically modified foods and reducing the Common Agricultural Policy. Maria, like the majority of non-fair-trade supporters, was unconvinced that the consumer could be sure that what they bought actually translated into better conditions for the producers:

> It may be very cynical and sceptical, but I don't think there's enough monitoring to tell who is getting the money anyway. So it's a market distortion as far as I'm concerned and it may actually do more harm than good. I wouldn't choose a product on the basis that it's fair-trade. I've thought about this, it's not that I haven't … unfortunately that's how I feel [laughs].

Maria's position on fair-trade is probably heavily influenced by her professional credentials and the fact that economists have, in general, challenged the claims of the fair-trade movement (see Sidwell, 2008). However, she was not alone in holding sceptical views about the possibility of using consumer power to challenge global trading relations, with the majority of non-fair-traders voicing some scepticism about the claims of the fair-trade movement.

There tended to be two main ways non-fair-traders questioned the effectiveness of the fair-trade consumer choice. First, unlike fair-trade supporters who believed that fair-trade was a more direct way of helping those in poverty because it would circumvent the corruption found in governments in the Third World, non-fair-traders thought that corruption in the developing world was unavoidable and therefore anything they did was unlikely to make any difference.

**Moderator:** Do you think we can make a difference to poverty through our consumption choices?

**Lisa:** Again you don't know how much goes to that country so I don't know.

**Jenny:** I think people are quite sceptical because we raise all this money and, like when we did Live Aid and all that and we raised phenomenal amounts of money and really in reality it hasn't made a huge difference.

**Karen:** It just doesn't get through.

**Jenny:** We know that the governments are corrupt and we know that the governments are really rich but the people who the money should have gone to are really poor. So I think there is this scepticism about whether the money is getting to the right place.

**Paul:** I think it's the scepticism 'cos you don't see it yourself and I'm sure that it has made a hell of a difference to a lot of people's lives but you just don't see it.

**Linda:** It's like you'd almost like to see the money that you've paid what's that gonna go and buy, you almost like want to see it leaving from your account.

**Jenny:** I wanna see a mud hut somewhere [laughs].

**Linda:** Yeah, that's what you want to see the book that you bought for the children or whatever.[8]

Despite the fact that the fair-trade movement relies heavily upon promotional strategies that aim to connect the consumer and producer in global chains of responsibility (e.g. through producer visits, and striking visual campaigns), non-fair-trade supporters do not tend to notice or be involved in networks where this information is distributed. But they, too, want to *see* the direct connection that the fair-trade supporters feel they get. While fair-trade supporters feel that they have the privileged position of seeing on some level how their cup of coffee makes a difference, these participants do not think it is possible to *see* or make a difference. They draw on their experiences of having donated to large charitable appeals like Comic Relief and Live Aid, and use the lack of visibility of the impact of this action as a reason for not supporting fair-trade. We ought to remember that the situation of the focus group may have exaggerated participants' tendency to reject fair-trade as they searched for a consensus as a group of non-fair-trade consumers, although we do find similar arguments in individual/household interviews. Therefore, in keeping with Malpass et al.'s (2007b) 'scandalous suggestion', for now let us listen to these statements as reasonable and well-reasoned arguments from citizens who are voicing objections to how much they, as individuals, can be expected to be responsible for.

This leads us into the second main way non-fair-traders challenged the suggestion that they ought to be using their individual consumption to alleviate poverty in the Third World. Unlike fair-traders, non-fair-traders had difficulty connecting their individual choices to a wider collective movement, which meant that they were less likely to see consumption as an effective individual action.

| | |
|---|---|
| Steven: | I mean, you also think you're just one person, aren't you, at the end of the day, and if I buy that [fair-trade] that's not gonna help a farmer keep in business, is it. |
| Michael: | No, if you don't buy it, it's still not gonna affect anything personally. |
| Joe: | No, he's only gonna lose like 10p or something for a packet of coffee, so I'm not actually gonna pay much more. |
| Kim: | But if a million people changed their minds with you, then I suppose it would. |
| Steven: | Yeah, I know, I understand that … but then you only think of yourself, don't you. |
| Kim: | Yes, I guess so. |
| Steven: | The money doesn't filter down, 'cos it'll come into the country and the government will say well we'll have some of that, otherwise we'll shut you down and what do they do? That's the problem, you get people like Mugabe obviously who just runs their country, and all the money just rises to him basically. |
| Jesse: | That's right. |
| Michael: | Yes, his empire's still going up and up. |
| Steven: | If the government can't make a difference then what difference can we make? That's the way you see it.[9] |

In this extract it is interesting to see how Steven rejects the idea of consumer-citizenship. If the government is unable to tackle the corruption in African countries then what difference can he make by paying an extra 10 pence for a packet of coffee? While Steven clearly has doubts about the capacity of the UK government to improve the situation for farmers, he does not see this as opening up new avenues for the expression of individual consumer power as the literature on consumer reflexivity tends to assume. Although Kim points out that if a million people switched to fair-trade then this might have an impact, Steven has trouble imagining his individual consumption as part of a wider collective. As an individual, Steven is not empowered as a customer of transnational corporations nor does he have the ability or responsibility to tackle the problem of poverty in the corrupt developing world.

Rather than taking up their responsibilities as citizen-consumers, individuals tended to argue that their consumption, which was often intimately tied to other personal commitments and practices, say parenthood, for example (see previous chapter), could not be expected to bear the level of responsibility that policy makers have placed upon it. In many cases, they called for some organised body, generally either supermarkets or governments, to act in order to improve the conditions for workers.

Hazel:    But is it down to us to do fair-trade or is it down to governments to insist on fair-trade by companies?

Linda:    Yeah, if people don't know about it then obviously no-one's been educated enough about buying it, 'cos considering that not a lot of us knew about it and we're just a handful of us, you know what does everybody else not know about it.

Hazel:    But why should two different chocolate bars 50–75 per cent exactly the same, one is fair-trade and the other one isn't, so is it down to us to decide what's fair-trade or shouldn't it just be somebody else deciding it … that we shouldn't do fair-trade, it shouldn't be down to the consumer it should be up to the governments to fair-trade with other countries, not us buying one kind of chocolate over another.[10]

We see here how Hazel argues for governmental action over individual consumer choices. Interestingly, we find a parallel here between the attitudes of fair-trade and non-fair-trade supporters towards the role of the government in the alleviation of poverty in the developing world.

Both call for greater governmental intervention and policy changes, but while fair-trade supporters believe that the amalgamated impact of their purchases will send a message that will cause a catalyst for this greater political change, non-fair-trade supporters are arguing that governments and big businesses ought to act regardless of their preference for one type of chocolate over another. In a sense, the non-fair-traders are supporting the removal of 'choice'. However, they are calling for the removal of choice by changing trading relations. This does not necessarily imply a switch to fair-trade, which is a particular consumer label.

Like the respondents in Malpass et al.'s study, non-fair-trade consumers articulated a 'justifiable scepticism towards the whole frame of "responsibility" that [was] being addressed to them' (Malpass et al., 2007b: 247). As the analysis of the Omnibus Survey suggested, those who do not believe that consumption is an effective way of alleviating poverty in the Third World are not necessarily uninterested or apathetic consumers, but may be individuals who are expressing reasonable doubts about the practicality and legitimacy of altering their consumption practices in line with debates about global responsibility. Academic and policy discourses have often assumed that consumers ought to be willing to acknowledge their responsibilities as citizens, and have entered into the moral language of blame when individuals do not do so. However, as Malpass et al. point out, what these discourses are often unable or unwilling to hear is the degree to which citizens (not consumers) are able to challenge and question these assumptions (ibid.: 253). If those who promote fair-trade consumption are serious about attributing new responsibilities and powers to citizen-consumers, a dialogue must be opened for these citizens to discuss, contest and contribute to the debate as citizens, rather than assuming that all individual consumers are equally willing and able to participate.

## Conclusion

In this chapter, I have looked at how individuals in the UK rate the effectiveness of fair-trade consumption relative to other political and individual actions. It is surprising that so little research has been conducted in this area given the tendency for academics, campaigners and policy makers to understand fair-trade consumption as a consequence of the conditions of late modern society marked by the decreasing faith in the power of national governments to control the business and trading practices of multinational corporations. The UK provides a distinctive context for the exploration of consumer power, and it will be important for comparative research to be conducted to assess the applicability of these findings to other contexts. In particular, countries with a social-democratic welfare regime are likely to attribute different roles to the citizen-consumer, with the state as a trusted partner in the regulation of fair-trade goods. I have demonstrated that it is not necessarily the case that British fair-trade supporters use fair-trade consumption instead of engaging in more traditional forms of political participation or charitable giving, but rather they use fair-trade as an important extension to an already-existent repertoire of collective and individual campaigning activities. On the other hand, I have argued that those who are not committed fair-trade supporters, despite the fact that they may be unknowingly consuming fair-trade on a regular basis, are likely to question both the effectiveness of fair-trade as an individual 'political' action and the assumption that they should be expected to be responsible for the alleviation of poverty through their consumption practices.

Although fair-trade supporters and the fair-trade movement tend to stress the non-exclusivity of fair-trade consumption, we have seen that those who are most likely to believe that buying fair-trade goods is an effective individual action do have distinctive socio-economic and demographic characteristics (women, older people and those in higher socio-economic groups), as well as attitudes of concern for poverty in developing countries. However, fair-trade support cannot be explained by socio-demographic profile alone, and attitudes and opinions are equally important if we are to understand why someone might choose fair-trade. Those who prioritised paying taxes over fair-trade were more likely to believe that the government ought to be providing more aid to developing countries than working towards a fairer trading system, suggesting that these people were rejecting the dominant discourses, which have framed trade as a more important means of development than aid. On the other hand, those who prioritised fair-trade held a consistent underlying belief in the power of trade (whether through individual action or through government regulation) rather than aid to make a difference to world poverty. Individuals who are educated to degree-level (controlling for level of concern) were more likely than those less highly educated to support the rather conventional, and arguably passive choice of taxes as an 'effective' outcome. This, along with the fact that education was not important for fair-trade support, raises doubts over those debates that have stressed the importance of greater education in order to mobilise individuals as citizen-consumers.

This chapter has found further support for the suggestion that those who are committed fair-trade supporters have existing sympathies for the aims of the fair-trade movement. Those who are unconcerned about poverty in the developing world and do not have an opinion about the role the government ought to be playing in the alleviation of global poverty are the most likely to believe that there is nothing they can do that will have any impact. Despite increasing calls to consumers to use their consumption to enact their citizenly duties, the likelihood of believing you cannot have an impact has not significantly changed over the four years of the Omnibus Survey – in other words, fair-trade does not open up new opportunities and convince the apathetic to become engaged but rather converts the converted. Indeed, the likelihood of prioritising 'campaigning for change' over fair-trade has decreased over time, which suggests that those individuals who are already disposed to engage in individual or collective activism are the ones who are being persuaded to choose fair-trade.

While the likelihood of prioritising 'paying taxes' and 'campaigning for change' over fair-trade decreased over the four-year period of the Omnibus Survey, offering some limited support for the suggestion that individuals are using the sphere of consumption to enact their citizenly responsibilities rather than traditional spheres of politics, we must interpret this finding cautiously for several reasons. First, despite the fact that some individuals evaluated buying fair-trade as an effective individual action, it is not necessarily the case that these individuals actually regularly purchased fair-trade, given the sales figures of fair-trade products over the same period. Second, it may not be that those who are committed to fair-trade will be buying fair-trade instead of engaging in the traditional sphere of politics, but more likely that they will be buying fair-trade in addition to more traditional political actions.

This chapter has demonstrated that the *individual* citizen-consumer voting through their individual purchases, so frequently hailed by fair-trade organisations, does not reflect how fair-trade supporters understand this action. Although it is clear from the comments of the committed fair-trade supporters in Chelmsford that they believe that buying fair-trade will send a message to those in power to improve global trading relations, this is because they are able to conceptualise the aggregate impact of their purchases. Because of their involvement in a collective culture organised around local town networks, fair-trade supporters are able to imagine a community of other fair-trade supporters who together are campaigning for change. Fair-trade supporters know that in order for fair-trade to be effective a large number of people will have to buy it, and even then they stress the importance of a continued need for campaigning around trade justice issues, as well as political and economic intervention in the market. This is perhaps why the practice of being a fair-trade supporter involves campaigning to shift systems of collective provision rather than trying to convince every individual that fair-trade is an important and effective citizenly action.

Non-fair-trade supporters, on the other hand, tended to reject the concept of the citizen-consumer and the suggestion that individuals can have an impact on global poverty through their consumption practices. While they may be able to see the moral value of fair-trade consumption and recognise that it may be an effective action if enough people do it, they raised serious questions about this model of responsibility. They questioned whether fair-trade offered a superior alternative to already-existing efforts to reduce poverty in the developing world, given the lack of global visibility and the corruption in Third World governments. They also asked whether global citizenship was a burden their consumption ought to be expected to bear. Non-fair-traders tended to believe that alleviating poverty was something that governments and global businesses ought to have responsibility for. While some might hear this statement as an attempt by apathetic consumers to shift the blame from themselves onto others, this chapter has suggested that we ought to listen to these views because they are being made by citizens who are challenging those (i.e. fair-trade organisations, fair-trade supporters, supermarkets, local and national government, schools, churches) who are defining how they ought to be using their 'vote'.

They rejected the notion of consumer 'choice' as a meaningful tool for alleviating poverty in the developing world and yet regarded the concept of fair-trade as worthy. On the one hand, we might think that because non-fair-traders have expressed a desire for governments and businesses to take responsibility for the alleviation of poverty, the shifting of systems of collective provision towards fair-trade-only lines by an ever-increasing number of supermarkets, businesses and public buildings is answering their demands. On the other hand, however, we might argue that by shifting systems of collective provision, the opportunity is being removed for citizen-consumers to engage in a democratic debate about the effectiveness of the various ways of alleviating global poverty (beyond the fair trade model) and a discussion about whose responsibility this important task should be.

# 8
# Conclusion: The Ideology of the Citizen-Consumer

At the fifth Fairtrade Towns conference in Malmö, the founder of the first Fairtrade Town, Bruce Crowther, read an emotive extract from Harriet Lamb's *Fighting the Banana Wars and Other Fairtrade Battles* (2008), which told of how a woman named Maria from Costa Rica had lost her baby because he was born with deformities, owing to the widespread use of pesticides on banana plantations in the 1980s (see Lamb, 2008: 6–7). After finishing this extract, Crowther turned to the audience and asked, after hearing this, 'how can one possibly go out and buy a banana that isn't fair-trade?'

It is often assumed that as soon as consumers are given the information that their consumption is environmentally or socially damaging, they will be motivated to act. However, this book has demonstrated that the situation is not quite as simple as this. Consumption is a complex process, which is collectively constituted and embedded within routine and normative practices. As we have seen, the fair-trade movement is quite aware of this, despite its persistent representation of the fair-trade consumer as a citizen-consumer acting voluntarily in the marketplace. The citizen-consumer is a powerful symbol, which is used to publicly represent and motivate support for fair-trade because it serves a number of important functions for different individuals and institutions. However, by representing fair-trade consumption in this way, this book has revealed that a moral hierarchy of value is created in which the fair-trade choice is defended as the only course of action that a concerned and ethical consumer ought to make (as exemplified by Crowther's question). It could be argued that such an approach ignores the 'lay normativities' of those whose consumption is motivated through alternative logics and moralities. This book has listened to the normative and practical challenges of the 'ordinary' consumer and has questioned whether individual consumption should be made to bear the level of responsibility that is often placed upon it. This concluding chapter will summarise the key debates presented throughout this volume, as well as draw the reader's attention to their wider relevance for policy makers keen to promote sustainable consumption behaviour and future academic debates on (ethical) consumption practices.

## The complexity of consumption

In this book, I have challenged the dominant image of the fair-trade citizen-consumer who uses his/her individual shopping choices to 'vote' for a better world. Fair-trade consumption is embedded within a wider socio-political context, which shapes and coordinates this behaviour. Rather than the consumer operating as an individual actor, this figure is constrained or enabled through various collective structures, such as infrastructures of provision, social norms and institutional frameworks. We have seen how the fair-trade movement creates opportunities for consumers within their social networks and how collective cultures of fair-trade support can create dispositions towards fair-trade consumer goods, as well as deeper engagement in the fight for global justice. We have also seen how interventions within the market and fair-trade 'choice-editing' have been made possible because of a complex set of interactions between various actors from the state, market and civil society, at the same time creating a growing number of 'accidental' fair-trade consumption acts. Not all those who buy fair-trade do so because they want to 'vote' for a better world, and not all those who fail to buy fair-trade do so because they do not care about global poverty. This book has demonstrated that consumption is a complex process that is neither fully reflexive nor constrained, and therefore the attribution of sovereign power to individual consumer choice ought to be re-evaluated.

This book has argued that a practice-theoretical approach can be usefully employed to account for the differentiation of consumption practices. In such an approach the focus shifts away from the individual to explore the capacities of social networks, social norms surrounding appropriate behaviour, infrastructures of provision, and institutional configurations of responsibility. In so doing, it becomes apparent that the fair-trade consumer does not exist as an abstract or generalised figure across all contexts but rather is constituted through complex and contingent interactions between each of these elements at different times and places. By focusing on the development of the fair-trade consumer movement across three countries, the reader has learnt how the consumer is differentially enabled to act because of the variations in the institutionalisation of fair-trade. For example, there were distinct differences in the mainstream provisioning of fair-trade, the networks of fair-trade support at the local and national level, the role of different market, state and civil society actors in the promotion of fair-trade, and the ideas about what fair-trade ought to comprise of.

Through a close focus on the practices of fair-trade and non-fair-trade supporters living within a Fairtrade Town in the UK, it was demonstrated how consumption connects to, and emerges from, an individual's engagement in a whole range of social practices. Interest in fair-trade builds gradually over time, as people interact with others and develop 'understandings, procedures and engagements' around how to 'do' fair-trade support. Collective cultures, such as Fairtrade Towns, help to generate the social recognisability of the practice, as well as deepen people's commitment to the fair-trade movement. Fair-trade support is not only about consuming fair-trade goods but involves organising events, raising awareness of trade justice, and shaping the availability of fair-trade within the local environment. It therefore extends beyond individual consumption routines and moves into forms of civic participation. Of course, the actions of the fair-trade supporter are influenced by the existing situation within one's town or country. For example, in Sweden, where the state plays an important role in the organisation of fair-trade provisioning at the municipal level, fair-trade supporters appeared less likely to engage in the campaigning seen elsewhere, which, particularly in areas where there was limited availability of fair-trade (as in areas in the USA), involved visiting stores, community organisations and public offices, asking them to stock or use more fair-trade items. In all contexts, being a fair-trade supporter involved more than just consuming fair-trade for one's personal consumption. This suggests that attention must be given to the wider practice of fair-trade support that is orienting people towards fair-trade goods, as well as other activities. By paying attention to how people learn about and maybe go on to support fair-trade, we can learn a great deal more about the fair-trade phenomenon than through a narrow focus on fair-trade consumption acts.

Indeed, we have seen that consuming fair-trade is not necessarily a prerequisite for being a fair-trade supporter – you can be a fair-trade supporter without always consuming fair-trade, and you can regularly consume fair-trade without being a fair-trade supporter. The latter has been made possible because of the actions of committed fair-trade supporters who have campaigned for changes to systems of local provisioning and because of the efforts of a coalition of interested actors (from state, market and civil society) who have promoted the morality of the fair-trade movement for different reasons. That is not to say that all those who consume fair-trade understand this action as a positive choice or 'vote' for fair-trade. Rather it may be that fair-trade coffee is all that is available or that fair-trade bananas are placed on a promotional offer and are therefore cheaper than alternatives. Non-fair-trade supporters have a range of interests and are involved in a multitude of social practices – just like fair-trade supporters – and these can work to guide them away from the fair-trade consumer label because it is not relevant to their existing commitments and concerns. Importantly, it was not the case that these individuals were 'unethical' consumers or uninterested in issues affecting the developing world, but rather that their consumption was informed by different logics and moralities, which placed an emphasis on the care of family members and friends, animal welfare or self-preservation. Their shopping routines were therefore not understood as an arena for the expression of the care for distant others.

Those who want to motivate sustainable consumption behaviour need to move away from the model of the consumer as an individualist chooser. Consumers are not infinitely malleable, and the provision of information alone is inadequate to change people's behaviour. Placing consumer choice at the centre of policies to change patterns of consumption ignores how the consumer is constrained by normative and collective processes that are themselves stabilised and reproduced through the routine performance of social practices. Rather than resort to models of the active citizen-consumer, this book suggests it is more realistic to focus upon the everyday social flow and 'do-ability' of consumer practices and performances, considering the socio-political contexts and conditions under which these performances are made possible (Halkier, 2010). Although many policy documents draw on the abstract figure of the active consumer when discussing sustainable consumption behaviour (Jackson, 2005; Southerton, Warde & Hand, 2004), we have seen that the fair-trade movement is quite aware that consumption is a collectively derived process – for example, their support of Fairtrade Towns and their use of fair-trade promotional periods that aim to bring a community of fair-trade supporters together in the celebration of the movement. Fair-trade cultures work to generate attachments to fair-trade goods among a particular section of the population and provide opportunities to intervene in the structuring of markets. We may therefore wonder why they publicly persist with the representation of the fair-trade consumer as an individual citizen-consumer, when they clearly rely on the capacity of social networks, support from a range of institutional actors and infrastructures of provision to change patterns of consumption. It seems likely that this is, at least in part, a strategy meant to deflect those criticisms of fair-trade that view it as an attack on the logic of the free, neo-liberal market.

## The possibilities and limitations of the citizen-consumer

The image of the individual citizen-consumer has for centuries offered a powerful symbol of the potential for social change. Importantly, this figure does not emerge automatically but has to be 'made' through mobilisation in the state, market and civil society, as well as in response to distinct socio-political conditions (Trentmann, 2006). Coalitions of interested groups have come together at different periods in modern history in order to mobilise a particular vision of consumer power to generate popular support for their movement aims and/or to influence governmental policy. In this way, the fair-trade citizen-consumer identity does not represent a novel morality, as some have claimed, but rather the continuation of a long tradition. Consumers have always been integral to the structuring of global markets, and attention must be paid to how those who seek to represent the 'consumer' construct very particular images of this figure for specific purposes. The fair-trade citizen-consumer draws on a coalition of interested organisations who jointly construct an image of consumer power in order to achieve sometimes quite different social, economic and political aims. The retailer who promotes fair-trade can represent itself as a responsible business answering the calls from their customers who have demanded more fair-trade; the municipality that supports fair-trade can promote their identity as a good place to live and work because they listen to and care about their community and take action on their behalf; and the fair-trade organisation can use this figure to claim they are acting in line with the wishes of thousands of people when they campaign for changes to trade policies or for fair-trade procurement. For the local fair-trade supporter, this image of the citizen-consumer provides a motivational resource to continue campaigning within their social networks. This creates an opportunity for fair-trade organisations to enrol willing and free marketing volunteers to increase sales and, in some cases, as within the UK, to join the wider movement for trade justice through lobbying activities.

Therefore the fair-trade citizen-consumer is an influential icon around which many different organisations from the state, market and civil society gather and seek to represent. It builds and bonds communities of diverse actors, and creates the opportunity for those organised within fair-trade networks to feel part of a wider movement. It enables some individuals to act in accordance with their values and feel good about themselves, their town, their supermarket and their local organisations, as well as providing resources for these individuals to engage within the political process as both citizens and consumers. In keeping with Littler's (2011) recent conclusions, I would agree that it is important to recognise the political potential of these forms of mobilisation around the fair-trade citizen-consumer, which generate enthusiasm and resources of hope for *some* individuals who feel empowered to make a difference. However, also in keeping with Littler's conclusions, there is a key danger in adopting such narratives of ethical consumption, which offer 'a celebratory individualism without locating its analysis in relation to larger political systems' (Littler, 2011: 33). Does the fair-trade citizen consumer move us towards more forms of equality or does it subtly 'entrench further inequalities and forms of exploitation?' (ibid.: 34).

To address these questions, this book has primarily turned to the non-fair-trade supporter because this figure is so often ignored in accounts of fair-trade consumption. As fair-trade has been promoted by a number of key institutions within society (such as local and national government departments and buildings, schools, churches and faith networks, chain-retail outlets and supermarkets, manufacturers and the media), those with no real commitment to the fair-trade movement are increasingly being encouraged to alter their consumption routines according to fair-trade principles. Fair-trade consumption is represented as an immediate action that everyone can and should participate in because it claims to be able to alleviate poverty and suffering in the developing world, and seems to require very little of the individual beyond switching to a sometimes more expensive brand of consumer good. However, this simple message assumes that our consumption routines are both infinitely malleable in the light of new information and are the product of completely conscious and unconstrained choices, as well as a suitable arena in which to honour our responsibilities to global others.

The fact that non-fair-trade supporters in the UK perceived there to be clear socio-economic, cultural and moral boundaries between themselves and fair-trade consumers raises some important questions about the politics of inclusion and exclusion that the citizen-consumer identity can evoke. Individuals sensed that their 'choice' to consume or not consume fair-trade was subject to an evaluative judgement regarding which ways of life and definitions of morality are worth valuing. This inevitably creates power struggles within the social field as individuals attempt to justify why they are worthy of recognition. Evaluations of fair-trade consumption by the non-fair-traders in Chelmsford revealed issues of social inequality and highlighted the differential levels of access to valued resources because of the sometimes higher price of fair-trade goods. However, it was demonstrated that the relationship between social class and fair-trade consumption is a complicated one because we are dealing with individuals' 'lay normativities', as well as a blurry boundary between the exclusivity and ordinariness of fair-trade left by the historical trajectory of mainstream fair-trade provisioning in the market. Indeed, many of the non-fair-trade supporters had in fact regularly bought fair-trade because of changing systems of provision, even if they did not identify themselves as fair-trade consumers/supporters. These accidental fair-trade consumers revealed a 'justifiable scepticism' about the effectiveness of consuming fair-trade in order to alleviate poverty in the developing world.

Chapter 7 revealed that those who were least likely to believe that fair-trade consumption is an effective individual action held distinctive characteristics (other things being equal, those in lower socio-economic groups, younger age categories and men), and either believed that there was nothing they could do as an individual consumer/citizen to alleviate global poverty, or felt that this was a task that ought to be left to governmental aid. Analysis of the Omnibus survey suggests that fair-trade is not opening up new opportunities for the uninterested to become engaged, but rather converts the converted. Importantly, fair-trade supporters did not view consumption as a substitute to engaging in the 'traditional' political process, and tended to imagine the amalgamated impact of their collective purchases rather than the power of the individual citizen-consumer. Non-fair-traders did not identify with this concept of collective consumer action and instead raised serious questions about the effectiveness of *individual* consumption choices as a means of alleviating poverty in the developing world. They felt that because of the ingrained injustices within our global trading system (corrupt Third World governments, the organisation of world trade and the limited visible effect of existing charitable efforts like Live Aid) the impact of their consuming a different cup of coffee was likely to be negligible. Fair-trade supporters were equally aware of the problems of corruption within the Third World, and indeed also highlighted the limited effect of fair-trade consumption as a means of tackling the huge issue of global poverty. However, their involvement in Fairtrade Town networks provided them with some 'proof' of the effectiveness of fair-trade in improving the lives of a small number of fair-trade producers, as well as reassuring them that they are part of a collective of like-minded individuals who are working together for the same ends.

It is essential to stress that even the most committed fair-trade supporters raised doubts about the effectiveness of the power of the consumer to alleviate global poverty. Indeed, consumption was not was seen as the only, or even the most important, way to register their support for the fair-trade movement. For the fair-trade supporters, consuming fair-trade was an addition to a repertoire of actions, and there was a shared belief in the continued need for government aid and structural interventions to improve the global trading system. The non-fair-trade supporters, too, called for more government action, but they believed that the government ought to act regardless of their own preference for a particular brand of chocolate. While there has been a tendency to assume that those who do not engage in a topic or practice of interest lack the necessary information or understandings in order to participate, the approach taken in this book has interrogated the assumed passivity of non-participation. I have argued that we should not understand non-fair-trade supporters as apathetic or uninterested individuals, but rather as individuals who are capable of articulating reasonable and well-reasoned arguments, in the light of their understandings of existing social structures and global conditions. There are clear limits to the citizen-consumer identity, and both fair-trade and non-fair-trade supporters recognised this.

In recent years, we have seen a number of moral and political consumption campaigns around issues of sustainable living and the need to adopt more environmentally friendly forms of transport and energy use in order to save the planet, as well as healthy living programmes that are aimed at tackling problems of obesity and poor health. By appealing to the figure of the citizen-consumer who ought to act regardless of their material, cultural and affective circumstances – because it is as simple as switching your brand of coffee or buying more fruit and exercising – there is a danger of ignoring the normative dimensions of individuals' responses to these campaigns, as well as the reasonable challenges from citizens to the model of individual consumer responsibility they are presented with. Those who are responsible for implementing ethical and sustainable consumption campaigns, and indeed future studies exploring these campaigns, need to take account of people's 'lay normativities'. By listening to what citizens actually think, such campaigns may have more success in convincing people towards adopting more sustainable lifestyles and perhaps avoid further entrenchment of social inequality.

## Fair-trade choice-editing

Fair-trade is a powerful market device that has been shown to generate support from diverse sections of the community through promotional campaigns, such as Fairtrade Towns and the fair-trade promotional period. The interplay between different actors (consumers, municipalities, businesses, fair-trade organisation) with diverse objectives works to symbolically sustain the image of the active citizen-consumer and, in so doing, frames fair-trade choice-editing as a legitimate and called-for action. On the citizen-consumer's behalf, fair-trade options have become institutionalised across a variety of locations. The UK represents the largest market for Fairtrade-certified sales at present, and rather than explaining this with reference to a model of individualised consumer choice, this book has shown that it can largely be explained through the increase of mainstream provisioning of Fairtrade in supermarkets, the collective cultures and networks of fair-trade support and the growth of Fairtrade public procurement. Grassroots fair-trade networks developed in the 1970s in the UK, and this history has shaped the capacity of the movement to generate support from a number of different actors across diverse locations. Interventions in the marketplace could not have occurred without this level of support shown by a coalition of institutions. Directing their efforts to this collective level, the fair-trade movement in the UK has been very successful in changing people's consumption behaviours.

In Sweden, societal support for fair-trade has been more managed by the FFTS, who have developed different schemes to mobilise support from consumers (Fairtrade Ambassador scheme) and municipalities (Fairtrade Cities). In this context, fair-trade choice-editing has been realised through provisioning policies at the local state level. Unlike the UK, there have been no 100 per cent Fairtrade switches by major retailers, but some leading brands have switched to Fairtrade, including Zoegas coffee and Danisco sugar. The mainstreaming project is not yet as pronounced in Sweden as in the UK, although the desire is there and it has the potential to be so.

In the USA, on the other hand, consumer support for fair-trade lags behind (because building fair-trade businesses was the key focus of FTUSA for a number of years), and there are, at present, only a small number of Fair Trade towns and limited or varying availability within the mainstream stores. The history of the fair-trade movement in the USA reveals a number of tensions surrounding how best to realise fair-trade principles on the ground, which, along with the sheer size of the USA, is slowing the capacity of the movement to create collective cultures and shift provisioning systems. But this is clearly the aim of FTUSA, as its 'Fair Trade for All' strategy makes clear.

It is important to be aware of these differences between the movements and to reflect upon the way the relationship between the consumer, the state, the market and civil society is coordinated within different contexts. Comparative research is a particularly powerful tool for revealing 'distinct patterns for the institutionalisation of ... consumption and the role of consumers' (Kjærnes, Harvey & Warde, 2007: 191), and more ought to be done to explore the variations in fair-trade consumer cultures across the world, which are constantly evolving in nationally (and locally) distinctive ways.

I want to end this book with a critical observation about fair-trade choice-editing identified through my research within the UK. It may be that this message is quite distinctive to the UK context, given the way the fair-trade consumer has been mobilised as a powerful actor voting with every purchase, and in view of the penetration of the Fairtrade label into mainstream markets. However, because the UK is often looked to for ideas for campaigning by other countries[1] and was the pioneer in the mainstreaming project for supermarket-own fair-trade, it does occupy an important role within the future development of the international fair-trade consumer movement. The symbol of individual consumer power is utilised across the international movement, and those switches to Fairtrade that have occurred are often conducted in the name of the consumer.

The fair-trade movement relies on being able to demonstrate that it has broad consumer support for its aims, in order to legitimise its advocacy role within debates about wider trade issues, as well as to successfully intervene in the market and shift systems of collective provision. On the one hand, the fair-trade consumer movement has generated a great deal of support from a number of different sections of society, which has led to the mainstream switches to Fairtrade and the changes to procurement policies we have seen. On the other hand, it does not automatically follow that the collective acts created by these 'switches' should be counted as representative of support for the fair-trade movement and then used in order to justify further fair-trade interventions into the marketplace and lobbying in the name of the consumer. The mainstreaming of fair-trade products changes people's behaviours because they are likely to be consuming fair-trade on a regular basis, but this is not the same as thousands of citizen-consumers choosing fair-trade because they are supportive of the fair-trade movement's aims, as it is so often represented.

I put this point to the FTF, and their response was as follows:

**Hannah:**    I think if you speak to any producer, any farmer the one thing they will always say is that we want to sell more.... So there's a massive need to scale up to really increase the volume so that we increase the benefits going back to producers. ... So there's something about volume and that's what you see from the big switches ... people may not, it's not a conscious purchase but that price and premium is still going back to producers.

**Interviewer:**    So what you're saying is the fact that it's helping the producers justifies the fact the people don't know?

**Hannah:**    Our primary role is always empowering producers through trade, that's what we were set up to do, and in order to do that, fair-trade, as a movement has activated people, it's increased understanding, it's getting people thinking about development issues.... I think as well the big mainstream switches means you're reaching fairly different consumers, very different shoppers, people who do not shop in Oxfam, or buy Traidcraft products at the back of a church, but they're starting to see that mark and you would hope that questions start to be asked. We're also starting to see some great, very creative point of sale material ... some quite powerful messaging and producer imagery and stories being told in supermarkets and coffee shops, so again you're reaching people that we haven't reached before and giving them the opportunity to start thinking about it, and to find out more when they're interested.[2]

Despite the discourses surrounding consumer choice and power, the fair-trade movement is, in many ways, acting 'behind the backs of consumers' (Barnett et al., 2011: 22), leaving it up to the consumer to find out more 'when they're interested'. Of course, this relies on the consumer noticing that a product is fair-trade and paradoxically drawing on the representations of consumer power offered by the producer imagery at point of sale displays. This imagery is itself subject to some critique, as we saw in Chapter 4, for romantically commodifying producers and the environments in which they live, in order to empower consumers to feel they can make a difference (Varul, 2008a; Wright, 2004). For the FTF, the mainstream switches are reasonable because fair-trade is helping producers. However, as indicated in the Introduction, the fair-trade model is not a panacea for trade injustices and can look remarkably similar to 'conventional' trade, especially in its mainstream guise (Barrientos & Dolan, 2006; Dolan, 2008; Jaffee, 2007; Lyon, 2006; Lyon & Moberg, 2011; Raynolds, Murray & Wilkinson, 2007). From the consumer perspective, this book has challenged the model of the individual citizen-consumer for a host of theoretical, moral and political reasons. Meanwhile, multiple citizen-consumer votes are being counted, which is somewhat problematic given that many fair-trade consumers were unaware they were taking part in a ballot in the first place.

# Appendix: The National Omnibus Survey Questions (Module 236)

*Source*: Office for National Statistics (2005 [Technical Report: 105])

- Which item on this card best describes how you feel about levels of poverty in developing countries?
  1. Very concerned
  2. Fairly concerned
  3. No strong feelings one way or another
  4. Not very concerned
  5. Not at all concerned
  6. Don't Know (Spontaneous only)
- On this card is a list of ways in which the UK Government could contribute to reducing poverty in developing countries. In which three ways, if any, you think they should be contributing to reducing poverty, starting with the most important and then the next most important and so on. [I used their first answer, which is the one they thought was most important.]
  1. Providing financial support and other types of aid such as training and/or expertise
  2. Working for a fairer world trading system
  3. Encouraging increased private sector investment
  4. Reducing conflict and war
  5. Working to improve the effectiveness of international organisations like the World Bank, the UN and the European Union
  6. Working to cancel the debts owed by developing countries
  7. Other (please specify)
  8. None of these
- In which ways, if any, do you think you as an individual can most effectively contribute to reducing poverty in developing countries? Please choose up to three ways. Starting with the most important and then the next most important and so on.
  1. Paying taxes – a proportion of which is spent on International Aid by the Government
  2. Donating to charities or other appeals on behalf of developing countries
  3. Supporting socially responsible business and investment
  4. Buying Fair trade goods
  5. Working in a developing country to promote development
  6. Being involved in church or campaign groups working on behalf of developing countries
  7. Putting pressure on politicians to increase the assistance which the Government gives to developing countries
  8. Travelling to a developing country as a tourist
  9. Other (please specify)
  10. Do not think can contribute effectively as an individual to reducing poverty in developing countries (Spontaneous only)

# Notes

## 1 Introduction: The Rise of the Fair-Trade Citizen-Consumer

1. The reader should note that there are different meanings attached to the different ways of writing this word; when 'fair trade/fair-trade' is separated into two words without capital letters, it refers to the wider fair-trade movement, which encompasses labelled and non-labelled products, as well as the wider movement seeking to secure trade justice for the world's poorest producers. When 'Fair Trade' is capitalised in two words, it refers to the labelled Fair Trade products certified in the USA by Fair Trade USA and organisations certified by the Fair Trade Federation, as well as the Fair Trade towns' movement in the USA. When 'Fairtrade' is capitalised in one word, it refers to Fairtrade labelled goods and the towns'/cities' movement in the UK and Europe.
2. Of course, as Shove (2003) points out (and this book demonstrates), it is not always possible to make a clear distinction between spectacular and ordinary consumption.

## 2 Constructing the Fair-Trade Citizen-Consumer

1. Interestingly, the appeal to the consumer as culpable for slavery was also employed in the 1820s in America in the free-produce movement, which promoted the consumption of goods produced by the labour of free men in a similar vein to the fair-trade movement today (Glickman, 2004; 2006).
2. A buycott refers to the positive purchasing of specific products/services for ethical reasons as opposed to avoidance of specific products/services (boycott).
3. The LSA was a consumers' league that was organised by both men and women as a way of translating their Catholic religion 'into daily practices which would ultimately affect a broader transformation of society according to religious principles' (Chessel, 2006a: 82).
4. So, for example, advice for women to plan ahead, buy in advance and try to encourage shops to close early on Saturdays and on the Sabbath reflected and promoted the 'behavioural norms of the bourgeoisie' rather than taking into consideration the consumption practices of working women (Chessel, 2006b: 63).
5. The Equitable Pioneers of Rochdale are usually credited with the founding of the Co-operative movement in 1844 (Birchall, 1997; Fairbairn, 1994; Furlough & Strikwerda, 1999). The Pioneers consisted of a group of Owenites, weavers, Chartists and temperance campaigners who came together to establish a retail co-operative in Rochdale, as the first step in the creation of a utopian self-supporting community. The Co-operative movement 'grew out of the critique and rejection of an increasingly individualistic, market-oriented and

competitive mode of production/consumption in Eighteenth-century England' (Gurney, 1996: 11–12).

6. Gurney (1996) points out that the divi was particularly important for women on low incomes who could use their accumulated divi for special purchases.

7. The local store, visited daily for basic provisions, was a 'social nexus' where women met friends and neighbours and where they could be sure they would be treated civilly regardless of their income (Gurney, 1996: 62).

8. Other activities included tea parties, soirées, festivals and choirs, field days, galas and outings, demonstrations and marches (Gurney, 1996: 65). Many of these tactics have been employed by the present-day fair-trade movement, such as the fair-trade promotional period, which showcases fair-trade products and tries to secure the commitment of already-existing supporters to the movement (see Chapter 4).

9. Allusion to the 'blood stain'd luxury' (see Davies, 2001) or the 'blood-sweetened beverage' [tea] (see Hochschild, 2005) appeared as dominant tropes within the abolitionist literature.

10. Modelled on the Consumer's Union of the United States, the Consumers' Association was established in Britain in 1956 in order to provide advice to consumers about how to discriminate between the increasing world of consumer goods through the comparative testing of commercial products. The CA was a coalition of professional people – economists, engineers, scientists, academics, business executives and civil servants – from across the political spectrum who were 'united by their faith in expertise and motivated by the common feeling that the consumer was insufficiently considered by British manufacturers' (Hilton, 2003: 199). The CA produced a monthly magazine, *Which?*, offering best buy advice. By 1961 the number of subscribers to *Which?* had reached a quarter of a million (ibid.: 210).

11. Cohen focused particularly on the ways that women and African-Americans used consumption as a tool for their own social and political campaigns over the three periods of history.

12. See Chapters 3 and 4 for a discussion of the emergence of the fair-trade citizen-consumer in Sweden (a social-democratic state), where it is the government that becomes a key target for the consumption of fair-trade goods.

13. It is possible to identify this post-moralism in the writings of cultural theorists – for example, the work of the CCCS, who suggested that consumption was a space in which identities could be created and dominant norms could be challenged (Clarke et al., 1975; Hall, 1980; Hebdige, 1979; Willis, 1978); from the growing interest in the sphere of advertising, which promotes consumption as a meaningful social activity in itself (Nixon, 1996; 2003; Sassatelli, 2007); and in the work of anthropologists such as Miller (1987; 2001) and Douglas and Isherwood (1979) who have suggested that, rather than promote a selfish individualism, material culture can 'enhance their [individuals'] humanity and develop their sociality' (Miller, 2001: 232).

# 3   The International Fair-Trade Consumer Movement

1. Although the UK actually has the largest market for Fairtrade-certified retail sales at present, sales in the US are only marginally lower than the UK and

as awareness grows within this country, sales are likely to increase beyond those of the UK.

2. The Solidaridad organisation was a collaborative venture between Catholic and Protestant churches.
3. Interview with Andi Trindle, Atlantic Specialty Coffee, California, April 2011.
4. See Anderson (2009) for a critical history of the Co-op's involvement with fair-trade in the UK.
5. Interview with Hannah Reed, Fairtrade Foundation, May 2011.
6. When the organisation first formed in 1986, it was called 'Nationella Föreningen U-SAM, U-landsgruppers samarbetsförening', and it changed its name in 1997 to 'Världsbutikerna för Rättvis Handel'. In 2011, it changed its name again to 'Organisationen Fair Trade Återförsäljarna' (Organisation of Fair Trade Retailers).
7. Although Åkerlund (2010) notes that initial discussions about the formation of a national labelling scheme were not met with much enthusiasm by the World Shops who were threatened (*hotade*) by the concept.
8. The LO is the largest trade union organisation in Sweden, and they explain their involvement with fair-trade as one way they can ensure better conditions for workers in different parts of the world (LO, 2011). Although Micheletti (2003: 121) has claimed that unions are no longer a dominant actor in political consumerist activities in Sweden, the case of fair-trade suggests otherwise.
9. Sackeus AB is the largest fair-trade importing organisation in Sweden today and it deals mainly with the popular church coffee, Cafe organico, which accounts for 80 per cent of its turnover (Björner, 2006: 51).
10. Author observations in ICA, Coop, and Hemkop stores in Stockholm and Lund in May and June 2011.
11. Interview with Swedish Fairtrade expert, May 2011.
12. While the FFTS may not be engaged in advocacy work, Åkerlund (2010) points out that the Swedish Church does engage in advocacy work. She calls on consumers to recognise their potential to challenge the system beyond buying fair-trade.
13. Details on the long list of financial supporters of FTUSA's work can be found in their annual reports (FTUSA, 2009a: 40–1).
14. Interview with Katie Barrow, FTUSA, April 2011.
15. Interview with David Funkhouser, FTUSA, April 2011.

# 4  Promoting Fair-Trade

1. This is not to mention the growing number of other fair-trade 'place' initiatives, such as Fairtrade Churches, Fairtrade Schools, Fairtrade Universities and Fairtrade Workplaces.
2. They may include provisions for the domestic consumption of fair-trade goods (such as in Kumamoto in Japan and Alfenas in Brazil) or the requirement to become a twin town with a Fairtrade Town in the North (as in New Koforidua in Ghana, which is twinned with Garstang in the UK and Media in the USA). Criteria for Fairtrade Towns in the South are currently under discussion (International Fairtrade Towns Conference, 2011).

3. The information about Chelmsford has been gathered from the ONS Website for Official Labour Market Statistics (Nomis, 2009). Population and earning statistics were gathered in 2008, the labour market statistics refer to the period between April 2008 and March 2009, and the educational statistics to the period between January and December 2008.

4. All names have been changed to protect the anonymity of the respondents.

5. The history of the Chelmsford campaign has been gathered from the minutes of the CFAG and through discussions with the group's members.

6. Extract from focus group with Chelmsford community representatives (from local political parties, the cathedral and Women's Institute) conducted in April 2008. Speaking in this extract was the representative from the Labour & Co-op Party.

7. However, the aim with fair-trade is not to create a commonwealth that will unite the working classes across the globe, but rather to raise awareness of the plight of developing world producers and draw attention to the responsibility of those attending fair-trade events towards these producers.

8. Jenny was a 42-year-old youth worker who was instrumental in gaining 'Fairtrade church' status for her church, as well as a member of CFAG.

9. Thirty-six churches have committed to support fair-trade in Chelmsford, with ten of these also making their own unique applications for 'Fairtrade Church' status. Other community organisations involved with fair-trade include the local Amnesty group, Soroptimists, Women's Institute, Friends of the Earth, Conservative Club, and the Chelmsford Liberal Democrats, Green Party and Co-op Party.

10. The number of Co-operative stores selling fair-trade in Chelmsford (17) has remained relatively constant throughout the campaign, so when they put in their first application for Fairtrade Town status, the Co-operative stores made up the majority of their required number of retail stores (14 out of 23).

11. Just one person out of the 42 non-fair-trade supporters spoken to throughout this study (either in focus groups or individual interviews) was aware that Chelmsford was a Fairtrade Town. He worked for Chelmsford Borough Council so was made aware of the status through his job. Although he was aware of using Fairtrade at work, he did not actively look for Fairtrade products when he shopped for his family as he felt it was not available.

12. This focus group consisted of a group of mothers (aged 32–45) who were all taking a break from employment to raise their children.

13. For example, in Garstang, local dairy farmers joined together with fair-trade campaigners in both a local and global campaign.

14. The information about Lund has been gathered from the Lunds Kommun Website (2011a; 2011b) and Lunds Kommun Newsletter (2011c).

15. IM was founded in 1938 and is inspired by Christian-Humanist Values. Today its work spans 13 countries and it has 30,000 members.

16. The details of the Lund campaign were gathered from interviews in June 2011 and from Scott-Jacobsson (2007).

17. ICA is the biggest supermarket chain in Sweden, but each store is an individual franchise so they have some discretion over what products it stocks.

18. A film by Swedish film-maker Fredrik Gertten (2009), which highlights abuses in the banana industry. The film and its film-maker became embroiled in a

legal battle, which involved the Swedish Parliament who came to the film-maker's defence.

19. Interview with Lund Fairtrade City Coordinator, June 2011.
20. Interview with representative from Berkeley City Council, April 2011. Other facts about Berkeley have been gathered from Berkeley City (2011).
21. The details of the Berkeley campaign were gathered from interviews with Fair Trade Berkeley supporters in April 2011.
22. Interview with representative from Berkeley City Council, April 2011.
23. Since my visit in April 2011, Rachel informs me that all stores supporting Fair Trade in Berkeley have now placed decals in their windows to highlight Berkeley's Fair Trade Town status and their support of it.
24. Interview with USA Fair Trade Town Coordinator, Billy Linstead Goldsmith, April 2011.
25. Collaborations between fair-trade and local produce in Fairtrade Town campaigns are common. For example, they were found in the first Fairtrade Town, Garstang, and are the sixth Fairtrade Town goal in Belgium.
26. For example, businesses are keen to support fair-trade because it will increase their sales and potential customer-base (as well as demonstrate their corpo-rate social responsibility or CSR credentials); municipalities want to support fair-trade because it will promote their identity as a responsible place; activ-ists want to support fair-trade because it offers them the opportunity to act upon an issue they feel strongly about in their daily life; consumers join Fairtrade Towns because they want to feel part of a collective movement for change; fair-trade organisations recognise Fairtrade Towns as a chance to increase the sales of fair-trade and therefore the benefits to producers in the developing world; and Buy Local campaigns support Fairtrade Towns because of the potential to reach new, sympathetic supporters through a broadly similar repertoire of activities and events.
27. Social capital has been variously understood as the way actors within social networks are able to secure benefits by virtue of their membership (Portes, 1998: 6). Social capital is not a 'single entity' but rather a variety of 'produc-tive' entities that make 'possible the achievement of certain ends that in its absence would not be possible' (Coleman, 1988: S98).
28. I met fair-trade supporters from other US Fair Trade Towns at the Inter-national Fairtrade Towns conference (2011) who described the differences between their town and Berkeley. For example, Roger from Minnesota described how in his town there was very limited availability of fair-trade, with just one coffee shop that served fair-trade and Wal-Mart offering fair-trade coffee. This meant that fair-trade activities in his town were organised among faith networks. The sheer size of the US means that further research ought to be conducted before generalisations are made about the form of Fair Trade Town campaigns.
29. Nectar points are part of the Sainsbury's loyalty reward scheme, which awards points according to how much consumers spend in store. The points can then be converted to money off future shopping trips.
30. Multiple Olympic Gold medallist from the UK.
31. However, Trentmann points out that although the promotion of empire goods reflect an imperial ethics of consumerism, they also were based on reciprocity because both producers and consumers were united by the shared

need to sell and consume goods, unlike fair-trade, which imagines the producers in the South helped by consumers in the North (Trentmann, 2007: 1082–7).

32. Extract from focus group with Chelmsford community representatives (from local political parties, the cathedral and Women's Institute) conducted in April 2008. Speaking in this extract was the representative from the Women's Institute.

33. While at the International Fairtrade Towns conference (2011), I was struck by the way the fair-trade producers' presence was held up as something extraordinary to be continually applauded, as well as how the audience took numerous pictures of the fair-trade speakers – this did not happen when 'ordinary' fair-trade supporters and speakers were presenting.

34. While one focus group respondent was aware that fair-trade wine had been discounted in the Co-op, he did not know why it had been discounted, which suggests that the Co-op did not do enough to connect the Fairtrade Fortnight message with its promotional discount. In fact, the discount was used by Michael as a reason to question the fair-trade movement because he wondered how it could be fair-trade if they were selling it more cheaply than other wines.

35. Reshmi was an 'Asian or Asian British–Indian' Female (see note 7, Chapter 6), aged 45, educated to A-level, who worked in a clerical position at the local council. Emma was aged 37, educated to A-level, and used to be an insurance underwriter. Dave was aged 21, educated to NVQ level 1 and was unemployed (previous job in a fish and chip shop). Karl and Diane were a couple in their mid-20s, both educated to degree level and working in professional jobs. All participants in this focus group mainly did their shopping at Sainsbury's.

36. Interview with Hannah Reed, UK Fairtrade Towns Coordinator, May 2011.

37. It should not be forgotten that fair-trade is only one of the consumer labels on the market, with Rainforest Alliance and Utz Certified offering alternative approaches to sustainable development, as well as numerous other projects (such as those led by the Speciality Coffee Association of Europe/America, and the 'Cup of Excellence') that are aimed at improving the prices that producers receive for their crop. All these initiatives are attempting to help farmers trade their way out of poverty – and yet these models have not received the government and institutional endorsement that the fair-trade model has.

## 5  The Practice of Fair-Trade Support

1. Bourdieu did hint at the importance of the internal differentiation of practices in *Distinction*, for example, his discussion of the meaning of sporting practices revealed how past experience, as well as the type of team, the place and the equipment used etc. were likely to differentiate the practice (Bourdieu, 1984: 211).

2. Reckwitz notes that, for some, this processual focus may seem too close to everyday discussions about agents and their behaviour. Instead, he argues that practice theory 'implies a considerable shift in our perspective on body,

mind, things, knowledge, discourse, structure/processes and the agent' (see Reckwitz, 2002: 250–7).

3. The majority of the 19 interviews were conducted in respondents' homes with the individuals/couples responsible for shopping decisions within their household. Of these interviews, 11 were conducted with fair-traders and eight with non-fair-traders, and they lasted between 45 and 90 minutes each. Fair-trade supporters were recruited from either the Chelmsford Fairtrade Town group or at one of the fair-trade events I attended during Fair-trade Fortnight 2008. Over half of the fair-trade supporters were nearing or past retirement age, and while every attempt was made to seek fair-traders outside this age limit (I spoke with a young couple in their thirties, two men in their thirties and two women in their forties), the make-up of the Chelmsford fair-trade group and related networks was heavily weighted towards the older age brackets. Having attended a number of fair-trade events in Chelmsford, I feel that the sample achieved reflects the nature of fair-trade support in Chelmsford, as well as general trends in civic participation (Department for Communities and Local Government, 2008; Putnam, 2000). The non-fair-trade supporters were more difficult to identify, but I met a number of non-fair-trade supporters through my focus group interviews (see Chapter 6) and used a snowball sampling method to identify others who were willing to participate in an interview.

4. Reader should note that all ages refer to ages of respondents at the time of interview in the period March–July 2008, and that all names have been changed to protect the anonymity of respondents.

5. Traidcraft is a fair-trade company in the UK, which relies on volunteers to sell fair-trade products on their behalf, often at church. See Chapter 3 for the role of Traidcraft in the development of fair-trade in the UK.

6. For example, Leon, a 34-year-old musician, understood his consumption of fair-trade as working to protect the environment in developing countries because if crops were not profitable for producers they may start damaging the environment through deforestation. And Oliver, a retired senior local government official, understood his consumption of fair-trade as a way of 'stabilising the world' and ensuring that producers and their families stay in their own countries rather than becoming refugees in other parts of the world.

7. Mouze states that 'Unlike modern scientists, yogis are not interested in the chemical content (protein, vitamins, etc.) of the food. Instead, food is traditionally classified according to its effect on the body and mind, using the three Gunas: *Sattva* (the quality of love, light and life), *Raja* (the quality of activity and passion, lacking stability) and *Tamas* (the quality of darkness and inertia, dragging us into ignorance and attachment)' (Mouze, 2009). He also states that vegetarianism is an important issue with a yogic diet. 'Not only are fish and meat specifically listed among the "food injurious to the yoga" by the Hatha Yoga Pradipika (I, 59), but eating the flesh of dead animals violates the first principle of yogic ethics (yamas) as laid down by Patanjali in the Yoga Sutras, that of non-violence (ahimsa). Yogis believe that the fear of death permeates every cell of the body of an animal when it is slaughtered, and therefore, the traditional yogic diet is lacto-vegetarian and avoids eggs as well as all animal flesh' (ibid.).

8. For example, on the evening of the interview, they admitted they had bought a pizza because this was quick and easy to prepare, meaning they had time to talk to me.
9. This provides an interesting contrast with the slave-grown sugar campaign, discussed in Chapter 2.

## 6   The Normalisation and Exclusivity of Fair-Trade Consumption

1. Bennett et al. (2009) suggest that omnivorousness – an openness to engage in a range of cultural activities – is the most dominant expression of cultural capital in Britain today. While there is a class pattern to consumption behaviour and cultural participation, 'many aspects of cultural life are shared by people who inhabit diverse social positions'. Importantly, the lower classes do not feel excluded from cultural activity; however they can sometimes feel aggrieved if they believe they are being looked down upon because of their non-participation (ibid.: 252).
2. These authors highlight the moral significance of work in these representations – with fair-trade farmers who are 'engaged in their work *and enjoying it*' (Adams & Raisborough, 2008: 1175), and the proximate white working class who are workshy, lazy, lacking in taste and denigrated by the use of terms such as 'chav' and 'pikey' (see Lawler, 2005; Nayak, 2006; McRobbie, 2004). In this way, they remind us of the persistence of an 'old bourgeois attitude' – 'the bourgeois has always been ready to acknowledge virtue in the servant class when it finds it: pliant, loyal, living patiently in the attic, carrying on dutifully a service' (Thompson, 1980: 46–7, cited in Adams & Raisborough, 2008: 1178).
3. Two of the non-fair-trade focus groups consisted of existing friendship networks (a group of men and women in their thirties, and a group of non-employed mothers) and two were composed of strangers (one group of five men and four women of varying ages and professions, and one group of Sainsbury's shoppers comprising four men and four women). The sampling of these focus groups was perhaps not ideal, but it should be remembered that 'there has been an over-emphasis on the degree of control researchers have over relevant characteristics of individuals in their groups and often the exact composition of the groups will reflect circumstance rather than planning' (Kitzinger & Barbour, 1999 cited in Bloor et al., 2001: 21). The fair-trade supporter focus groups were organised around the context of participants' interest in fair-trade – one group were members of the Chelmsford Star Co-op Society, one group were attached to the fair-trade group at the local university, one group were the dedicated members of CFAG, and one group were members of the CFAG but not heavily involved in the group's activities.
4. The selection of coffees and chocolates included at least one fair-trade option as well as an organic option in order to provide an alternative 'ethical' choice.
5. As we saw in Chapter 5, the fair-trade supporters stressed the non-exclusivity of fair-trade consumption in the individual interviews, and although not illustrated in Helen and Mark's narrative, the majority of non-fair-trade  supporters

understood the fair-trade consumer as an individual with distinctive socioeconomic, cultural and moral characteristics.

6.  Fran and Ling used to work in catering, Lindsey used to be a secretary, and Amanda used to be a sales assistant. Lindsey and Fran were 45 years old, Ling was 36 years old and Amanda was 33 years old. Amanda had no formal qualifications, while the rest were educated to NVQ or A Level.

7.  Dave was 21 years old, living with his parents, educated to NVQ level and currently unemployed (he used to work in a fish and chip shop); Emma was a 37-year-old insurance underwriter educated to A level; Nicole was a 42-year-old administrative assistant, educated to A level with five children; Karl was a 26-year-old IT professional educated to degree level; and Diana was a 25-year-old academic officer, educated to degree level with no children.

8.  All focus group participants were given a short questionnaire to fill out at the beginning of the session. Ethnic group was self-defined from the following options: White British; Any other White background; Mixed – White and Black Caribbean; Mixed – White and Black African; Mixed – White and Asian; Any other Mixed background; Asian or Asian British – Indian; Asian or Asian British – Pakistani; Asian or Asian British – Bangladeshi; Asian or Asian British – Any other Asian background; Black or Black British – Black Caribbean; Black or Black British – Black African; Black or Black British – Any other Black background; Chinese; Any other (please define). The majority of the respondents were White British unless otherwise stated.

9.  At the time of these interviews, legislation was proposed to increase the vehicle tax on 'gas-guzzling' 4x4s and sports cars as well as increasing the tax for other more 'regular' vehicles (Milmo, 2008), and discussions were also under way proposing the end of free plastic bags at supermarket checkouts and the introduction of a 5p charge (Sparrow, 2008).

10.  Hazel was a business analyst and Lisa was a part-time secretary. They were both educated to A-level and Lisa had a dependent child under five years.

11.  See note 4 above for details on the women in this exchange.

12.  Such as Cafe Revive in Marks and Spencer's, Starbucks, supermarket cafes, the local swimming centre cafe; several participants worked at Chelmsford Borough Council offices and had drunk Fairtrade coffee and tea at work.

13.  Jackie holds an administrative role and Keith was a member of the clergy. They are both educated to degree level and are in their fifties.

14.  Linda is a 66-year-old retired sales assistant; Kathy is a 46-year-old sales assistant; Sandra is a 61-year-old retired administrative clerk; Tim is a 35-year-old library assistant; and Peter is a 59-year-old retired supervisor at a car manufacturer. Peter and Tim hold degrees and the women are educated to NVQ or BTEC level.

15.  Matt is a 67-year-old part-time education consultant, who is educated to degree level and in involved with the Chelmsford Co-operative Society.

# 7  The Politics of Fair-Trade Consumption

1.  After 2008, the question was no longer included on the 'public attitudes to development' module.

2. These questions can be found in the Appendix.
3. Income is measured in the Omnibus using a single-income question, which bands income into discrete categories. Micklewright and Schnepf (2007) suggest that when using banded income categories in regression analysis it is common practice to convert the categorical variable into a continuous one by allocating individuals to the mid-point of their income groups, with individuals in the top unbounded interval being assigned to an estimate of the group mean using an external source. Therefore in the regression analysis, I used estimates from the Family Resources Survey to estimate the incomes of men and women in the unbounded category.
4. Income was taken out of the second model because it was insignificant and remained so, even when socio-economic status was not included in the regression.
5. Although, as indicated in more recent years of the Omnibus, charitable giving has decreased as fair-trade increased, so it may be that if we were to run this regression with more recent figures, we would find a significant change over time for charitable donations versus buying fair-trade.
6. Focus group with key community representatives conducted in April 2008. Lyn is a representative from the Women's Institute, Beth is a Green Party candidate, and Peter is a Labour and Co-op Party political advisor.
7. Sandra was a 61-year-old retired administrative clerk who was educated to BTEC level and is a Quaker. Milena is Mexican and was 31 years old; she was educated to degree level and is a full-time mum who used to work as an interpreter.
8. Lisa was 27 years old and a part-time secretary, with a dependent child; Jenny was 27 years old and an operations manager; Linda was 27 years old and a hairdressing salon manager; Paul was 32 years old and worked as an IT systems analyst; Karen was 33 years old and worked as a business modeller. Karen had a degree, Lisa, Jenny and Paul were educated to A-level and Linda had NVQ qualifications.
9. Kim was South African, aged 40, educated to degree level, employed as a social worker; Jesse was aged 64 with no formal educational qualifications, retired but used to be a deputy warden; Joe was 'Black or Black British – any other Black Background' (see note 7, Chapter 6), aged 39, educated to A-level, and worked full-time as a gas engineer, with three dependent children; Michael was aged 37, educated to NVQ level, and worked full-time as a carpenter, with two dependent children; Steven was aged 33, educated to degree level, and worked full-time as a local council officer.
10. Linda was 27 years old and a hairdressing salon manager. Hazel was aged 30 and worked as a business analyst.

# 8  Conclusion: The Ideology of the Citizen-Consumer

1. Both Fairtrade Fortnight and the Fairtrade Towns movement were pioneered in the UK, and from discussions with a number of fair-trade supporters throughout the international phase of this research there was a sense in which people look to the UK for ideas. The UK was described to the author

as 'the Mecca of Fairtrade', and campaigning ideas have been translated to other contexts – such as the different themes for Fairtrade Fortnight utilised in other countries (the 'Big Swap' in Fairtrade Fortnight in the UK in 2010 was then used as the theme in Australia later that year), and of course Fairtrade Towns.

2. Interview with Hannah Reed, Fairtrade Towns Coordinator at the FTF, May 2011.

# Bibliography

Adams, M. and Raisborough, J. (2008) 'What Can Sociology Say about FairTrade?', *Sociology*, Vol. 42(6): 1165–82.

Åkerlund, K. (2010) 'Det är människor som gör det av' (It's People Who Do It), http://www.skr.org/download/18.3eea013f128a65019c280008294/Det+%C3%A4r+m%C3%A4nniskor+som+g%C3%B6r+det+%28Karin+%C3%85kerlund%29.pdf, accessed on 15 November 2011.

Andersen, J. and Tobiasen, M. (2006) 'Who are these Political Consumers Anyway?', in M. Micheletti, A. Follesdal and D. Stolle (eds) *Politics, Products and Markets*, pp. 203–22. New Brunswick and London: Transaction Publishers.

Anderson, M. (2009) 'Fair Trade and the British co-operative movement', in L. Black and N. Robertson (eds) *Consumerism and the Co-operative movement in modern British history*, pp. 240–59. Manchester: Manchester University Press.

Atley, L. (1978) 'From Social Conscience to Social Action', *Social Service Review*: Vol. 52(3): 362–82.

Barnett, C., Cafaro, P. and Newholm, T. (2005) 'Philosophy and Ethical Consumption', in R. Harrison, T. Newholm and D. Shaw (eds) *The Ethical Consumer*, pp. 11–24. London: Sage.

Barnett, C., Cloke, P., Clarke, N. and Malpass, A. (2005) 'Consuming Ethics: Articulating the Subjects and Spaces of Ethical Consumption', *Antipode*, Vol. 37(1): 23–45.

Barnett, C., Cloke, P., Clarke, N. and Malpass, A. (2007) 'The Subjects and Spaces of Ethical Consumption', http://www.open.ac.uk/socialsciences/_assets/5gsrrxm9zyaajpugzg.pdf, accessed on 16 June 2009.

Barnett, C., Cloke, P., Clarke, N. and Malpass, A. (2011) *Globalizing Responsibility*, Oxford: Wiley-Blackwell.

Barrientos, S. and Dolan, C. (eds) (2006) *Ethical Sourcing in the Global Food System*, London: Earthscan.

Barrientos, S., Conroy, M. and Jones, E. (2007) 'Northern Social Movements and Fair Trade', in L. Raynolds, D. Murray and J. Wilkinson (eds) *Fair Trade: The Challenges of Transforming Globalization*, pp. 51–62. London and New York: Routledge.

Basu, A. and Hicks, R. (2008) 'Label Performance and the Willingness to Pay for Fair Trade Coffee', *International Journal of Consumer Studies*, Vol. 32(5): 470–8.

Bauman, Z. (1998) *Work, Consumerism and the New Poor*, Buckingham: Open University Press.

Beck, U. (1992) *Risk Society*, London: Sage.

Beck, U. (1994) 'The Reinvention of Politics: Towards a Theory of Reflexive Modernization', in U. Beck, A. Giddens and S. Lash (eds) *Reflexive Modernization*, pp. 1–55. Cambridge: Polity.

Becker, H. (1963) *Outsiders: Studies in the sociology of deviance*, New York: The Free Press.

Bennett, T., Savage, M., Silva, E., Warde, A., Gayo-Cal, M. and Wright, D. (2009) *Culture, Class, Distinction*, London and New York: Routledge.

Bennett, W. L. (2004) 'Branded Political Communication', in M. Micheletti, A. Follesdal and D. Stolle (eds) *Politics, Products and Markets*, pp. 101–26. New Brunswick and London: Transaction Publishers.

Berkeley City (2011) 'Community Profile Data Budget Book FY 2012–2013', http://www.ci.berkeley.ca.us/uploadedFiles/City_Manager/Level_3_-_General/2011%20Community%20Profile%20FINAL.pdf, accessed on 29 October 2011.

Birchall, J. (1997) *The International Co-operative Movement*, Manchester: Manchester University Press.

Björner, M. (2006) 'Country Case Study, Sweden', in L. Shaw (ed.) *Co-operation, Social Responsibility and Fair Trade in Europe*, pp. 47–66. Oldham: Co-operative College.

Black, C. (1887) 'Caveat Emptor', *Longman's Magazine*, Vol. 10(58): 409–20.

Black, L. (2004) 'Which?craft in Post-War Britain', *Albion*, Vol. 36(1): 52–82.

Bloor, M., Frankland, J., Thomas, M. and Robson, K. (2001) *Focus Groups in Social Research*, London: Sage.

Boström, M. and Klintman, M. (2006) 'State-centered Versus Nonstate-driven Organic Food Standardization', *Agriculture and Human Values*, Vol. 23(2): 163–80.

Bourdieu, P. (1984) *Distinction*, New York and London: Routledge.

Bourdieu, P. (1990) *The Logic of Practice*, Cambridge: Polity.

Bowes, J. (2011a) 'A Brilliant Idea', in J. Bowes (ed.) *The Fair Trade Revolution*, pp. 1–18. London: Pluto Press.

Bowes, J. (2011b) 'Honesty, Openness and Social Responsibility', in J. Bowes (ed.) *The Fair Trade Revolution*, pp. 125–39. London: Pluto Press.

Breckman, W. G. (1991) 'Disciplining Consumption', *Journal of Social History*, Vol. 24(3): 485–505.

CAF (Charities Aid Foundation) (2010) *The World Giving Index 2010*, http://www.cafonline.org/pdf/WorldGivingIndex28092010Print.pdf, accessed on 2 December 2011.

Callon, M. (ed.) (1998) *The Laws of the Markets*, Oxford: Blackwell.

Callon, M., Méadel, C. and Rabeharisoa, V. (2002) 'The Economy of Qualities', *Economy and Society*, Vol. 31(2): 194–217.

Carter, A. (2001) *The Political Theory of Global Citizenship*, London and New York: Routledge.

Chan, T. K. and Goldthorpe, J. (2007) 'Social Stratification and Cultural Consumption', *European Sociological Review*, Vol. 23(1): 1–19.

Chatriot, A., Chessel, M. and Hilton, M. (2006) 'Introduction', in A. Chatriot, M. Chessel and M. Hilton (eds) *The Expert Consumer*, pp. 1–18. Farnham: Ashgate.

Chessel, M. (2006a) 'Women and the Ethics of Consumption in France at the Turn of the Twentieth Century', in F. Trentmann (ed.) *The Making of the Consumer*, pp. 81–98. Oxford: Berg.

Chessel, M. (2006b) 'Consumers' Leagues in France: A Transatlantic Perspective', in A. Chatriot, M. Chessel and M. Hilton (eds) *The Expert Consumer*, pp. 53–70. Farnham: Ashgate.

Clarke, N., Barnett, C., Cloke, P. and Malpass, A. (2007a) 'Globalising the Consumer', *Political Geography*, Vol. 26(3): 231–49.

Clarke, N., Barnett, C., Cloke, P. and Malpass, A. (2007b) 'The Political Rationalities of Fair-Trade Consumption in the United Kingdom', *Politics & Society*, Vol. 35(4): 583–607.

Clarke, J., Hall, S., Jefferson, T. and Roberts, B. (1975) 'Subcultures, Cultures and Class', in K. Gelder and S. Thornton (eds) (1997) *The Subcultures Reader*, pp. 100–11. London and New York: Routledge.

Clarke, J., Newman, J., Smith, N., Vidler, E. and Westmarland, L. (2007) *Creating Citizen-Consumers*, London: Sage.

Cochoy, F. (2007) 'A Sociology of Market Things', in M. Callon, Y. Millo and F. Muniesa (eds) *Market Devices*, pp. 109–29. Oxford: Blackwell.

Coffin, J. (1991) 'Social Science Meets Sweated Labour', *The Journal of Modern History*, Vol. 63(2): 230–70.

Cohen, L. (2003) *A Consumers' Republic*, New York: Alfred A. Knopf.

Coleman, J. S. (1988) 'Social Capital in the Creation of Human Capital', *The American Journal of Sociology*, Vol. 94(Supplement): S95–S120.

Co-operative Bank (2007) *The Ethical Consumerism Report 2007*, Manchester: ECRA/Co-op.

Cowe, R. and Williams, S. (2001) *Who are the Ethical Consumers?* Manchester: Cooperative Bank.

Dankers, C. (2003) *Environmental and Social Standards, Certification and Labelling for Cash Crops*, Rome: FAO Publication.

David, C. and Kim, H. A. (2010) 'Developing Markets, Building Networks: Promoting Fair Trade in Asia', in K. Macdonald and S. Marshall (eds) *Fair Trade, Corporate Accountability and Beyond*, pp. 57–74. Farnham: Ashgate.

Davies, K. (2001) 'A moral purchase: femininity, commerce and abolition' in E. Eger, C. Grant, C. Gallchoir and P. Warburton (eds) *Women, writing and the public sphere*, pp. 133–59. Cambridge: Cambridge University Press.

Department for Communities and Local Government (2008) 'Cohesion Research Statistical Release 5', http://www.communities.gov.uk/documents/statistics/pdf/994541.pdf, accessed on 3 May 2009.

DFID (2005) *Trade Matters*, http://www.dfid.gov.uk/tradematters/tradematters.pdf, accessed on 19 March 2009.

De Pelsmacker, P., Driesen, L. and Rayp, G. (2005) 'Do Consumers Care about Ethics? Willingness to Pay for Fair-Trade Coffee', *Journal of Consumer Affairs*, Vol. 39(2): 363–85.

De Pelsmacker, P., Janssens, W., Mielants, C. and Streckx, E. (2007) 'Marketing Ethical Products', in E. Zaccaï (ed.) *Sustainable Consumption, Ecology and Fair Trade*, pp. 109–26. London: Routledge.

Dickinson, R. and Carsky, M. (2005) 'The Consumer as Economic Voter', in R. Harrison, T. Newholm and D. Shaw (eds) *The Ethical Consumer*, pp. 25–36. London: Sage.

Dickson, M. (2005) 'Identifying and Profiling Apparel Label Users', in R. Harrison, T. Newholm and D. Shaw (eds) *The Ethical Consumer*, pp. 155–72. London: Sage.

Dolan, C. (2008) 'Arbitrating Risk through Moral Values: The Case of Kenyan Fairtrade', in G. De Neve, P. Luetchford, J. Pratt and D. C. Wood (eds) *Hidden Hands in the Market*. pp. 271–96. Bradford: Emerald Group Publishing.

Doran, C. (2009) 'The Role of Personal Values in Fair Trade Consumption', *Journal of Business Ethics*, Vol. 84(4): 549–63.

Douglas, M. and Isherwood, B. (1979) *The World of Goods*, New York: Basic Books.

Esping-Andersen, G. (1990) *The Three Worlds of Welfare Capitalism*, Cambridge: Polity.

European Commission (1997) *The Common Agricultural Policy: Attitudes of EU Consumers to FairTrade Bananas*, Brussels: Directorate-General for Agriculture, http://ec.europa.eu/public_opinion/archives/ebs/ebs_116_en.pdf, accessed on 30 January 2009.

Fagan, A. (2006) 'Buying Right', in J. Dine and A. Fagan (eds) *Human Rights and Capitalism*, pp. 115–41. Cheltenham: Edward Elgar.

Fairbairn, B. (1994) 'The Meaning of Rochdale', *Occasional Paper Series: University of Saskatchewan*, http://ageconsearch.umn.edu/bitstream/31778/1/re94fa01.pdf, accessed 9th June 2006.

Fairtrade Advocacy Office (2009) *A Charter of Fair Trade Principles*, http://www.fairtrade-advocacy.org/images/charterfairtradeprinciples.pdf, accessed on 14 October 2011.

Fair Trade Federation (2011) 'About us', http://www.fairtradefederation.org/ht/d/sp/i/177/pid/177, accessed on 14 October 2011.

Fairtrade Foundation (2002) *Fairtrade Towns Initiative*, London: The Fairtrade Foundation.

Fairtrade Foundation (2008a) 'Fairtrade Fortnight 2008 Review', http://www.fairtrade.org.uk/includes/documents/cm_docs/2008/f/ft_review_08_prf7.pdf, accessed on 20 March 2009.

Fairtrade Foundation (2008b) 'General Action Guide', http://www.fairtrade.org.uk/includes/documents/cm_docs/2008/f/fortnight2008_action_guide.pdf, accessed on 20 March 2009.

Fairtrade Foundation (2008c) 'Response to Adam Smith Institute Report', http://www.fairtrade.org.uk/press_office/press_releases_and_statements/feb_2008/response_to_adam_smith_insititute_report.aspx, accessed on 25 June 2009.

Fairtrade Foundation (2009a) 'Cadbury Dairy Milk Commits to Going Fairtrade', http://www.fairtrade.org.uk/press_office/press_releases_and_statements/march_2009/cadbury_dairy_milk_commits_to_going_fairtrade.aspx, accessed on 7 December 2011.

Fairtrade Foundation (2009b) 'Frequently Asked Questions', http://www.fairtrade.org.uk/what_is_fairtrade/faqs.aspx, accessed on 14 September 2009.

Fairtrade Foundation (2009c) 'Sales of Fairtrade Certified Products in the UK', http://www.fairtrade.org.uk/what_is_fairtrade/facts_and_figures.aspx, accessed on 14 September 2009.

Fairtrade Foundation (2010a) 'Annual Report and Financial Statements for the Year Ended 31 December 2009', http://www.fairtrade.org.uk/includes/documents/cm_docs/2010/a/annual_report_and_financial_statements_2009.pdf, accessed on 14 October 2011.

Fairtrade Foundation (2010b) 'Fairtrade is Unique', http://www.fairtrade.org.uk/what_is_fairtrade/fairtrade_is_unique.aspx, accessed on 20 January 2011.

Fairtrade Foundation (2011a) 'Global Survey Shows UK Leads the Way on Fairtrade', http://www.fairtrade.org.uk/press_office/press_releases_and_statements/october/global_survey_shows_uk_leads_the_way_on_fairtrade.aspx, accessed on 9 December 2011.

Fairtrade Foundation (2011b) 'Annual Review 2010/2011', http://fairtrade.clikpages.co.uk/annualreview2011/, accessed on 28 October 2011.

Fairtrade Labelling Organisation (2010) 'Annual Report 2009–10', http://www.fairtrade.net/fileadmin/user_upload/content/2009/resources/FLO_Annual-Report-2009_komplett_double_web.pdf, accessed on 14 October 2011.

Fairtrade Labelling Organisation (2011a) 'Annual Reports', http://www.fairtrade. net/annual_reports.html, accessed on 6 December 2011.

Fairtrade Labelling Organisation (2011b) 'Fairtrade Labelling Initiatives', http:// www.fairtrade.net/labelling_initiatives1.0.html, accessed on 14 October 2011.

Fairtrade Labelling Organisation (2011c) 'Q&A on Fairtrade International and Fair Trade USA', http://www.fairtrade.net/897.0.html, accessed on 14 October 2011.

Fair Trade USA (2009a) 'Transfair USA Annual Report 2009', http://fairtradeusa. org/sites/default/files/ANNUAL%20REPORT%202009.pdf, accessed on 14 October 2011.

Fair Trade USA (2009b) 'Transfair USA Celebrates Fair Trade Month in October with 31 Days, 31 Ways', http://fairtradeusa.org/press-room/press_release/ transfair-usa-celebrates-fair-trade-month-october-31-days-31-ways, accessed on 25 November 2011.

Fair Trade USA (2009c) 'Fairtrade Flows against Economic Tide', http:// fairtradeusa.org/press-room/press_release/fairtrade-flows-against-economic-tide, accessed on 25 November 2011.

Fair Trade USA (2010) 'Fair Trade Up, Charitable Giving Down', http://fairtradeusa. org/press-room/press_release/fair-trade-charitable-giving-down, accessed on 1 December 2011.

Fair Trade USA (2011a) 'Fair Trade USA Names Green Mountain Coffee Roasters, Inc. World's Largest Purchaser of Fair Trade Certified Coffee', http:// fairtradeusa.org/press-room/press_release/fair-trade-usa-names-green-mountain-coffee-roasters-inc-world-s-largest-pur, accessed on 14 October 2011.

Fair Trade USA (2011b) 'Fair Trade for All', http://fairtradeforall.com/, accessed on 1 December 2011.

Follesdal, A. (2006) 'Political Consumerism as Chance and Challenge', in M. Micheletti, A. Follesdal and D. Stolle (eds) *Politics, Products and Markets*, pp. 3–20. New Brunswick and London: Transaction Publishers.

Föreningen för Fairtrade Sverige (2007) 'Rättvisemärkt – de tio första åren' (Fairtrade – First Ten Years), http://www.fairtrade.se/obj/docpart/a/a8a4f055 5b4f5c6d6ddeba4ec51cdc2e.pdf, accessed on 14 October 2011.

Föreningen för Fairtrade Sverige (2010a) 'Verksamhetsberättelse (Annual Report) 2010', http://www.fairtrade.se/obj/docpart/4/49f4ff14cf79ceb5f8651f5c9d 366a7c.pdf, accessed on 14 October 2011.

Föreningen för Fairtrade Sverige (2010b) 'Fairtrade-rapporten 2010: Sverige kan göra mer', (Sweden Can Do More), http://www.fairtrade.se/cldoc/pressmeddelanden/ 1016.htm, accessed on 14 October 2011.

Föreningen för Fairtrade Sverige (2010c) 'Aktivitetsguiden 2010' (Activity Guide, 2010), http://www.fairtrade.se/obj/docpart/1/1dfb870ea9b01435a3402cefd 0519878.pdf, accessed on 25 November 2011.

Föreningen för Fairtrade Sverige (2010d) 'Fairtrade Fokus 2010', http://www. fairtrade.se/obj/docpart/9/972eac79ee32ee22d374848bb5f6f064.pdf, accessed on 25 November 2011.

Föreningen för Fairtrade Sverige (2011) 'Ambassadörs-handbok', http:// www.fairtrade.se/obj/docpart/3/3919c66b71b3eb35f7d5ddfd93ae9665.pdf, accessed on 14 October 2011.

Finch, H. and Lewis, J. (2003) 'Focus Groups', in J. Ritchie and J. Lewis (eds) *Qualitative Research Practice*, pp. 170–98. London: Sage.

Fridell, G. (2006) 'Fairtrade and the International Moral Economy', in T. Shallcross and J. Robinson (eds) *Global Citizenship and Environmental Justice*, pp. 81–94. Atlanta: Rodopi.

Furlough, E. and Strikwerda, C. (1999) 'Economics, Consumer Culture, and Gender', in E. Furlough and C. Strikwerda (eds) *Consumers against Capitalism?*, pp. 1–66. Oxford: Rowman & Littlefield Publishers.

Gabriel, Y. and Lang, T. (2006) *The Unmanageable Consumer*, London: Sage.

Gertten, F. (2011) 'Move Forward', Paper presented at 5th International Fair Trade Towns Conference, Malmö, 19 November.

Giddens, A. (1984) *The Constitution of Society*, Cambridge: Polity.

Giddens, A. (1990) *The Consequences of Modernity*, Cambridge: Polity.

Giddens, A. (1991) *Modernity and Self-Identity*, Cambridge: Polity.

Giddens, A. (1994) 'Living in a Post-Traditional Society', in U. Beck, A. Giddens and S. Lash (eds) *Reflexive Modernization*, pp. 56–109. Cambridge: Polity.

Glickman, L. (2004) 'Buy for the Sake of the Slave', *American Quarterly*, Vol. 56(4): 889–912.

Glickman, L. (2006) 'Through the Medium of Their Pockets', in A. Chatriot, M. Chessel and M. Hilton (eds) *The Expert Consumer*, pp. 21–36. Farnham: Ashgate.

Global Exchange (2008) 'Top Reasons to Oppose the WTO', http://www.globalexchange.org/campaigns/wto/OpposeWTO.html, accessed on 9 March 2009.

Globescan (2009) *Fairtrade Labelling Organizations International Label Perceptions Survey Findings Report US*, Project: 2284, Toronto: GlobeScan.

Goodman, M. K. (2004) 'Reading Fairtrade: Political Ecological Imaginary and the Moral Economy of Fair Trade Goods', *Political Geography*, Vol. 23(7): 891–915.

Gronow, J. and Warde, A. (2001) (eds) *Ordinary Consumption*, London: Routledge.

Gurney, P. (1996) *Co-operative Culture and the Politics of Consumption in England, 1870–1930*, Manchester: Manchester University Press.

Gurney, P. (1999) 'Labor's Great Arch: Cooperation and Cultural Revolution in Britain, 1795–1926', in E. Furlough and C. Strikwerda (eds) *Consumers against Capitalism?* pp. 135–72. Oxford: Rowman & Littlefield Publishers.

Halkier, B. (2010) *Consumption Challenged*, Farnham: Ashgate.

Hall, S. (1980) 'Encoding/Decoding', in Centre for Contemporary Cultural Studies (ed.) *Culture, Media, Language*, pp. 128–38. London: Hutchinson.

Harvey, M. (2007) 'Instituting Economic Processes in Society', in M. Harvey, R. Ramlogan and S. Randles (eds) *Karl Polanyi*, pp. 163–84. Manchester: Manchester University Press.

Heater, D. (1999) *What is Citizenship?*, Cambridge: Polity.

Hebdige, D. (1979) *Subculture: The Meaning of Style*, London: Methuen.

Heckman, S. (1995) *Moral Voices, Moral Selves*, Cambridge: Polity.

Hilton, M. (2003) *Consumerism in 20th-Century Britain*, Cambridge: Cambridge University Press.

Hochschild, A. (2005) *Bury the Chains*, London: MacMillan.

Högberg, B. (2011) 'Rättvis handel – en tillbakablick' (Fairtrade – Looking Back), http://www.rattvishandel.net/fairtrade/historia.aspx, accessed on 14 October 2011.

Horowitz, D. (1985) *The Morality of Spending*, Baltimore: Johns Hopkins University Press.

Horowitz, D. (2004) *The Anxieties of Affluence*, Amherst and Boston: University of Massachusetts Press.

International Fairtrade Towns Conference (2011) 'Beyond 1000 Fair Trade Towns', Malmö, 19–20 November.

International Fairtrade Towns Network (2011a) 'What is a Fair Trade Town?', http://www.fairtradetowns.org/about/what-is-a-fairtrade-town/, accessed on 25 November 2011.

International Fairtrade Towns Network (2011b) 'International Fairtrade Towns List', http://www.fairtradetowns.org/about/, accessed on 15 October 2011.

Jackson, P. and Thrift, N. (1995) 'Geographies of Consumption', in D. Miller (ed.) *Acknowledging Consumption*, pp. 203–36. London: Routledge.

Jackson, T. (2005) *Motivating Sustainable Consumption*, http://www.sd-research.org.uk/wp-content/uploads/motivatingscfinal_000.pdf, accessed on 2 December 2011.

Jaffee, D. (2007) *Brewing Justice*, Berkeley: University of California Press.

Jaffee, D., Kloppenburg, J. and Monroy, M. (2007) 'Bringing the "Moral Charge" Home', *Rural Sociology*, Vol. 69(2): 169–96.

Janowitz, M. (1994) 'Observations on the Sociology of Citizenship', in B. S. Turner and P. Hamilton (eds) *Citizenship, Critical Concepts: Volume 1*, London and New York: Routledge.

Jensen, N. (2006) *Nation States and the Multinational Corporation*, Princeton: Princeton University Press.

Kjærnes, U., Harvey, M. and Warde, A. (2007) *Trust in Food*, Basingstoke: Palgrave Macmillan.

Klein, N. (2000) *No Logo*, London: Harper Perennial.

Krier, J. (2007) *Fair Trade 2007*, http://www.fairtrade-advocacy.org/documents/FairTrade2007_newfactsandfigures.pdf, accessed on 19 November 2009.

Lamb, H. (2007) 'The Fairtrade Consumer', in S. Wright and D. McCrea (eds) *The Handbook of Organic and Fair Trade Food Marketing*, pp. 54–81. Oxford: Blackwell.

Lamb, H. (2008) *Fighting the Banana Wars and Other Fairtrade Battles*, London: Rider.

Lamont, M. (1992) *Money, Morals and Manners*, Chicago: University of Chicago Press.

Lawler, S. (2005) 'Disgusted Subjects', *The Sociological Review*, Vol. 3(3): 429–46.

Lindsey, B. (2003) 'Grounds for Complaint', CATO Institute, Trade Briefing Paper 16, http://www.cato.org/pubs/tbp/tbp-016.pdf, accessed on 25 November 2011.

Littler, J. (2009) *Radical Consumption*, Buckingham: Open University Press.

Littler, J. (2011) 'What's Wrong with Ethical Consumption', in T. Lewis and E. Potter (eds) *Ethical Consumption*, London: Routledge.

Littrell, M. and Dickson, M. (1999) *Social Responsibility in the Global Market*, London: Sage.

Littler, J., Barnett, C. and Soper, K. (2005) 'Consumers – Agents of Change?' *Soundings*, Vol. 31: 147–60.

LO (2011) 'Rättvisemärkt för schysta arbetsvillkor' (Fairtrade for decent working conditions) http://www.lo.se/home/lo/home.nsf/unidView/9D57EA95DC49817DC125764A00443F09, accessed on 14 October 2011.

Low, W. and Davenport, E. (2006) 'Mainstreaming fair trade: adoption, assimilation, appropriation', in *Journal of Strategic Marketing*, Vol. 14: 315–27.

Low, W. and Davenport, E. (2007) 'To Boldly Go … Exploring Ethical Spaces to Re-politicise Ethical Consumption and Fair Trade', *Journal of Consumer Behaviour*, Vol. 6(5): 336–48.

Lunds Kommun (2011a) 'Facts about Lund', http://web.lund.se/templates/Page_21315.aspx, accessed on 17 October 2011.

Lunds Kommun (2011b) 'Statistik', http://www.lund.se/Politik–forvaltning/Kommunfakta/Statistik, accessed on 17 October 2011.

Lunds Kommun (2011c) 'Lund i siffror' (Lund in Figures), http://www.lund.se/Global/F%C3%B6rvaltningar/Kommunkontoret/Utvecklingsavd/Statistik%20om%20Lund/Lund%20i%20siffror/1102%20Lund%20i%20Siffror.pdf, accessed on 17 October 2011.

Lyon, S. (2006) 'Evaluating Fair Trade Consumption', in *International Journal of Consumer Studies*, Vol. 30(5): 452–64.

Lyon, S. and Moberg, M. (eds) (2010) *Fair Trade and Social Justice*, New York and London: New York University Press.

MacIntyre, A. (2007) *After Virtue*, London: Duckworth Publishers.

Malpass, A., Cloke, P., Barnett, C. and Clarke, N. (2007a) 'Fairtrade Urbanism?', *International Journal of Urban and Regional Research*, Vol. 31(3): 633–45.

Malpass, A., Barnett, C., Clarke, N. and Cloke, P. (2007b) 'Problematizing Choice', in M. Bevir and F. Trentmann (eds) *Governance, Consumers and Citizens*, pp. 231–56. Basingstoke: Palgrave Macmillan.

Maniates, M. (2002) 'Individualization: Plant a Tree, Buy a Bike, Save the World?', in T. Princen, M. Maniates and K. Conca (eds) *Confronting Consumption*, pp. 43–66. Cambridge, MA: MIT Press.

Marshall, T. H. (1950) *Citizenship and Social Class*, Cambridge: Cambridge University Press.

McCracken, G. (1988) *Culture and Consumption*, Bloomington: Indiana University Press.

McRobbie, A. (2004) 'Notes on "What Not To Wear" and Post-Feminist Symbolic Violence', *The Sociological Review*, Vol. 52(2): 99–109.

Micheletti, M. (2003) *Political Virtue and Shopping*, New York and Basingstoke: Palgrave Macmillan.

Micheletti, M. (2010) *Political Virtue and Shopping: Second Edition*, New York and Basingstoke: Palgrave Macmillan.

Micklewright, J. and Schnepf, S. (2007) 'How Reliable are Income Data Collected with a Single Question?', Southampton Statistical Sciences Research Institute, Applications & Policy Working Paper A07/08, http://eprints.soton.ac.uk/49499/01/s3ri-workingpaper-a07-08.pdf, accessed on 14 September 2009.

Micklewright, J. and Schnepf, S. (2009) 'Who Gives Charitable Donations for Overseas Development?', *Journal of Social Policy*, Vol. 38(2): 317–41.

Midgley, C. (1992) *Women against Slavery*, London and New York: Routledge.

Miller, D. (1987) *Material Culture and Mass Consumption*, Oxford: Basil Blackwell.

Miller, D. (1995) 'Consumption as the Vanguard of History', in D. Miller (ed.) *Acknowledging Consumption*, pp. 1–52. London: Routledge.

Miller, D. (1998) *A Theory of Shopping*, Cambridge: Polity.

Miller, D. (2001) 'The Poverty of Morality', *Journal of Consumer Culture*, Vol. 1(2): 225–43.

Miller, N. and Rose, N. (1997) 'Mobilising the Consumer', *Theory, Culture and Society*, Vol. 14(1): 1–36.

Milmo, D. (2008) 'Gas-guzzlers Hit with High Taxes', 12 March, http://www.guardian.co.uk/business/2008/mar/12/budget.4x4s.greencars.exciseduty, accessed on 30 January 2009.

Moberg, M. and Lyon, S. (2010) 'What's Fair? The Paradox of Seeking Justice through Markets', in S. Lyon and M. Moberg (eds) *Fair Trade and Social Justice*, pp. 1–24. New York and London: New York University Press.

Mouze, C. (2009) 'Yogic Eating', http://www.yoga-magazine.net/diet.htm, accessed on 1 November 2009.

Muniesa, F., Millo, Y. and Callon, M. (2007) 'An Introduction to Market Devices', in M. Callon, Y. Millo and F. Muniesa (eds) *Market Devices*, pp. 1–12. Oxford: Blackwell.

Murray, D. and Raynolds, L. (2007) 'Globalization and its Antinomies', in L. Raynolds, D. Murray and J. Wilkinson (eds) *Fair Trade: The Challenges of Transforming Globalization*, pp. 3–14. London and New York: Routledge.

Murrmann, M. and Weir, L. (2002) 'Coffee Measure Tests Berkeley's Taste for Fair Trade', http://journalism.berkeley.edu/projects/election2002/stories/000111.html, accessed on 29 October 2011.

Nayak, A. (2006) 'Displaced Masculinities', *Sociology*, Vol. 40(5): 813–31.

Needham, C. (2007) *The Reform of Public Services under New Labour*, Basingstoke: Palgrave MacMillan.

Newholm, T. (2005) 'Case Studying Ethical Consumers' Projects and Strategies', in R. Harrison, T. Newholm and D. Shaw (eds) *The Ethical Consumer*, pp. 107–24. London: Sage.

Nicholls, A. and Opal, C. (2005) *Fair Trade: Market-driven Ethical Consumption*, London: Sage.

Nixon, S. (1996) *Hard Looks*, London: University College London Press.

Nixon, S. (2003) *Advertising Cultures*, London: Sage.

Nixon, S. (2008) Review of 'The Expert Consumer, Associations and Professionals in Consumer Society', *Contemporary British History*, Vol. 22(2): 289–90.

Nomis (2009) 'Labour Market Profile Chelmsford', https://www.nomisweb.co.uk/reports/lmp/la/2038431770/report.aspx?town=chelmsford, accessed on 14 September 2009.

O'Neill, B. (2008) 'Roasting the Masses', 27 August, http://www.guardian.co.uk/commentisfree/2008/aug/27/oliver.foodanddrink, accessed on 9 August 2009.

Office for National Statistics (2002) Social Survey Division, *ONS Omnibus Survey, July 2002* (computer file). Colchester, Essex: UK Data Archive (distributor), September 2003. SN: 4716.

Office for National Statistics (2003) Social Survey Division, *ONS Omnibus Survey, July 2003* (computer file). Colchester, Essex: UK Data Archive (distributor), August 2005. SN: 5154.

Office for National Statistics (2004) Social Survey Division, *ONS Omnibus Survey,* *July 2004* (computer file). Colchester, Essex: UK Data Archive (distributor), January 2007. SN: 5573.

Office for National Statistics (2005) Social Survey Division, *ONS Omnibus Survey,* *August 2005* (computer file). *2nd Edition.* Colchester, Essex: UK Data Archive (distributor), September 2007. SN: 5665.

Organic Consumers Association (2010) 'Tell TransFair that Fair Trade is a Movement, not a Brand', http://organicconsumers.org/transfairusa/, accessed on 14 October 2011.

Otero, A. (2007) 'À la recherche d'un commerce équitable Sud–Sud: quelles opportunités?' (Looking at South–South Fair trade – What Opportunities?), Paper presented to the 2007 World Social Forum, Nairobi, Kenya, January, http://fairtrade.socioeco.org/en/documents.php#list_docs_id_doc_7611, accessed on 14 October 2011.

Peterson, R. and Kern, R. (1996) 'Changing Highbrow Taste: From Snob to Omnivore', *American Sociological Review,* Vol. 61(5): 900–7.

Pirotte, G. (2007) 'Consumption as a Solidarity-based Commitment', in E. Zaccaï (ed.) *Sustainable Consumption, Ecology and Fair Trade,* pp. 127–43. London: Routledge.

Portes, A. (1998) 'Social Capital', *Annual Review of Sociology,* Vol. 24(1): 1–24.

Putnam, R. (2000) *Bowling Alone,* New York and London: Simon & Schuster.

Rainforest Alliance (2011a) 'Alleviating Poverty', http://www.rainforest-alliance. org/about/poverty, accessed on 14 October 2011.

Raynolds, L. (2002) 'Consumer/Producer Links in Fair Trade Coffee Networks', *Sociologia Ruralis,* Vol. 42(4): 404–24.

Raynolds, L. and Long, M. (2007) 'Fair/Alternative Trade: Historical and Empirical dimensions', in L. Raynolds, D. Murray and J. Wilksonson (eds) *Fair Trade: The Challenges of Transforming Globalization,* pp. 15–32. London and New York: Routledge.

Raynolds, L., Murray, D. and Wilkinson, J. (eds) (2007) *Fair Trade: The Challenges of Transforming Globalization,* London and New York: Routledge.

Reckwitz, A. (2002) 'Toward a Theory of Social Practices', *European Journal of Social Theory,* Vol. 5(2): 243–63.

Renard, M. and Pérez-Grovas, V. (2007) 'Fair Trade Coffee in Mexico: At the Center of the Debates', in L. Raynolds, D. Murray and J. Wilksonson (eds) *Fair Trade: The Challenges of Transforming Globalization,* pp. 138–56. London and New York: Routledge.

Rosenthal, J. (2011) 'The Greatest Challenge', in J. Bowes (ed.) *The Fair Trade Revolution,* pp. 157–72. London: Pluto Press.

Sainsbury's (2009) 'Corporate Responsibility: Sourcing with Integrity', http://www. j-sainsbury.co.uk/cr/index.asp?pageid=36, accessed on 19 November 2009.

Salamon, L. and Anheier, H. (1996) 'Social Origins of Civil Society', Working paper from *The Johns Hopkins University Institute for Policy Studies,* http://www. ccss.jhu.edu/pdfs/Publications/origins.pdf, accessed on 14 October 2011.

Sassatelli, R. (2006) 'Virtue, Responsibility and Consumer Choice', in J. Brewer and F. Trentmann (eds) *Consuming Cultures, Global Perspectives,* pp. 219–50. Oxford: Berg.

Sassatelli, R. (2007) *Consumer Culture,* London: Sage.

Savage, M., Bagnall, G. and Longhurst, B. (2001) 'Ordinary, Ambivalent and Defensive: Class Identities in the Northwest of England', *Sociology*, Vol. 35(4): 875–92.

Sayer, A. (2005a) *The Moral Significance of Class*, Cambridge: Cambridge University Press.

Sayer, A. (2005b) 'Class, Moral Worth and Recognition', *Sociology*, Vol. 39(5): 947–63.

Scammell, M. (2000) 'The Internet and Civic Engagement', *Political Communication*, Vol. 17(4): 351–5.

Scammell, M. (2003) 'Citizen Consumers: Towards a New Marketing of Politics?', in J. Corner and D. Pels (eds) *Media and the Restyling of Politics*, pp. 117–36. London: Sage.

Schatzki, T. (1996) *Social Practices*, Cambridge: Cambridge University Press.

Schatzki, T. (2001) 'Introduction: Practice Theory', in T. Schatzki, K. Cetina and E. von Savigny (eds) *The Practice Turn in Contemporary Theory*, pp. 1–14. London: Routledge.

Schatzki, T. (2002) *The Site of the Social*. Pennsylvania: Pennsylvania State University Press.

Scott-Jabobsson, L. (2007) 'En rättvisare stad' (A Fairer City), http://web.lund.se/upload/Kommunkontoret/milj%C3%B6strategiska/Fairtrade/Fairtrade%20City%20rapport,%20LS-J%20sep%202007.pdf, accessed on 4 December 2011.

Shaw, D., Newholm, T. and Dickinson, R. (2006) 'Consumption as Voting', *European Journal of Marketing*, Vol. 40(9/10): 1049–67.

Shove, E. (2003) *Comfort, Cleanliness and Convenience*, Oxford: Berg.

Sidwell, M. (2008) *Unfair Trade*, London: The Adam Smith Institute.

Skeggs, B. (1997) *Formations of Class and Gender*, London: Sage.

Sklar, K. (1998) 'The Consumers' White Label Campaign of the National Consumers League, 1898–1918', in S. Strasser, C. McGovern and M. Judt (eds) *Getting and Spending*, pp. 17–36. Cambridge: Cambridge University Press.

Soper, K. (2004) 'Rethinking the "Good Life": The Consumer as Citizen', *Capitalism, Nature, Socialism*, Vol. 15(3): 111–16.

Soper, K. (2008) 'Alternative Hedonism and the Citizen-Consumer', in K. Soper and F. Trentmann (eds) *Citizenship and Consumption*, pp. 191–205. Basingstoke: Palgrave Macmillan.

Soper, K. (2009) 'Introduction', in K. Soper, M. Ryle and L. Thomas (eds) *The Politics and Pleasures of Consuming Differently*, pp. 1–24. Basingstoke: Palgrave Macmillan.

Soper, K. and Trentmann, F. (2008) 'Introduction', in K. Soper and F. Trentmann (eds) *Citizenship and Consumption*, pp. 1–16. Basingstoke: Palgrave Macmillan.

Southerton, D., Warde, A. and Hand, M. (2004) 'The Limited Autonomy of the Consumer', in D. Southerton, H. Chappells and B. Van Vliet (eds) *Sustainable Consumption*, pp. 32–48. Cheltenham: Edward Elgar.

Sparrow, A. (2008) 'Brown May Legislate Against Free Plastic Bags', 29 February, http://www.guardian.co.uk/politics/2008/feb/29/greenpolitics.plasticbags, accessed on 30 January 2009.

Stewart, D., Shamdasani, P. and Rook, D. (2007) *Focus Groups*, London: Sage.

Stolle, D., Hooghe, M. and Micheletti, M. (2005) 'Politics in the Supermarket: Political Consumerism as a Form of Political Participation', *International Political Science Review*, Vol. 26(3): 245–69.

Sussman, C. (2000) *Consuming Anxieties*, Stanford, CA: Stanford University Press.
Tallontire, A., Rentsendorj, E. and Blowfield, M. (2001) *Ethical Consumers and Ethical Trade*, London: Natural Resources Institute.
Taplin, L (2009) 'An Evaluation of Impact of the European Fairtrade Towns Movement', Commissioned by the Fairtrade Foundation UK, http://fairtradetowns.gn.apc.org/wp-content/uploads/final-report-l-taplin-may-09.pdf, accessed on 19 November 2009.
Teddlie, C. and Tashakkori, A. (2009) *Foundations of Mixed Methods Research*, London: Sage.
*The Economist* (2006) 'Good Food', 9 December, Vol. 381(8507): 11.
Thompson, E. P. (1991) *Customs in Common*, London: The Merlin Press.
TNS (2008) *Public Attitudes to Development*, TNS Report prepared for COI on behalf of the Department for International Development, http://s3.amazonaws.com/zanran_storage/www.dfid.gov.uk/ContentPages/4813334.pdf, accessed on 2 December 2011.
Trägårdh, L. (2007) 'The "Civil Society" Debate in Sweden', in L. Trägårdh (ed.) *State and Civil Society in Northern Europe*, pp. 9–36. New York and Oxford: Berghahn Books.
Trentmann, F. (2006) 'Knowing Consumers – Histories, Identities, Practices: An Introduction', in F. Trentmann (ed.) *The Making of the Consumer*, pp. 1–30. Oxford: Berg.
Trentmann, F. (2007) 'Before "Fair Trade": Empire, Free Trade, and the Moral Economies of Food in the Modern World', *Environment and Planning*, Vol. D25: 1079–1102.
Utz Certified (2011) 'What is Utz Certified?' http://www.utzcertified.org/en/aboututzcertified/whatisutzcertified, accessed on 14 October 2011.
Varul, M. (2008a) 'Consuming the Campesino', *Cultural Studies*, Vol. 22(5): 654–79.
Varul, M. (2008b) 'Fair Trade Consumerism as an Everyday Ethical Practice: A Comparative Perspective, Full Research Report', *ESRC End of Award Report*, RES-000-22-1891. Swindon: ESRC.
Varul, M. (2009) 'Ethical Selving in Cultural Contexts', *International Journal of Consumer Studies*, Vol. 33(2): 183–9.
Wålsten, L. (2011) 'Det finns inga skäl att gynna rättvisemärkt' (There is No Reason to Promote Fairtrade), http://www.svd.se/opinion/brannpunkt/ingen-vinst-med-kommunala-fairtradekop_6156101.svd, accessed on 25 November 2011.
Waitrose (2007) 'The Fairtrade Debate', http://www.waitrose.com/food/originofourfood/fairtrade/thefairtradedebate.aspx, accessed on 1 November 2009.
Warde, A. (2005) 'Consumption and Theories of Practice', *Journal of Consumer Culture*, Vol. 5(2): 31–153.
Wheeler, K. (2012) '"Change Today, Choose Fairtrade": Fairtrade Fortnight and the Citizen-Consumer', *Cultural Studies*, Vol. 26(4): 492–515.
Wijkström, F. and Zimmer, A. (2011) 'Introduction', in F. Wijkström and A. Zimmer (eds) *Nordic Civil Society at a Cross-roads*, pp. 9–26. Munich: Nomos.
Willis, P. (1978) *Profane Culture*, London: Routledge & Kegan Paul.
World Fair Trade Day (2011a) 'World Fair Trade Day 2011 Declaration', http://www.wftday.com/index.php/en/wftd-2011, accessed on 25 November 2011.

World Fair Trade Day (2011b) '9 Step Event Guide', http://www.wftday.com/index.php/en/wftd-2011/9-step-guide, accessed on 25 November 2011.

Wright, C. (2004) 'Consuming Lives, Consuming Landscapes', *Journal of International Development*, Vol. 16(5): 665–80.

Yeo, S. (1974) 'On the Uses of Apathy', *European Journal of Sociology*, Vol. 15(2): 279–311.

Zukin, S. (2008) 'Consuming Authenticity', *Cultural Studies*, Vol. 22(5): 724–48.

# Index